# IATEFL 2008

## Exeter Conference Selections

42nd International Conference
Exeter
7–11 April 2008

Edited by Briony Beaven

Editorial Committee: Ingrid Gürtler, Amos Paran, Silvana Richardson

Published by IATEFL
Darwin College
University of Kent
Canterbury
Kent CT2 7NY

Copyright for whole volume © IATEFL 2009

First published 2009

British Library Cataloguing in Publication Data
Education
Beaven, Briony (Ed.)
    IATEFL 2008 Exeter Conference Selections

ISBN 1 901905 22 3

For a complete list of IATEFL publications, please
write to the above address, or visit the IATEFL
website at www.iatefl.org

Copy-edited by Simon Murison-Bowie, Oxford.
Designed and typeset by Keith Rigley, Charlbury.
Printed in Britain by Information Press, Eynsham.

# Contents

# Editor's introduction

The 42nd Annual International IATEFL Conference was held at the University of Exeter Streatham Campus, UK. Delegates enjoyed a wealth of professionally stimulating talks and workshops with the opportunity to look at the bigger picture both professionally and physically—walks between session venues frequently revealed panoramas of the attractive city of Exeter and the delightful countryside vista of the surrounding hills.

With four days of concurrent sessions as well as ten pre-conference one-day events organised by various IATEFL Special Interest Groups (SIGs), delegates needed to plan their individual programmes carefully to benefit fully from the cornucopia of offerings on various topics. One very strong topic thread of this conference, however, immediately becomes apparent on looking at the contributions to this volume. Language policy and its close connection to social issues in ELT such as diversity, equality, racism, and the values transmitted by coursebooks appears at present to be a major area of focus for the IATEFL community.

For the second time IATEFL and the British Council collaborated in an online, distance element. Building on the good work done in Aberdeen, the online part of the conference was a bigger, better and more complete affair with plenty of audio and video material made available to remote participants, and much lively discussion in the SIG discussion forums. Thanks once again to the British Council for their generous support of this initiative.

A new feature of our annual conference was a tribute session in which sadness at the loss of colleagues and truly happy memories of them were exchanged. The three principal people mentioned were David Riley, Business English materials writer for Macmillan, Arthur Brookes, CUP handbook author, and Cheryl Benz, teacher educator and team leader for the TESOL 2006 conference in Florida, USA.

Exeter delegates were also able to enjoy a number of extra-curricular events including visits to several of Devon's beautiful manor houses and a very successful evening of Pecha Kucha, ably hosted by Lindsay Clandfield, in which presenters are allowed twenty slides, each shown for only twenty seconds. Another social programme highlight was David Crystal's evening devoted to language play, with unforgettable renderings of the work of well-known comedians by David and members of his family.

This issue of *Conference Selections* is divided into twelve chapters. So many interesting and valuable summaries were submitted this year that I have dispensed with chapter introductions in favour of this longer Editor's introduction in order to allow more of the summaries to be included. Nevertheless, owing to limitations of space, many worthwhile contributions have had to be omitted.

As has become customary, Chapter 1 consists of personal views of the whole conference from two delegates. If the conference reviewers commented on a talk for which there is a summary in this *Conference Selections*, their texts have been annotated accordingly.

Chapter 2 opens with Zoltán Dörnyei's plenary on motivation in which he sets out an approach to conceptualising motivation that is centred on the learner's vision. Linking the human 'self' with actions, he proposes that learners can be motivated to move consistently towards their goals through the creation of a strong, plausible, ideal language self which is linked to concrete plans and strategies aimed at achieving this vision of self as an effective L2 speaker. Other reports in this chapter also deal with helping language learners to find their own motivation for learning languages and related matters such as learner beliefs, learner attitudes and learner autonomy.

IATEFL conference presenters regularly address issues concerned with the training and professional development of teachers and this conference was no exception. Twelve reports on initial training, in-service training, online teacher education, different modes of and techniques for development, and trainer training are gathered together in Chapter 3.

In Summary 4.3, Catherine Walter and Michael Swan suggest a radical rethink of much of the current orthodoxy exemplified in teaching learners the so-called 'reading sub-skills'. According to Walter and Swan much of this teaching is misplaced and unnecessary; classroom time would be better spent in helping learners with specific linguistic features that can make texts hard to decode. Other contributions to Chapter 4 introduce specific techniques for encouraging learners to engage with texts. Learners face not only semantic difficulties but also cultural challenges when dealing with written texts in English. The relationship between text and culture is considered in summaries about training learners in critical literacy and about raising learners' awareness of features of some writing genres. The report of the symposium on critical approaches to coursebooks points out that teachers, too, need to read critically, remembering that coursebooks contain cultural messages, often implicit rather than explicit.

Alastair Pennycook's plenary focuses on topical issues about the global spread of English. He stresses that globalisation reaches far beyond the traditional concerns of economics. Pennycook notes that new technologies and methods of communication are enabling multiple movements of people, signs, sounds and images in multiple directions. He reminds us that as English teachers we are involved in political, social, cultural, moral and economic global matters, like it or not. It is clear that his concerns are shared by other presenters at our conference. Of the ten points he discusses several are taken up by other writers in Chapter 5. Lai, Troudi, Habbash and Jibowo all reflect on English as a translocal language and language as a social activity. Qian and Nambu consider the role of translation in classrooms. The *ELT Journal* Debate explores the extent to which methodology should be specific to particular social and cultural contexts. Rosa Jinyoung Shim's plenary, which closes this chapter, takes up the theme of World Englishes and puts it in a particular context, South Korea, in order to examine closely the difficulties inherent in implementing a critical pedagogy which accepts a non-native speaker variety as the goal of English education.

Chapter 6 contains six summaries on aspects of working with Young Learners. The authors are concerned with the learners' exposure to English both inside and outside their classrooms, with new resources for young learners, with techniques for coping with learners with a behavioural disorder and with young learners' perceptions regarding desirable characteristics of English teachers.

Attempts to measure 'quality' in language teaching and language teacher education make use of different criteria according to different priorities. Summaries in Chapter 7 address the quality assurance areas of meeting student expectations, ensuring standardisation and alignment of levels, and making classes fully relevant to the needs of adults. Gary Motteram's closing summary suggests that another benchmark of quality might consist of making the providers' construction of the learning process explicit and inviting students to engage critically with this.

Year on year we see an increase in technology applications in ELT and as Jody Skinner notes in his summary (8.1) about making use of a virtual learning environment, such applications can free us from the restrictions of space and time, help us organise courses and track student progress, and increase student participation and autonomy. The rest of Chapter 8 consists of reports on solving teaching problems through technology, teaching through different media and channels, frameworks for online education and a survey of the many teaching tools available via Google.

Approaches to teaching writing skills figure extensively, as would be expected, in Chapter 9, English for Academic Purposes, though Platzer and Verdonk question the emphasis on writing in a business university, while reports by Clare Anderson and Singhanat Nomnian tackle the subjects of commitment and linguistic identity amongst EAP students.

The shortest chapter in this volume, Chapter 10, links research and practical actions in the sphere of assessment and examinations. Under the microscope are functional progression in the CEFR, research into TOEIC and IELTS and an account by Peter Beech of getting trainee teachers to use tasks from past examination papers as the basis for their teaching practice.

One of the reports in Chapter 11 is titled 'Nuts and bolts' and this chapter comprises articles on basic, practical areas of ELT, such as grammar, vocabulary, use of dictionaries and role-play. Comparing the fruits of this conference with those of conferences only a few years ago one is aware of changing priorities in ELT; earlier volumes of *Conference Selections* tended to contain many more articles about our professional 'nuts and bolts'. It is to be hoped that in the well-justified and important current focus on socio-cultural issues in teaching and learning we do not lose sight of classroom teachers' need for the provision of stimulation and variety through new insights into teaching language as systems. Certainly, however, this chapter should reassure us that the basics are still receiving useful attention with, for example, Christian Jones outlining his findings on two contrasting techniques for teaching discourse markers and Robert Ledbury suggesting handy techniques for learners to work on affixation.

Finally, Chapter 12 brings together several articles on social and curricular issues, ending with Radmila Popović's plenary on forging peace through ELT. Popović is well aware of the difficulties facing anyone attempting to conduct peace education through ELT, such as lack of interest on the part of teachers, lack of time owing to standardised syllabuses and lack of support from administrative or senior pedagogical staff. She enumerates further challenges, for instance the need for special teaching skills, the vagueness of the subject matter and the problems of power relationships in classrooms. Nevertheless, by reporting realistically on teachers' efforts at peace education to date and by providing a workable framework for teaching peace through language she is able to considerably hearten those who hope that ELT can be a force for good beyond mere language instruction.

It was a privilege to edit this year's *Conference Selections* with so much evidence of members of our profession aiming to do their work as well as possible, seeking excellence at the micro-and the macro-levels of ELT areas of legitimate concern. I hope you will enjoy reading it as much as I enjoyed editing it.

I turn here briefly to some organisational matters before concluding. Last year's innovation of a topic index is retained. Its aim is to help readers quickly locate summaries and papers of particular interest to them. Some articles deal with two or more topics, which may be traced and followed up by using the chapter titles as well as the topic index and by searching out further cross-chapter links.

The job of editing could not be accomplished without the work of the Editorial Committee. Newer members of IATEFL may not know that these reviewers read all the reports 'blind', that is, they do not know who wrote the reports. Based on these 'blind' readings, members of the Editorial Committee make recommendations to the Editor as to which reports to include; they also make useful suggestions for the editing process. So my thanks go to Ingrid Gürtler, Amos Paran and Silvana Richardson, who together make up an exceptionally dedicated, thorough and perceptive panel. I would also like to thank our copy-editor Simon Murison-Bowie, and Keith Rigley for design and layout.

NOTE: References are given in full for plenary papers, but are limited to three in other reports. Readers wishing to follow up references can obtain details on application to the authors, or to the Editor, only in cases where no contact information is given.

**Briony Beaven**
*Freelance, Munich, Germany, September 2008*
Email: brionybeaven@t-online.de

# 1 Two personal views of the conference

## 1.1 Sparks and dank corners

**Jeff Stanford** *Freelance, Bath, UK*

Why do I like IATEFL? I meet fellow professionals, who give me a sense of belonging and who share their energy or witty jadedness. I meet potential sparks who beckon me along some new path, and occasionally I visit some dank corners which remind me of what not to do in my own professional life. I was only at IATEFL for a day and a half this year, but that was time enough to find some sparks and a few dank corners which I'll share here with those of you who didn't make it to the conference.

### Sparks

A pleasant venue is vitalising. The Exeter University campus was lovely. Exuberant verdancy. Meandering paths through the campus. Increasingly better coffee. Nicely spread out rooms which were never too hard to find. Some exhibitors didn't like being split into two separate rooms this year but I enjoyed the enforced stroll from one to the other.

You hardly notice good admin staff when they do their job well. That's how it felt this year. Pleasant human signposts dotted around the campus, cheerful information-givers, a real sense of welcome.

Other people's enthusiasm is contagious. Scrivener's engaging review of Postman and Weingartner's *Teaching as a Subversive Activity* was refreshing. Their 1969 book was about the need for enquiry-based learning, challenging students to think and build their own constructs rather than digest prescribed formulas. Scrivener's talk was humorous and modest in its reminder of how we as teachers can usefully challenge the status quo, both by thinking for ourselves and by helping students think for themselves.

Another aspect of the conference which was a big plus for me was the online element: http://exeteronline.britishcouncil.org. If you didn't make it to the conference you can go there now and enjoy recordings of many of the sessions, pick up handouts and join in the many forum discussions. What a great way to be using technology! I missed the real-life Pecha Kucha session in which several well-known EFL speakers spoke for 6 minutes 40 seconds each on different aspects of EFL. But I saw the video afterwards and realised how short can be beautiful and fun!

For the last year I've been meaning to get a second life, but just wasn't convinced. For the uninitiated, second life (http://secondlife.com/) is a virtual world where, in the form of avatars, we can collaborate and network socially. I've sat cynically on the fence for the last year, regurgitating common jibes about getting a first life, but talking to more devotees at this conference finally pushed me into creating my own second life presence and I'm actually excited about experiencing my first second life activity.

Graham Stanley provided a persuasive introduction to this. And yes, I can finally see how the lifelike appearance of second life worlds could make learning fun. I wonder what second life red wine tastes like!

## Dank corners

Poor ideas or good ideas poorly expressed lower the spirits. One novice speaker at the conference read a dense academic text about discourse problems in non-native speaker writing. The topic was full of promise but the lack of presentation skills was worrying and got me wondering whether the guidance for presenters can be improved or rein-forced. At the end I was delighted to see a more experienced speaker give the speaker advice on how to make information more accessible: a helpful reminder to make my presentations as accessible as possible.

The session on becoming an expert teacher attracted me because I like and respect the ideas of Rose Senior and Scott Thornbury. Somehow the session [Editor: see 3.7 in this volume] didn't work for me, though. There was an artificial antipathy between the two speakers, which wasn't convincing as they really seemed to agree with each other. My conclusion: they needed a more controversial topic to get their teeth into.

So it was a short conference for me, but enjoyable and memorable. Maybe the whole thing should be run on second life next time? Definitely not. I need real sparks and dank corners.

Email: jeffstanford@wordflair.com

## 1.2 Connecting themes relating to learner autonomy

**Jo Mynard** *Kanda University of International studies, Japan*

I felt this year's IATEFL conference was a good one to attend for those of us inter-ested in learner autonomy. Firstly, there was the Learner Autonomy Special Interest Group pre-conference event (PCE), which featured presentations related to learner autonomy by Leni Dam (Denmark), Vance Stevens (UAE), Adrian Holliday (UK), Richard Pemberton (UK), and Lienhard Legenhausen (Germany). In addition to the PCE, there were many other learner autonomy related presentations, workshops and forums throughout the conference. Issues were debated by participants who contrib-uted either physically at the conference, virtually through the British Council online forums and in writing through the journal *Independence*. In this short report, I will attempt to summarise and connect some of the themes which emerged from the con-ference in relation to learner autonomy.

## Theme 1: Teacher education for learner autonomy

One theme which emerged from a number of talks I attended was the need for im-proved and continuing teacher education in order to promote learner autonomy. People discussed how teacher education workshops and initial training should mirror what happens in the language classroom. I was also involved in discussions with other delegates about the importance of supporting the self-esteem of practising teachers as well as student teachers so that they are able to face change—including changing themselves. I am particularly interested in how technology can promote learner autonomy. Throughout the week, I became more convinced of the need for teachers to be autonomous learners of technology so that they could inspire their learners to be autonomous.

## Theme 2: Narratives

Many presentations drew on narratives in order to explore themes related to learner autonomy. There were narrative accounts of self-access principles around the world, narrative accounts of interactions where participants' interpretations were clouded by cultural assumptions, and discussions about the usefulness of drawing on teacher narratives as a way to improve the theory of learner autonomy from the bottom up. Narratives from educators were shared in order to raise issues for teacher education. It was also interesting to see that most of the British Council online forum posts themselves were in fact narratives.

## Theme 3: Motivation and learner autonomy

There is an overlap between the fields of learner autonomy and motivation and I was pleased to be able to attend the symposium on good language learners [Editor: see 2.2 in this volume] to examine the relationship more closely. Ema Ushioda highlighted internally regulated motivation as being a powerful factor contributing to autonomous language learning. Yoshiyuki Nakata looked at needs analysis as a starting point for identifying areas of intrinsic motivation. Conducting a needs analysis is often the starting point when practitioners begin to promote autonomy in language learners, but often in terms of language learning or future career needs only.

Zoltán Dörnyei, in his plenary session [Editor: see 2.1 in this volume], discussed motivation and the self. He described the concept of 'possible selves': a mental representation of a future possibility and a powerful motivating factor. I thought about how this could be incorporated into goal setting activities with learners when helping them become more autonomous. He went on to describe how the ideal self could only be an effective motivator if certain conditions are present including being accompanied by appropriate strategies. This is something that practitioners interested in promoting learner autonomy would also draw on.

## Theme 4: The role of the educator

The role of the educator provoked lively discussions. It was suggested that depending on the learning situation, the teacher might not necessarily be part of the classroom. Instead, the teacher's role might be a resource students can come to when they decide they need it. Anna Gorevanova's talk described a programme in Uzbekistan where students work independently in self-access centres, making appointments with learning advisors only when they need to. There were also discussions about how the role of the teacher extends beyond the classroom and how it is becoming quite common for teachers and learners to establish a dialogue through diaries, email, blogs or discussion forums.

## Conclusions

This is just a taster of the various issues related to learner autonomy which were deliberated on throughout the conference. Many other related issues came up over the four days and of course we didn't have all the answers! It was useful however to hear the voices of educators (and learners) from various parts of the world and learning contexts. I look forward to further stimulating conversations at conferences and on online forums in the future.

Email: mynardjo@hotmail.com

# 2 Psychology matters

## 2.1 Motivation and the vision of knowing a second language

**Zoltán Dörnyei** *University of Nottingham, UK*

'Motivation' is one of the most important concepts in psychology as motivation theories attempt to explain nothing less than *why humans behave and think as they do*. The notion is also of great importance in language education as it is one of the most common terms teachers and students use to explain what causes success or failure in learning. Indeed, motivation provides the primary impetus to initiate second/foreign (L2) learning and later the driving force to sustain the long and often tedious learning process. Without sufficient motivation, even individuals with the most remarkable abilities cannot accomplish long-term goals, and neither are appropriate curricula and good teaching enough on their own to ensure student achievement.

In this paper I describe a new approach to conceptualising motivation that is centred around the learner's *vision*; this approach and how it has emerged in L2 motivation research is described in more detail in a recent anthology (Dörnyei and Ushioda 2009; see especially Dörnyei 2009). Here I provide a brief overview, focusing mainly on the practical aspects of the theory. I start with a brief summary of the 'L2 Motivational Self System', which provides the theoretical link between motivation and vision, within a historical background.

### Three phases of L2 motivation research

L2 motivation research has been a thriving area within applied linguistics with several books and literally hundreds of articles published on the topic during the past four decades. It is useful to divide this period into three phases:

- *The social psychological period* (1959–1990), which was characterised by the work of social psychologist Robert Gardner and his students and associates in Canada (e.g. Gardner 1985; Gardner and Lambert 1972; Gardner and MacIntyre 1993). The best-known concepts stemming from this period were integrative and instrumental orientation/motivation, the former referring to the desire to learn an L2 of a valued community so that one can communicate with members of the community and sometimes even become like them, the latter to the concrete benefits that language proficiency might bring about (e.g. career opportunities, increased salary).

- *The cognitive-situated period* (during the 1990s), which was characterised by work that drew on cognitive theories imported from educational psychology, mainly conducted outside Canada. The best-known concepts associated with this period were intrinsic and extrinsic motivation, attributions, self-confidence/efficacy and situation-specific motives related to the learning environment, e.g. motives related to the L2 course, teachers, peers. (For overviews, see Dörnyei 2001b; Williams and Burden 1997.)

- *New approaches* (past decade), which have been characterised by an interest in motivational change and in the relationship between motivation and identity. The best-known concepts originating in this period have been the process-oriented conceptualisation of motivation (Dörnyei 2000, 2001b), motivation as investment (Norton 2000) and the concepts of the ideal and ought-to L2 selves, which will be described in detail below.

## Motivation and the self

In 2005, I proposed a new approach to the understanding of L2 motivation (Dörnyei 2005), conceived within an 'L2 Motivational Self System', which attempts to integrate a number of influential L2 theories (e.g. by Gardner 2001; Noels 2003; Norton 2001; Ushioda 2001) with findings of 'self research' in psychology. This initiative was rooted in an important trend in self psychology: over the past two decades self theorists have become increasingly interested in the active, dynamic nature of the self-system—the 'doing' side of personality—thus placing the self at the heart of motivation and action (Cantor 1990). This dynamic self concept has created an intriguing interface between personality and motivational psychology.

Within the dynamic approach of linking the human self with human action, the notion of 'possible selves' offers one of the most powerful, and at the same time the most versatile, motivational self-mechanism, representing the individuals' ideas of what they *might* become, what they *would like to* become, and what they are *afraid of* becoming (Markus and Nurius 1986). Thus, possible selves involve a person's specific image of his or her self in future states. It needs to be stressed that possible selves are more than mere long-term goals or future plans in that they involve tangible *images* and *senses*. Accordingly, imagery is a central element of possible selves theory—if we have a well-developed possible future self, we can imagine this self in vivid, realistic situations. A good example of this imagery aspect is how athletes regularly imagine themselves completing races or stepping onto the winning podium in order to increase their motivation. As Markus and Nurius (1986) emphasise, possible selves are represented in the same imaginary and semantic way as the here-and-now self, that is, they are a *reality* for the individual: people can 'see' and 'hear' a possible self. (See also Ruvolo and Markus 1992.) Thus, in many ways possible selves are similar to *dreams* and *visions* about oneself.

## Ideal selves, ought-to selves and the L2 Motivational Self System

From the point of view of education, one type of possible self, the *ideal self*, appears to be a particularly useful concept, referring to the representation of the characteristics that someone would ideally like to possess—i.e. a representation of hopes, aspirations or wishes. (See Higgins 1987, 1998.) It requires little justification that if someone has a powerful ideal self—for example a student envisions him/herself as a successful businessman or scholar—this self image can act as a potent self-guide, with considerable motivational power. This is expressed in everyday speech when we talk about someone following or living up to their dreams.

A complementary self-guide that has educational relevance is the *ought-to self*, referring to the attributes that one believes one ought to possess—i.e. representation of someone's sense of personal or social duties, obligations or responsibilities. (See Higgins 1987, 1998.) This self-image is particularly salient in some Asian countries where students are often motivated to perform well to fulfil some family obligation or to bring honour to the family's name.

Ever since I first came across the concept of possible selves, and in particular the ideal and the ought-to selves, I have been convinced that these concepts would be highly useful for understanding the motivation to learn a foreign language. Having considered the theoretical implications of these ideas from an L2 perspective and having conducted some relevant empirical research, in 2005 I proposed (Dörnyei 2005) a tripartite construct of L2 motivation that was made up of the following three components:

- *Ideal L2 Self,* which concerns the L2-specific facet of one's *ideal self:* if the person we would like to become speaks an L2, the ideal L2 self is a powerful motivator to learn the L2 because we would like to reduce the discrepancy between our actual and ideal selves.

- *Ought-to L2 Self,* which concerns the attributes that one believes one *ought to* possess to *avoid* possible negative outcomes, and which therefore may bear little resemblance to the person's own desires or wishes.

- *L2 Learning Experience,* which concerns situation specific motives related to the immediate learning environment and experience (e.g. the positive impact of success or the enjoyable quality of a language course).

(For more details on the evolution of this model, see Dörnyei 2009, in press.) Thus, the L2 Motivational Self System covers the internal desires of the learner, the social pressures exercised by significant or authoritative people in the learner's environment and the actual experience of being engaged in the learning process.

## Conditions for the motivating capacity of the ideal and ought-to selves

While future self-guides such as the ideal and the ought-to selves provide incentive, direction and impetus for action in order to reduce the discrepancy between the desired selves and the actual self, past research has shown that the motivational capacity of these future self-guides is not automatic but depends on a number of conditions. Accordingly, the Ideal L2 Self is an effective motivator only if:

- the learner *has* a desired future self-image;
- which is *elaborate* and *vivid;*
- which is perceived as *plausible* and is in harmony—or at least does not clash—with the expectations of the learner's family, peers and other elements of the social environment;
- which is *regularly activated* in his/her working self-concept;
- which is accompanied by relevant and effective *procedural strategies* that act as a *roadmap* towards the goal;
- which also contains elaborate information about the *negative consequences* of *not* achieving the desired end-state.

These conditions offer a useful framework for developing some practical implications of motivation theory: designing methods and strategies to realise these conditions in the language classroom can form the basis of an effective programme for introducing a motivational teaching practice.

## Generating and enhancing a vision for language learning

Motivational strategies have received attention in applied linguistics for several decades and a comprehensive collection of practical motivating techniques has been offered by Dörnyei (2001a), covering a wide range of issues from classroom management and task presentation to student self-motivation. However, the approach discussed below opens up a whole new avenue for promoting student motivation by means of increasing the elaborateness and vividness of self-relevant imagery in the students. That is, the approach suggests that an effective way of motivating learners is to create in them an *attractive vision* of their ideal language self. This motivational programme consists of six components, which are described below.

### Construction of the Ideal L2 Self: creating the vision

The (obvious) prerequisite for the motivational capacity of future self-guides is that they *need to exist*. Therefore, the first step in a motivational intervention that follows the self approach is to help learners to construct their Ideal L2 Self—that is, to *create an L2-related vision*. The term 'constructing' the Ideal L2 Self is, in fact, not entirely accurate because it is highly unlikely that any motivational intervention will lead a student to generate an ideal self out of nothing—the realistic process is more likely to involve *awareness raising* about and *guided selection* from the multiple aspirations, dreams, desires, etc. that the student has already entertained in the past. Thus, igniting the vision involves increasing the students' mindfulness about the significance of the ideal self in general and guiding them through a number of possible selves that they have entertained in their minds in the past, while also presenting some powerful role models to illustrate potential future selves.

### Imagery enhancement: strengthening the vision

Even if a desired self image exists, it may not have a sufficient degree of elaborateness and vividness to be an effective motivator. Methods of imagery enhancement have been explored in several areas of psychological, educational and sport research in the past, and the techniques of *creative* or *guided imagery* can be utilised to promote ideal L2 self images and thus to *strengthen the students' vision*. (For reviews and resources, see for example, Berkovits 2005; Fezler 1989; Gould *et al.* 2002; Hall *et al.* 2006; Horowitz 1983; Leuner *et al.* 1983; Singer 2006; Taylor *et al.* 1998). Undoubtedly, further research is needed in applied linguistics to review the imagery enhancement techniques utilised in other fields with regard to their potential applicability to promoting L2 motivation and the vision to master a foreign language. The details of an effective 'language imagery programme' are still to be worked out, but let there be no doubt about it: 'Our capacity for imagery and fantasy can indeed give us a kind of control over possible futures!' (Singer 2006: 128).

## Making the Ideal L2 Self plausible: substantiating the vision

Possible selves are only effective insomuch as the learner perceives them as *possible*, that is, conceivable within the person's particular circumstances. Thus, in order for ideal self images to energise sustained behaviour, they must be anchored in a sense of realistic expectations—they need to be *substantiated*, resulting in the curious mixed aura of imagination and reality that effective images share. This process requires honest and down-to-earth reality checks as well as considering any potential obstacles and difficulties that might stand in the way of realising the ideal self. Inviting successful role models to class can send the powerful message to students that, although everybody faces certain hurdles in reaching their ideal selves, it can be, and has been, done.

## Developing an action plan: operationalising the vision

Future self-guides are only effective if they are accompanied by a set of concrete *action plans*. Therefore, the ideal self needs to come as part of a 'package' consisting of an imagery component *and* a repertoire of appropriate plans, scripts and self-regulatory strategies. Even the most galvanizing self image might fall flat without ways of *operationalising the vision*, that is, without any concrete learning pathways into which to channel the individual's energy. This is clearly an area where L2 motivation research and language teaching methodology overlap: an effective action plan will contain a goal-setting component (which is a motivational issue) as well as individualised study plans and instructional avenues (which are methodological in nature).

## Activating the Ideal L2 Self: keeping the vision alive

Very little is said in the literature about activating and re-activating the ideal self, but this is an area where language teachers have, perhaps unknowingly, a great deal of experience. Classroom activities such as warmers and icebreakers as well as various communicative tasks can all be turned into effective ways of *keeping the vision alive*, and playing films and music, or engaging in cultural activities such as French cheese parties or 'Cook your wicked western burger' evenings can all serve as potent ideal-self reminders. Indeed, good teachers in any subject matter seem to have an instinctive talent to provide an engaging framework that keeps the enthusiasts going and the less-than-enthusiasts thinking.

## Considering failure: counterbalancing the vision

For maximum effectiveness, the desired self should be *offset by the feared self*: we do something because we want to do it *and also* because not doing it would lead to undesired results. In language teaching terms this process of *counterbalancing the vision* would involve regular reminders of the limitations of not knowing foreign languages as well as regularly priming the learners' ought-to L2 self to highlight the duties and obligations they have committed themselves to.

## Conclusion

The L2 Motivational Self System suggests that there are three primary sources of the motivation to learn a foreign/second language: (a) the learner's vision of him/herself as an effective L2 speaker, (b) the social pressure coming from the learner's environment, and (c) positive learning experiences. This paper elaborated on the first of these sources. I firmly believe that it is possible for teachers to consciously generate L2-learning vision in learners and I would like to encourage colleagues to develop a repertoire of techniques to ignite and enhance this vision. The six main areas of relevant motivational strategies presented in this talk are intended to offer a framework for future language teaching methodological developments along this line. Good luck!

Email: zoltan.dornyei@nottingham.ac.uk

## References

Berkovits, S. 2005. *Guided Imagery: Successful Techniques to Improve School Performance and Self-Esteem*. Duluth, Minn.: Whole Person Associates.

Cantor, N. 1990. 'From thought to behavior: "having" and "doing" in the study of personality and cognition'. *American Psychologist* 45/6: 735–50.

Dörnyei, Z. 2000. 'Motivation in action: towards a process-oriented conceptualisation of student motivation'. *British Journal of Educational Psychology* 70: 519–38.

Dörnyei, Z. 2001a. *Motivational Strategies in the Language Classroom*. Cambridge: Cambridge University Press.

Dörnyei, Z. 2001b. *Teaching and Researching Motivation*. Harlow: Longman.

Dörnyei, Z. 2005. *The Psychology of the Language Learner: Individual Differences in Second Language Acquisition*. Mahwah, N.J.: Lawrence Erlbaum.

Dörnyei, Z. 2009. 'The L2 Motivational Self System' in Z. Dörnyei and E. Ushioda (eds.). *Motivation, Language Identity and the L2 Self*. Clevedon: Multilingual Matters.

Dörnyei, Z. in press. 'Researching motivation: from integrativeness to the ideal L2 self' in S. Hunston and D. Oakey (eds.). *Doing Applied Linguistics*. London: Routledge.

Dörnyei, Z. and E. Ushioda (eds.). 2009. *Motivation, Language Identity and the L2 Self*. Clevedon: Multilingual Matters.

Fezler, W. 1989. *Creative Imagery: How to Visualize in All Five Senses*. New York: Simon and Schuster.

Gardner, R. C. 1985. *Social Psychology and Second Language Learning: The Role of Attitudes and Motivation*. London: Edward Arnold.

Gardner, R. C. 2001. 'Integrative motivation and second language acquisition' in Z. Dörnyei and R. Schmidt (eds.). *Motivation and Second Language Acquisition*. Honolulu, HI: University of Hawaii Press: 1–20.

Gardner, R. C. and W. E. Lambert. 1972. *Attitudes and Motivation in Second Language Learning*. Rowley, Mass.: Newbury House.

Gardner, R. C. and P. D. MacIntyre. 1993. 'A student's contributions to second-language learning. Part II: affective variables'. *Language Teaching* 26: 1–11.

Gould, D., N. Damarjian and C. Greenleaf. 2002. 'Imagery training for peak performance' in J. L. Van Raalte and B. W. Brewer (eds.). *Exploring Sport and Exercise Psychology*, Second Edition. Washington, D.C.: American Psychological Association: 49–74.

Hall, E., C. Hall, P. Stradling and D. Young. 2006. *Guided Imagery: Creative Interventions in Counselling and Psychotherapy*. London: Sage.

Higgins, E. T. 1987. 'Self-discrepancy: a theory relating self and affect'. *Psychological Review* 94: 319–40.

Higgins, E. T. 1998. 'Promotion and prevention: regulatory focus as a motivational principle'. *Advances in Experimental Social Psychology* 30: 1–46.

Horowitz, M. J. 1983. *Image Formation and Psychotherapy*. Northvale, N.J.: Jason Aronson.

Leuner, H., G. Horn and E. Klessmann. 1983. *Guided Affective Imagery with Children and Adolescents*. New York: Plenum.

Markus, H. and P. Nurius. 1986. 'Possible selves'. *American Psychologist* 41: 954–69.

Norton, B. 2000. *Identity and Language Learning: Social Processes and Educational Practice*. Harlow: Pearson.

Noels, K. A. 2003. 'Learning Spanish as a second language: learners' orientations and perceptions of their teachers' communication style' in Z. Dörnyei (ed.). *Attitudes, Orientations, and Motivations in Language Learning*. Oxford: Blackwell: 97–136.

Norton, B. 2001. 'Non-participation, imagined communities and the language classroom' in M. P. Breen (ed.). *Learner Contributions to Language Learning: New Directions in Research*. Harlow, England: Longman: 159–71.

Ruvolo, A. P. and H. R. Markus. 1992. 'Possible selves and performance: the power of self-relevant imagery'. *Social Cognition* 10/1: 95–124.

Singer, J. L. 2006. *Imagery in Psychotherapy*. Washington, D.C.: American Psychological Association.

Taylor, S. E., L. B. Pham, I. D. Rivkin and D. A. Armor. 1998. 'Harnessing the imagination: mental simulation, self-regulation, and coping'. *American Psychologist* 53/4: 429–39.

Ushioda, E. 2001. 'Language learning at university: exploring the role of motivational thinking' in Z. Dörnyei and R. Schmidt (eds.). *Motivation and Second Language Acquisition*. Honolulu, HI: University of Hawaii Press: 91–124.

Williams, M. and R. Burden. 1997. *Psychology for Language Teachers*. Cambridge: Cambridge University Press.

## 2.2 Symposium on good language learners: motivation and beyond

**Convenor: Blanka Frydrychova Klimova** *University of Hradec Kralove, Hradec Kralove, Czech Republic* with

**David McLoughlin** *Meiji University, Tokyo, Japan*

**Carol Griffiths** *Min Zu Da Xue (Central University of Nationalities), Beijing, China*

**Chizuyo Kojima** *University of Exeter, UK*

**Yoshiyuki Nakata** *Hyogo University of Teacher Education, Hyogo, Japan* and

**Ema Ushioda** *University of Warwick, UK*

This symposium discussed some of the theoretical and practical issues behind the effective language learning process. Six symposium speakers explored how to help language learners find their own motivation for learning languages, considered the characteristics of good language learners, and outlined implications for further research and pedagogical practice in the language classroom. The symposium drew on research into intrinsic and internally regulated motivation, attribution theory, and learners' beliefs. In addition, strategies for enhancing learner motivation were offered, and factors other than motivation that play a role in effective language learning were presented.

Whether motivation is intrinsic or extrinsic, most recent theoretical and research insights suggest that, for effective and autonomous language learning use to take place, motivation needs to come *from within* and be internally regulated, rather than regulated *from without* by external social forces such as teachers, parents, grades, examinations or coursework demands. Such *internally regulated motivation* can include both intrinsic and extrinsic motivational factors working in concert (van Lier 1996); the key point, as **Ema Ushioda** noted, is that both forms of motivation are internalised and self-determined, emanating from within the learner, rather than controlled by external social forces. Yet paradoxically, social processes in themselves are pivotal in mediating the healthy internal growth and self-regulation of motivation. Understanding the complex relationship between social and individual processes is vitally important if we want to develop our students' motivation within, and enable them to sustain and regulate their own motivation. Ushioda outlined three key principles in promoting motivational growth and self-regulation: enabling full participation in the social setting; involving people in making choices and decisions within this setting; and promoting responsibility.

Of course, as teachers we know the importance of intrinsic motivation and wish to develop this in our learners. However, in the EFL school context, as **Yoshiyuki Nakata** argued, this is not as easy as it sounds. Brophy (2004) claims that all day, every day intrinsic motivation is an ideal but unattainable motivational state for teachers to seek to develop in their students. He argues that one of the important tasks on the agenda of the motivation researcher is to find how to help students come to appreciate the value of school curricula and learning activities. Examining this area, the case study presented in the symposium by Nakata concluded that teachers should first attempt to develop their students' affective aspect of intrinsic motivation and then focus on the cognitive aspect. To a greater or a lesser extent, this is perhaps in line with Ushioda's view above. As a practical way of doing this, Nakata proposed that teachers start by examining their learners' needs through a needs analysis survey and subsequently apply what they have learned to their practice. In this way, Nakata argued, teachers can decide what aspects of intrinsic motivation to focus on at different stages of the learning process.

Another approach to understanding learner motivation is attribution theory, which claims that our past successes and failures considerably shape our motivational disposition underlying future action. More than forty years of research has shown that the two most common types of attribution are effort and ability. Research has also identified three dimensions in which attributions can be identified—locus, stability and controllability (Weiner 2001). Locus refers to whether the cause lies within or without an individual. Thus, ability and effort are both classed as internal, whereas difficulty of task or attitude of teachers is categorised as external. Stability has to do with how long the attribution persists over time. Ability is seen as something that is stable, whereas effort is generally viewed as unstable. Finally, controllability refers to the degree of control an individual has over the cause. These properties map onto expectancy and value (or emotional states): stability maps onto expectancies for future success; locus maps onto feelings of pride and self-esteem; controllability maps onto feelings of guilt and shame. Furthermore, attributing failure to lack of aptitude can lead to future failure and disengagement from the learning process (a maladaptive attribution), whereas an attribution to effort can cause an individual to try harder in future (an adaptive attribution). However, as **David McLoughlin** indicated, there are cultural differences in the way people make attributions. For example, in North America and East Asia there appear to be quite different attitudes to effort and aptitude in achievement contexts. Taking such cultural differences into account, teachers should try to direct their students towards making attributions that are more adaptive and in this way to help them persist with their language learning.

Moreover, beliefs about language learning can also influence the way people study a foreign language with consequences for motivation and proficiency (Mantle-Bromley 1995). For example, misconceptions about language learning might hinder a learner's choice of strategies, which could further affect progress and motivation to learn. **Chizuyo Kojima** demonstrated a sample case study of four Japanese students who were engaged in further language study in the UK, and who are regarded as successful language learners. They were interviewed about their beliefs related to learning language. An alternative sample of less competent students who had studied English for six years before entering a university in Japan were given open-ended questionnaires that aimed at revealing their beliefs about language learning. The main outcomes were as follows: memorising new vocabulary should be approached with the use of appropriate learning strategies; English should be used as a means of communication and speaking Japanese should be avoided; a positive attitude towards learning English should be enhanced by a process of learning which is enjoyable; and finally, perfectionism should be avoided—making mistakes should be considered natural.

As language practitioners, therefore, we can contribute enormously to the motivational growths of our students. There exist countless strategies which can generate and maintain learners' motivation. **Blanka Frydrychova Klimova** outlined ten of them, which she has found the most useful in her teaching. These include establishing a good rapport with students; systematic revision and recycling of new vocabulary; reorganising pairs for speaking activities; doing a short piece of writing with students; supporting students' learning with some additional materials for home or self-study, such as a support language website; finding, adapting, and making materials; meeting students' immediate, on-going and future needs through in-class discussion, tests, or evaluation forms; giving students feedback on their performance; further developing students' language skills with which they entered the class; and being good to self and to others. Nevertheless, the most important teaching strategy seems to be *showing enthusiasm for teaching and for students' learning*, which inevitably leads to an atmosphere in which motivation for learning any foreign language can more easily be fostered.

Concluding the symposium, **Carol Griffiths** provided an overview of the factors that play a part in making a language learner a good learner. Griffiths pointed out that motivation is not the only individual factor that contributes to effective language learning and reminded the audience of other factors that have been the subject of much research and controversy: age, gender, aptitude for languages, learning style and personality. Furthermore, learners need to develop certain behaviours to be successful in their language learning: effective use of strategies, metacognitive awareness, and autonomy. As well as individual characteristics, there are also external factors that have a bearing on how successful a language learner will be: how the language is taught, where the learner is studying it, and the level of other students. Griffiths' summary highlighted the complexity of the question of what makes a good language learner and how much further research is required into motivation and other related areas.

Email: blanka.klimova@uhk.cz

## References

Brophy, J. E. 2004. *Motivating Students to Learn*. Second edition. Mahwah, N.J.: Lawrence Erlbaum.

Mantle-Bromley, C. 1995. 'Positive attitudes and realistic beliefs: links to proficiency'. *The Modern Language Journal* 79/3: 372–86.

van Lier, L. 1996. *Interaction in the Language Curriculum: Awareness, Autonomy and Authenticity*. Harlow: Longman.

Weiner, B. 2001. 'Intrapersonal and interpersonal theories of motivation from an attribution perspective' in F. Salili *et al.* (eds.). *Student Motivation: The Culture and Context of Learning*. New York: Kluwer Academic/Plenum Publishers.

## 2.3 Symposium on learner and teacher beliefs

**Convenor: Hilal Handan Atlı** *Bilkent University, Turkey* with
**Rachel Wicaksono** *York St John University, UK*
**Peng Ding** *Nottingham University, UK* and
**Chiung-Wen Chang** *Fooyin University, Taiwan*

This symposium brought together teachers from Britain, China, Taiwan and Turkey to explore the beliefs of learners and teachers regarding teaching and learning English.

**Rachel Wicaksono** (Co-research with Ding) reported on Chinese English language learners' beliefs about classroom participation, which influence their attitudes, motivation, and shape their learning experience. While watching a group of students from China learning English in both UK and Chinese classrooms, she wondered whether the experience of two different learning contexts would influence their beliefs about language learning, specifically the importance of active participation in 'speaking' classes.

To stimulate reflection and in oorder to collect data, Horwitz's (1988) *Beliefs about Language Learning Inventory* was modified to include some open-ended questions. Twelve students, studying English at the Science and Technology College of Nanchang University, China, were divided into two groups. The first group had studied English at York St John University for one month; the second group had no overseas learning experience. The students completed the questionnaire and data were analysed using both frequency statistics and text analysis. Despite the drawbacks of the very small sample, the results suggest that it is still too early to conclude that the experience of different language learning contexts is an important influence on beliefs about classroom participation, as differences between the two groups were not clear. Both groups said that their own motivation, feelings of anxiety and understanding of the expectations of teachers and peers influenced their beliefs. Overall, the data suggest a diverse and complex range of factors, which can be broadly categorised into intra-learner factors and inter-learner factors, though with interaction between these two categories.

The conclusion was that, while learners see their beliefs as 'inside them' (perhaps connected to what they think of as their 'personality' or their life goals), they also recognise that their beliefs are somewhat dependent on time and context. Rather than coming to a conclusion about the relationship between learning context and beliefs, teachers, curriculum designers and textbook writers should engage their students in discussion about their beliefs, and the relationship between beliefs and classroom behaviour.

**Peng Ding** showcased some distinctive attributes of several 'particularly enthusiastic' teachers in China and Europe, discussed their cultural significance and provided practical recommendations for maximising classroom enthusiasm for second/foreign language teachers. An enthusiastic teacher has an extreme intrinsic interest in the subject matter and Salmon (1988) emphasised that it is the teacher's *unique* personal 'fire' that students catch. This argument implies (a) that enthusiasm is infectious and (b) that one individual teacher may transmit enthusiasm differently from another.

Hence the following questions: How do Chinese learners, in a UK teaching context, perceive the differences between Chinese and European manifestations of enthusiasm? Does each individual enthusiastic teacher exhibit their own idiosyncrasies? In Ding's study a hybrid qualitative ressearch method was adopted; it included thirty semi-structured interviews and classroom observations. The participants were twelve Chinese secondary school English language teachers, who were trainees studying on an English language and applied linguistics course in a British university. They selected five teachers including four Europeans (one Hungarian, one English, one Scottish and one Slovakian, all of whom were engaged in teaching in UK university English departments) and one Chinese teacher (in the Chinese EFL context) as 'particularly' enthusiastic teachers.

It was found that these teachers shared six core attributes: intrinsic interest in the subject, caring for students' learning, sound subject knowledge, passion for teaching, genuineness (congruence) and rapport/interaction with students. These components are absolutely essential if teachers are to be perceived as 'enthusiastic' by their students; the absence of just one of these core components will significantly impede their efforts to convey enthusiasm.

It was also found that enthusiasm interacted with cultural parameters. Chinese cultural norms and educational conventions seem to have posed difficulties for Chinese teachers in developing and demonstrating enthusiasm fully and freely. Thus, Chinese EFL teachers demonstrated more 'subdued' and implicit enthusiasm than their Western counterparts. Besides these 'shared' attributes, each individual teacher also demonstrated their idiosyncratic characteristics. Four types of enthusiasm were proposed: inspirational, intellectually stimulating, showmanship and apparent enthusiasm. In many ways, inspirational enthusiasm appeared to be an ideal form. Five areas related to enthusiasm emerged as important for teachers to pay attention to maximise their enthusiasm: (1) establishing congruence, (2) presentation, (3) bringing about personal elements, (4) relationship with students, (5) content/skills, and (6) applying 'culture-awareness' strategies (Ding in press).

**Chiung-Wen Chang** investigated the beliefs and practices of native (NEST) and non-native English-speaking teachers (N-NEST) concerning teaching English in pre-schools in Taiwan. This study was conducted over an intensive period, providing a cross-sectional look at several native and non-native English-speaking kindergarten teachers and their classroom in action. Case studies were constructed by closely examining each teacher and their classroom, comparing them, and providing examples of the teachers' beliefs and their classroom practices.

Despite all the challenges that N-NESTs face, they bring many positive attributes to the classroom which enhance learning. The N-NEST participants in this study mentioned several such attributes which they have: sharing the same language with the students, having themselves been through the complex process of learning English, being aware of difficulties students encounter, and empathising with them.

Native-like pronunciation is a major key for successful interactions with native speakers, and one would naturally think that the younger the age, the easier it is to acquire a native-like pronunciation. It seems native speakers are best for teaching children. Nevertheless, native English speakers without adequate training have found themselves very much limited as to the help they could offer to young children. Their ability to help young learners could certainly be improved if more training were provided to these NESTs.

In conclusion, talking about NESTs versus N-NESTs overlooks some very important issues. A teacher's language proficiency is only one element of a professional language teacher. Another concern is whether the person has the appropriate preparation to be a teacher. We must look beyond the labels and see teachers as individuals, with particular strengths and areas for improvement.

**Hilal Handan Atlı** reported on a longitudinal classroom-based study investigating a novice teacher's beliefs regarding grammar teaching from the beginning of her career into her third year. To gain more insight into this topic and to investigate whether in-service training courses have an impact on a teacher's beliefs, two questions were asked: (1) Do a teacher's beliefs regarding grammar teaching change during and after the Cambridge ESOL In-service Certificate in English Language Teaching (ICELT) course? (2) Is any such change reflected in her teaching?

Data was collected through a qualitative research paradigm including an intrinsic case study where the informant, Eda, was chosen according to a non-probability sampling method. To unearth Eda's beliefs regarding grammar teaching during these three years Kagan's (1990) 'multi-method' evaluation was used; this involved a questionnaire and seven open-ended classroom observations followed by audio-recorded semi-structured interviews. The same questionnaire was given three times during this period. At the beginning, Eda's responses were believed not to be true, though evidence later emerged to prove them to be so. Findings showed there were no major changes in Eda's beliefs at the end of the study. Her beliefs about teaching grammar were formed during her school years without her necessarily approving the teaching style.

Through classroom observations and interviews it was discovered that Eda did not have a sufficiently large 'repertoire' of classroom techniques at the beginning of the course. Therefore, she did not know how to implement her beliefs in her teaching and subconsciously imitated the style of teaching she was exposed to, especially when she did not feel secure in the classroom. ICELT sessions, having supervised classroom observations, doing literature review for assignments, and the coursebook methodology helped Eda to increase her awareness. Subsequently, she was better able to implement her beliefs in her teaching. The implications for in-service teacher training courses are that trainers should help teachers to better understand their classroom behaviour and whether it reflects their beliefs and if not, what prevents them from putting them into practice. Such courses should help teachers to find ways to put their beliefs into action.

Email: hilal@bilkent.edu.tr

## References

Ding, P. in press. 'Teacher enthusiasm in action' in G. Strong and A. Smith. *Adult Learners: Content, Context, and Innovation*. Alexandria, Virginia: TESOL.

Horwitz, E. K. 1988. 'The beliefs about language learning of beginning university foreign language students'. *Modern Language Journal* 72/3: 283–94.

Kagan, D. M. 1990. 'Ways of evaluating teacher cognition: inferences concerning the Gold-ilocks principle'. *Review of Educational Research* 60: 419–69.

Salmon, P. 1988. *Psychology for Teachers: An Alternative Approach.* London: Hutchinson.

## 2.4 Attending to differences—language learning beliefs of Japanese students

**Paul A. Riley** *Kanto Gakuin University, Yokohama, Japan*

My presentation was based on research into the language learning beliefs of first year students at a single Japanese university. The research revealed that Japanese students enter university with many strong beliefs about how English is, or should be learned, and that many differences exist between the beliefs of university students and their native English speaker instructors with regards to language learning. For example, many students underestimate the benefits of practising spoken English with their classmates in pair work and group work activities, and believe English can only be acquired through communication with native speakers of English. On the other hand, many students also tend to underestimate the difficulty of the task of second language learning, and may become prematurely discouraged by their slow progress.

Beliefs about language learning can influence or affect:

- the learning strategies employed by students,
- the willingness of students to participate in class activities,
- the level of trust between students and teacher,
- student anxiety levels,
- a breakdown in the learning process,
- discontinuation of study.

Several studies have been carried out into student beliefs about language learning but very few studies have surveyed teachers to compare student beliefs with teacher beliefs. This study employed the questionnaire instrument of Sakui and Gaies (1999), with a 45-item questionnaire in Japanese for students and a 37-item English version prepared for teachers. A total of 661 students and 34 teachers participated in the study, responding to items on a four-point scale from 'strongly disagree' to 'strongly agree'.

The presentation focused on one particular aspect of the research study, namely the differences discovered between student responses and teacher responses. The strongest beliefs reported by the students and teachers were discussed, together with some of the significant differences revealed in the study. Significant differences were found for 20 of the 37 common questionnaire items. Space here only allows for a summary of the differences discussed, which is shown in Table 1. Recurring themes in the results of the study indicated differences in beliefs about error correction, the role of the L1 and translation, and the usefulness of practising English with classmates. We can see from Figure 2.4.1, for example, that the teachers seem to believe far less than students in the need for error correction and translation of English to Japanese, and believe more in the efficacy of students practising speaking English with classmates.

| Responses of general agreement (p<.001) | S % | T % |
|---|---|---|
| 13. If you are allowed to make mistakes in the beginning, it will be hard to get rid of them later on. | 53 | 18 |
| 14. Learning English is mostly a matter of learning grammar rules. | 16 | 0 |
| 32. Learning a word means learning the Japanese translation | 42 | 2 |
| 34. I can improve my English by speaking English with my classmates. | 77 | 100 |
| 38. I want my teacher to correct all my mistakes. | 41 | 3 |
| 41. To understand English, it must be translated into Japanese. | 24 | 0 |

*Figure 2.4.1: Example of student and teacher differences*

Implications of these results include the possibility that in a class of first-year Japanese university students, potentially one quarter may be relying on translation and may not believe they can improve their English by speaking with their classmates. In addition, close to half of the students may be expecting the teacher to correct all their mistakes. To attend to possible differences in beliefs and student expectations it is important for teachers to explain classroom activities and reassure students of the benefits of the techniques and tasks used by the teacher in the language classroom. Mantle-Bromley (1995) suggests a process of positive intervention and guidance which could encourage students and help to address the possible negative effects of many student-held beliefs about language learning. Wenden (1998) discusses a guidance procedure which includes elicitation of student beliefs and presentation of alternative views, followed by a process of reflection and experimentation.

Email: edril@kanto-gakuin.ac.jp

## References

Mantle-Bromley, C. 1995. 'Positive attitudes and realistic beliefs: links to proficiency'. *The Modern Language Journal* 79/3: 372–86.

Sakui, K. and S. Gaies. 1999. 'Investigating Japanese learners' beliefs about language learning'. *System* 27/4: 473–92.

Wenden, A. 1998. 'Metacognitive knowledge and language learning'. *Applied Linguistics* 19/4: 515–37.

## 2.5 Developing a conscious approach to group participation

**Denise Norton** *Deakin University English Language Institute, Melbourne, Australia*

### Introduction

The programme called here the 'conscious' approach to group participation was developed at Deakin University English Language Institute in response to a growing concern that international students faced difficulties in adapting to the group learning and assessment environment they encountered at tertiary level. Although students in EAP classes frequently worked in groups both in class and in completing assessment projects, students often failed to value group participation. The goal of the programme was to focus students' awareness on group participation as a specific learning goal, quite distinct from the goal of the language/ assessment task itself.

Using Ehrman and Dörnyei's (1989) work on the four phases of group development as the theoretical underpinning, a participation programme was trialled, with the four stages of the programme being linked both by timing and task development to the four phases identified by Ehrman and Dörnyei. These four phases are: the Formation Phase (characterised by politeness and a degree of harmony), the Transition Phase (characterised by conflict), the Performance Phase (when the group is at its most productive), and the Dissolution Phase (the end of the group) (Dörnyei and Murphey 2003). The programme was designed to guide students through these four stages of group formation, while at every stage encouraging students to consciously examine how they and others functioned within the group. In this way, it was hoped to increase students understanding of the roles that contribute toward successful group outcomes.

No specific language tasks were developed. Instead, where course-related language tasks involved (or could be adapted to) group performance, the pedagogical tasks were followed by reflective tasks in which students were directed to discuss or write about their experience of the group. The aim of the reflective tasks was to engage students actively in the development of their understanding of group dynamics and to provide a vehicle for internalising and reinforcing their learning.

### Programme stages

In the Formation stage, a language based group task was followed by a discussion of the roles students usually assumed in group work and of the various functions performed within a typical group.

In the Transition stage, students were asked to adopt a particular group role (such as Secretary or Manager) while performing the language tasks. In this way, students had the opportunity to experiment with a number of different roles. It was found that longer tasks (more than twenty minutes) severely strained groups dealing with the inherent conflict of the Transitional phase and produced an unacceptable amount of stress for those students experiencing 'role strain' (Dörnyei and Murphey 2003: 123). For this reason, it was decided to restrict the activities at this stage to twenty minutes or shorter in length. Other than this one restriction, tasks were chosen with a view to incorporating the language objectives of the class, and for their suitability for group participation.

Where groups had suffered a degree of conflict or role strain, written reflective tasks were found to offer a greater opportunity for the open and honest expression of students' experience than spoken feedback. It was found that the reflective task served a dual purpose; not only did it help to consolidate students' understanding of group behaviour, but it also prevented groups from becoming mired in their conflict.

In the Performance Phase, the groups worked independently on group assignments, with a written reflective task serving to give feedback to the teacher on the group dynamic.

It was found that students who participated in this programme bonded strongly with classmates and in the Dissolution Stage, the reflective class discussion allowed students to express feelings of loss at the dissolution of the class. Students at this stage frequently expressed a greater confidence in their ability to participate in group work, as well as strongly valuing the experience of working within a group.

## Conclusion

A greater confidence in managing group personalities and some familiarity with how various roles contribute to group performance may assist international students in adapting to the Australian tertiary environment. The 'conscious' approach to group participation presented here encourages students to experiment with various roles, with the reflective tasks serving not only to focus students' attention on the group dynamic, but to assist them in negotiating the inherent conflict involved in dealing with a diversity of personalities, attitudes and abilities.

Email: denise.norton@deakin.edu.au

## References

Dörnyei, Z. and T. Murphey. 2003. *Group Dynamics in the Language Classroom*. Cambridge: Cambridge University Press.

Ehrman, M. E. and Z. Dörnyei. 1998. *Interpersonal Dynamics in Second Language Education: The Visible and Invisible Classroom*. Thousand Oaks, Calif.: Sage.

Norton, D. 2008. 'Promoting group participation: a conscious approach to collaboration'. *EA Journal* 24/1: 24–32.

## 2.6 Individualisation of language teaching in mainstream schools

**Svetlana Hanusova** *Masaryk University, Brno, Czech Republic*

In its beginnings the systematic study of the process of second language learning focused on what was common to all learners. At present the emphasis is being shifted to individual differences, including age, intelligence, aptitude, motivation, anxiety, cognitive and learning styles, learner strategies, learner beliefs, learner autonomy and other aspects.

Experts point out that the learner-centred approach is highly elaborated on the theoretical level but that there is hardly any classroom research bridging the gap between practice and theory. Hadley holds that

> while experimental research often does not build individual difference factors into study designs, but treats them as part of 'error variance', teachers in the classroom must deal with individual differences on a daily basis.
> (Hadley 2001: 79)

In the Czech educational context, an individual approach has always been one of the main slogans. School practice, however, was traditionally largely based on administrative differentiation by school. Pupils in any one class have always been instructed in the same way, regardless of their preferences, needs and potential.

The Czech school system is currently undergoing a major educational reform. Every school has to design their own school educational programme based on the Framework Educational Programme provided by the Ministry of Education. Czech teachers are asked to become curriculum designers and developers, a new challenge for them. The Framework Educational Programmes emphasise the role of individualisation in the teaching process and encourage teachers to consider learner differences, needs and preferences.

I decided to carry out an action research project focusing on the teachers' views of the individualisation of English language teaching. As a facilitator I cooperated with school teachers. I wanted the participants to benefit from their participation in the study and, therefore, attempted to design an *empowering research* study, conducted *with* teachers, not *on* teachers (Cameron *et al.*1992 in Kumaravadivelu 2005). Besides contact sessions with the teachers, we also cooperated online, via the virtual learning environment Moodle, where I provided information, gathered data and discussed the process of experimental innovation with the participants.

I worked with 57 primary, secondary and language school teachers in the first phase. In the second phase, a focus group of 14 teachers cooperated on the intervention in their current practice at lower secondary schools.

In the first phase of the research study, I explored the teachers' views, beliefs and common practices so as to establish whether individual differences and the individualisation of language teaching belong to central concepts of their pedagogical thinking and practice. The results showed that teachers had very limited knowledge of individual differences and the ways to accommodate them in language teaching. The participants believed that individualisation and differentiation were desirable, but at the same time too demanding or even impossible for teachers under current circumstances.

In the second phase of the study I provided the participants with information concerning individual differences and several possible forms of differentiated instruction (Heacox 2002). Then I let them narrow the focus, select one type of learner differences, make a diagnosis and differentiate their instruction. I specified four areas of differentiation: working with a text, grammar practice, vocabulary practice and communicative activities.

The teachers were supposed to report on their progress regularly in online discussion forums. Most teachers decided to identify the learning styles of their learners. The process of searching for ways to accommodate identified differences appeared to be quite challenging. Approximately one half of the teachers had problems grasping the concept and realising innovations. It was necessary to monitor discussion contributions, encourage participants and provide advice.

In the final reflections most teachers acknowledged that their effort was well-invested and stated they wanted to continue with differentiation in the future. They reported that pupils were pleased by the teacher's interest in their learning styles and their interest in learning increased. Pupils with specific learning difficulties and gifted pupils particularly benefited from the innovations.

The results indicate a major shift in the teachers' opinions. Foreign language teachers who introduced some elements of individualisation and differentiation tended to resolve the conflict of desirability versus impossibility in favour of desirability. A crucial factor in the change of their initial reservations proved to be positive experience and peer support.

Email: svetlana.hanusova@gmail.com

## References

Hadley, A. O. 2001. *Teaching Language in Context.* Boston: Heinle & Heinle.

Heacox, D. 2002. *Differentiating Instruction in the Regular Classroom: How to Teach and Reach All Learners Grades 3 to 12.* Minneapolis: Free Spirit Publishing.

Kumaravadivelu, B. 2005. *Understanding Language Teaching. From Method to Postmethod.* New Jersey: Lawrence Erlbaum Associates.

## 2.7 Symposium on learner autonomy

**Convenor: Nkechi M. Christopher** *University of Ibadan, Nigeria* with
**Cem Balçıkanlı** *Gazi University, Turkey*
**Aylin Köyalan Coşkun** *Izmir University of Economics, Turkey*
**Xianghu Liu** *University of Exeter, UK*
**Khaldah Al Mansoori** *ITTIHAD University, UAE* and
**Xiaoli Jiang** *University of Warwick, UK*

Learner autonomy is concerned with building learners' capacity for learning and leading learners to take responsibility for their learning. It is considered the ultimate goal of teaching (Jie and Xiaoqing 2006) and the hallmark of successful learning (Little 2001) and is gradually gaining acceptance in non-liberal countries on which the speakers at the symposium focused. Four of the six speakers at the symposium presented research findings, with two focusing on perception of learner autonomy by student teachers and two on the nature of autonomous learning. Two talks gave recommendations on how to exploit learners' predisposition to learner autonomy.

## Student teachers' perception of learner autonomy

In her talk **Nkechi Christopher** presented findings on student teachers' perception of learner autonomy and its practicability in Nigeria. The study was predicated on the assumptions that learner autonomy has not been adopted in language teaching in Nigeria; the group studied were unaware of it; the adoption of a learner autonomy style of language teaching will need to be preceded by an acceptance of its principles and the willingness of teachers to shift from the transmission method. She discovered that the respondents were generally well-disposed to a conceptualisation of language learning based on the principles of learner autonomy. The respondents' level of agreement with learner autonomy principles was appreciable but less so on issues of involving learners in the planning, monitoring and teaching process. Similarly, respondents' rating of the use of some learner autonomy enhancing strategies showed the lowest score in learner involvement in the teaching process. On culture, more male respondents than female ones believed that learner autonomy will encourage learner rudeness to teachers. All the same, the respondents favoured introducing learner autonomy to teachers—more of them preferring it as part of continued professional development rather than during initial training. This researcher opts for the latter as teachers are more predisposed to learning during initial training and because in-service development is not an established culture for most teachers in Nigeria.

**Cem Balçıkanlı** took the discussion on student teachers' perceptions of learner autonomy further by reporting on student teachers' perspectives of learner autonomy in the Turkish context but as it relates to their own learning. He wanted to confirm the assertion that learners' active involvement in decisions concerning their own learning supports better learning by making learning more focused and purposeful (Little 1991; Dam 1995). Student teachers' perception and experience with learner autonomy is of great importance as it will inevitably determine the extent of application of learner autonomy principles in their practice. In a study carried out in the ELT Department of Gazi University, he administered a questionnaire developed by Camilleri (1997) to 102 student teachers and interviewed twenty in five groups. The study findings indicate that student teachers are extremely positive towards the adoption of learner autonomy and believe that teachers should adopt learner-centred approaches in teaching EFL. However, the respondents wanted learners left out of decisions on time, place and methodology of lessons as well as textbook selection (in line with the Turkish educational system). Deriving conclusions from other findings in the study, he recommends that teacher educators encourage their students to engage in out-of-class tasks so as to increase independence; involve their students in decision making on teaching process; encourage students to experience the use of strategies through indulgence in strategy training sessions; and use portfolio assessment to provide student teachers with more insight into the development of practical knowledge, teaching behaviour and thought processes.

## Assessment of autonomous learning

**Aylin Köyalan Coşkun** in her talk on autonomy through self-access centres reported her study of the self-access centre (SAC) at her university. The aim of the study was to investigate the effectiveness of the SAC in terms of learners' attitudes, behaviours and practices. She observed that learner autonomy has been gaining ground in ELT since the 1960s. This development stems from the fact that learning can only occur if learners take responsibility for their own learning and are able to appreciate their role in the process. On the other hand, students' needs, styles of learning, interests, psychological and personal factors, varying study habits and levels of motivation and a variety of cultural traits are to be taken into consideration. Therefore, it was assumed in the university's programme that when students were taught how to learn on their own in self-access centres, a great many language teaching problems could be solved. The study findings suggest that the SAC facilitates learning, encourages learners to change their approaches to learning, and is valued by both the teachers and the students. However, in spite of its benefits, the SAC has not necessarily led to autonomy.

In a presentation on a similar topic **Xianghu Liu** spoke on Chinese higher-education students' use of IT for autonomous learning. He investigated Chinese higher-education students' attitude to and use of computers for autonomous learning of English out of class. A questionnaire was administered to 160 participants and in-depth follow-up interviews with six participants and six of their teachers were conducted. In line with a theoretical framework in the literature (Kaltenböck 2001; Saita, Harrison and Inmam 1998; Healey 1999; Kenning 1996), the study findings demonstrate that the students had positive attitudes towards autonomous learning and that the use of computers in learning English is effective. Additionally, the students and their teachers considered CALL (computer assisted language learning), a more effective way of learning English than other approaches.

Since learner autonomy and learner motivation are important in EFL and are both enhanced by CALL, Liu suggested that information technology be exploited for solving English language learning problems such as inefficient learning strategies and poor oral and listening performance, that for long have constituted limitations on teaching English in China. Furthermore, he recommended that teachers be given better training; English textbooks accompanied by CD-ROMs and linked to relevant learning websites; and more funds invested on computer access and other learning facilities for higher-education students.

## Naturalisation of learner autonomy

**Khaldah Al Mansoori** took a far-reaching position in her talk on 'EFL autonomous learner: a strategy for life'. She believes that to become independent, more productive and to be able to cope in a fast-changing world, EFL learners should be empowered with learner autonomy strategies (Lamb 2004) through educational policy design and classroom practices. Her talk indicated that learner autonomy presupposes a life plan geared to attaining set goals. In her very engaging and thought-provoking presentation, she led the audience through a series of self-analysing questions for developing a 'strategy for life'.

Clearly defining the purpose of learning a foreign language should be preceded by evolving a personal plan drawn in line with one's values, beliefs and objectives. The plan serves as a clear roadmap, guiding the learner on the steps to be taken in life. Learners must become aware of where they are heading in life, be trained on how to start a plan and the place of the language they are learning in their plan. Based on

Steven Covey's concepts, there are three circles that are of great interest in the 'strategy of life':

Teachers should develop motivation and independence in their learners (Cottera 1999) and encourage the young learners to develop a plan, helping learners to cover all aspects of their life where the language being learned is important.

**Xiaoli Jiang's** talk on fostering learner autonomy through powerful proverbs was based on her doctoral research findings that Chinese students learning English successfully derived their determination from certain proverbs. She observed that the psychological, cultural and linguistic content as well as the motivating potential of Chinese proverbs might enhance the construction of learner autonomy concepts in teaching EFL in China and therefore should be used in the English classroom.

In conclusion, the talks at the autonomy symposium indicate that learner autonomy enjoys acceptability even in places where it is yet to take root; learners and teachers find autonomous learning effective in language learning; and learner autonomy will gain much acceptability in areas with traditions of dependency if learners are made to see where language learning fits into in their life plan. There are, however, some lingering questions.

Email: nmxtopher@gmail.com, balcikanli@gazi.edu.tr, aylin.koyalan@ieu.edu.tr, liuxh863@hotmail.com, onlyme_2020@hotmail.com, xiaoli.jiang@gmail.com

## References

Camilleri, G. 1997. *Learner Autonomy: The Teachers' Views.* Retrieved on 18, April 2007 from www.ecml.at/documents/pubCamilleriG_E.pdf

Covey, S. R. 1989. *The Seven Habits of Highly Effective People: Restoring the Character Ethic.* London: Simon and Schuster.

Kenning, M. 1996. 'IT and autonomy' in E. Broady and M. Kenning. *Promoting Learner Autonomy in University Language Teaching.* London: Association for French Language Studies: 121–38.

## 2.8 Learner autonomy: perspectives from Thai university teachers and their students

**Janchai Wongphothisarn** *University of Exeter, Exeter, UK*

### Introduction

Learner autonomy has become a desirable goal in many educational contexts across the globe, including Thailand, owing to the increasing emphasis on lifelong learning. Before learners can acquire lifelong learning skills, they need to become autonomous learners who can take control over their own learning and apply these learning skills to all manner of real-life scenarios. Helping learners to become autonomous is a key theme in the process of language learning and teaching as well as in other fields. In order to succeed in promoting learner autonomy in a Thai context, we need to understand how our learners perceive autonomous learning and their responsibilities in learning. Moreover, teachers' attitudes towards learner autonomy are significant and should be explored as they can indicate how ready the teachers are to promote and enhance the practice of learner autonomy.

### The study

The study which I presented at the conference was carried out to gain a better understanding of the perceptions of Thai teachers and students at university level towards learner autonomy. The study also aimed at exploring how Thai university teachers promote learner autonomy to their students. The results of the study can be used as initial indications for the implementation of a learner autonomy policy and for empowering learners for lifelong learning in the research context.

### Methodology

The study had two main research questions: what are the perceptions of Thai teachers and their students regarding autonomy in language learning? And how, if at all, do Thai teachers attempt to promote learner autonomy in their practice? The study was carried out within an interpretative paradigm using a qualitative approach. The participants were five Thai English teachers and six fourth-year students in the School of Humanities at the University of the Thai Chamber of Commerce, Bangkok. Semi-structured interviews were used to yield the data along with classroom observation.

### Selected findings

#### Teachers' perceptions of learner autonomy

The results reveal that teachers clearly had a good understanding of theoretical concepts relating to autonomous learning. When exploring their understandings of learning, the teachers frequently recounted that they did not believe that Thai students were well suited to this form of learning. They were of the opinion that their students were too attached to traditional ways of learning, and unwilling to migrate to a new way of learning, unless coerced by the prospects of rewards such as grades. The teachers were generally of the opinion that their role in an ideal situation would be one of a facilitator but that in reality this was neither appropriate nor possible due to the limitations of their students and their confidence in practising the facilitator role.

## Teachers' practices to promote learner autonomy

The teachers were asked what was needed to improve their students ability in autonomous learning and the skills they needed as teachers to achieve this. Interestingly the teachers placed emphasis upon making the students aware of learner autonomy, both its practical implementation and its merits in the longer term for their lives beyond formal structured education. The teachers mentioned that students need to be able to choose their own materials, and that the learning in class should be more problem based, challenging and stimulating. The notion of stimulation feeds into their desire to kickstart motivation from within the students themselves.

## Students' perceptions of learner autonomy

Most students affirmed that they had some idea about learner autonomy but could not define it with confidence. They seemed to have a narrow understanding of what it entails, restricting it to an idea of learning without teachers, using textbooks or e-learning. They also conveyed a generally negative attitude, ending their answers with the qualification that this narrow understanding of learner autonomy was not suitable for them or their peers. They were of the opinion that this form of learning was boring, with little interaction, required very high and possibly unrealistic levels of self discipline. Most of them preferred teacher-led learning.

## Conclusions

The policies in Thailand developed to promote learner autonomy are a recent introduction and will take time to bed down and yield their desired results. There needs to be change both in teaching practices and learner attitudes. It seems that the old way of learning in Thailand is quite deeply rooted, and that to fully implement the goals of the new policies it would be wise to encourage autonomous learning at an earlier stage of education than university level.

Email: J.Wongphothisarn@exeter.ac.uk

# 3 Professional development of teachers

## 3.1 Symposium on initial teacher training (ITT)

**Convenor: Sandra Piai** *University of St Andrews, Scotland* with
**Stephen Andrews** *University of Hong Kong, Hong Kong*
**Jennifer Book** *University of Sussex, England*
**Ewa Brodzinska** *University of Bangor, Wales*
**Anja Burkert** *University of Graz, Austria* and
**Aleksandra Wach** *Adam Mickiewicz University, Poland*

The ITT symposium brought together six presenters from six different countries all interested in different aspects of initial teacher education from developing language awareness through teaching practice (TP) to reflective tools. **Stephen Andrews** opened the symposium by discussing issues related to teacher language awareness (TLA), which focuses on the interface between what teachers know, or need to know, about language and their pedagogical practice. TLA has a procedural dimension ('awareness') as well as a declarative dimension ('knowledge') and, in order to be a 'language-aware' practitioner, prospective teachers need to be helped to 'enact' knowledge, i.e to develop the kinds of organised understanding and skills that support effective action. The major challenge for teacher educators is the 'knowledge transfer' challenge: making the bridge between the declarative and procedural dimensions of TLA, thus helping novice teachers learn to 'enact' knowledge.

Approaches to the design of TLA courses and strategies to address the challenge of knowledge transfer were presented. These focused on the approaches adopted on a pedagogic grammar (PG) course in Year 3 of a four-year undergraduate programme at the University of Hong Kong. Stephen Andrews suggested that the timing of the course played a key role in addressing the 'knowledge transfer' challenge. The course was closely integrated with a nine-week block of TP and, just before the practicum, students were assigned various tasks relating to their experiences of dealing with grammar in their TP schools. The PG course then started as soon as TP finished and provided students with opportunities to reflect on their own recent experiences of dealing with grammar in the secondary school classroom and to re-evaluate some of their grammar-related pedagogical decisions in the light of knowledge gained on the course. This process of reflection and re-evaluation was reinforced by the use of portfolio assessment.

**Ewa Brodzinska** then reported on a diary study carried out on four final-year BA students at Bangor University who had *never* taught EFL before. It considered how 'affect' influenced trainees at this delicate stage. The study adopted a five-step procedure and resulted in the identification of 13 'themes' that generated negative feelings and nine which boosted positive feelings shown in descending order according to frequency of mention, distribution and saliency (Allwright and Bailey 1991):

| Negative feelings | Positive feelings |
|---|---|
| 1. unforeseen events | positive reinforcement |
| 2. timing | positive student response |
| 3. assessment/observation | tutor—calming effect |
| 4. performance—actually teaching | thorough planning |
| 5. lack of subject knowledge—grammar | feedback |
| 6. lack of information on students in TP classes | general 'feel-good' factor |
| 7. speaking in public | personal study |
| 8. lack of teaching experience—familiarity with levels | tried & tested methods |
| 9. fear of making mistakes | teaching solo |
| 10. role of teacher—adjusting to this role | |
| 11. lack of student response | |
| 12. uncertainty about lesson content | |
| 13. assuming responsibility—taking the initiative | |

*Figure 3.1.1 The influence of affect on trainee teachers during their first TP experience*

It appears that the process of becoming an EFL teacher is charged with both positive and negative emotion. In terms of providing support for trainees, it is not merely a question of eliminating anxiety, but of minimising the sources of debilitating anxiety and optimising the sources of facilitating anxiety. The study also revealed a mismatch between the students' wants and needs, especially as regards subject knowledge. 'Grammar' constituted the greatest gap in knowledge and yet the trainees appeared more concerned about 'timing' issues. This, unfortunately, reflects the view that many EFL teachers are not adequately trained in the very subject they teach (Andrews 1994).

The European Portfolio for Student Teachers of Languages (EPOSTL), a document designed to be used for reflection and self-assessment in initial teacher education, was then introduced by **Anja Burkert**. EPOSTL was developed by a team of six teacher educators from five different European countries at the European Centre for Modern Languages of the Council of Europe (ECML) in Graz, Austria and consists of three main parts:

1. *personal statement*: to reflect on general questions of teaching and on the experiences of student teachers as learners,
2. *self-assessment section*: consisting of 196 'I can' descriptors relating to the core didactic competences a teacher should strive to attain to promote reflection and self-assessment,
3. *dossier*: to make the outcomes of student teachers' self-assessment transparent and record examples of work relevant to teaching.

Each of the 196 descriptors is followed by an open bar to be coloured by student teachers according to their own self-assessment. It is not expected that all bars are completed by the end of the programme as teaching is considered a lifelong learning process. Thus the descriptors should not be regarded as a checklist, but should act as stimuli for discussions and dialogue between student teachers, their educators and mentors.

Anja Burkert also reported on the results of a questionnaire study carried out among secondary school teachers in Styria, Austria in relation to EPOSTL, which showed that teachers consider reflection and self-assessment as important concepts in initial teacher education. However, these had played only a minor role in their own teacher education and, although teachers are well informed about the recent trends in language education, i.e. learner autonomy, teacher autonomy and intercultural awareness, they do not feel confident implementing these in their teaching.

Staying with the theme of reflection, **Sandra Piai** and **Jennifer Book** then described how they had introduced critical incidents to encourage trainee teachers on initial teacher training courses to reflect in greater depth by identifying a positive or negative critical incident in their TP. Trainees were given a three-part questionnaire covering self-evaluation, reflection and critical incidents to be completed after each TP. The questionnaire was structured to help trainees identify key areas. The critical incidents were the final part of the questionnaire as it was felt that, after evaluating and reflecting, a critical incident should emerge. Three groups participated: two completed all three parts of the questionnaire, whereas the control group completed only the self-evaluation and reflections. At the end of the course a further questionnaire was distributed to investigate whether identifying critical incidents had helped trainees' teaching practice and development.

Overall, questionnaires from the two groups who had identified the critical incidents were more detailed and reflective compared to those of the control group. Examples of critical incidents ranged from language awareness to classroom management issues and most of them tended to be negative incidents (with one exception). The trainees felt that identifying critical incidents had helped them reflect more deeply, although it had not always been easy to identify one critical incident. Sandra and Jennifer concluded that more guidance and input on reflection is needed before trainees embark on TP and more support is necessary in post-teaching feedback to help trainees identify positive as well as negative critical incidents.

Finally **Aleksandra Wach** presented findings of a questionnaire study conducted with a group of 71 teacher-trainees to discover (a) how they evaluated the EFL didactics course and their obligatory practicum and (b) their suggestions to improve the quality of the teacher training programme. Data from questionnaires indicated a clear need for a more thorough selection of schools and supervising teachers in the practicum. This is now being undertaken, albeit rather randomly. The supervising teacher was an important factor, very often influencing the trainees' overall evaluation of their school teaching experience, and perhaps even the choice of their future career. One common sense suggestion was that the obligatory practicum should be conducted in at least two different school settings, preferably at different levels, which is not the case at the present time.

Generally, the practicum was a valuable experience for almost all trainees, from which they said they had learned a lot. The EFL didactics course at the university was also appreciated, although a considerable number of trainees expressed criticism of the theoretical courses, suggesting the implementation of purely practical classes offering ready-made teaching ideas. The fact that SLA (Second Language Acquisition) theory and EFL methodology provide useful insights into the teaching profession was not wholly recognised as not all trainees saw a direct link between the EFL teaching course and their teaching practice. Aleksandra Wach suggested that in order to provide a stronger link between the two, more team-planning and more systematic peer-teaching sessions should be provided within the course, which would hopefully lead to the development of enhanced self-reflection and self-evaluation by the trainees. Only then will the trainees be able to discover the theory-practice link and fully realise what it takes to be a successful foreign language teacher.

Email: smp6@st-andrews.ac.uk, sandrews@hkucc.hku.hk, waleks@ifa.amu.edu.pl, ewabrodzinska@hotmail.com, anja.burkert@aon.at, J.B.Book@sussex.ac.uk

## References

Allwright, D. and K. M. Bailey 1991. *Focus on the Language Classroom—An Introduction to Classroom Research for Language Teachers.* Cambridge: Cambridge University Press.

Andrews, S. 1994. 'The grammatical knowledge/awareness of native-speaker EFL teachers: what the trainers say' in M. Bygate, A. Tonkyn and E. Williams (eds.). *Grammar and the Language Teacher.* Prentice Hall International: 69–89.

## 3.2 Second language teaching methods course for pre-service language teachers

**Sumru Akcan** *Boğaziçi University, İstanbul, Turkey*

### Introduction

Every teacher education course should have a rationale, an explanation of what type of course it is, and why it has been designed in that way (Wallace 2001). This study investigates the impact of a second language teaching methods course on teacher efficacy by assessing teacher candidates' knowledge and skills in language teaching methodology. It also explores the modes of teaching and learning in the course. The course is offered in the third year of an undergraduate teacher education programme at an English-medium university in Istanbul, Turkey. It meets for three hours a week for 14 weeks. The purpose of this course is to familiarise pre-service English teachers with various language teaching methods, including the theory underlying each method. Pre-service teachers also gain experience applying the methods through peer teaching during the course.

### Design of the course

The course syllabus consists of reading materials that focus on the historical background of language teaching methods, including the oral approach (e.g., audiolingual method, direct method), comprehension-based approach (e.g., total physical response), humanistic-based approach (e.g., community language learning), cognitive approach (e.g., the Silent Way), and communicative approach (e.g., content-based language instruction, task-based language instruction). Modes of teaching and learning in the course include peer teachings, discussions of video sessions about a particular method, and teaching philosophy papers written by the teacher candidates. The main course objectives are: (a) to evaluate critically different approaches and methods in the field of language teaching and (b) to help teacher candidates establish their own teaching philosophies at the end of the course.

## Research design

Data for the study were collected from 13 student teachers during the academic year 2006–2007 through (a) interviews with pre-service teachers, (b) evaluation of the teaching philosophy papers, and (c) evaluation of the feedback sessions on peer teaching. In this study, teacher efficacy is defined as 'the teacher's belief in his or her capability to organize and execute courses of action required to accomplish ... a task' (Tschannen-Moran *et al.* 1998: 233). An adapted version of TSES (Teachers' Sense of Efficacy Scale; Tschannen-Moran and Woolfolk-Hoy 2001), with four items for each of three dimensions, was used to assess pre-service teachers' efficacy. The three dimensions are: teachers' efficacy for engaging student learning, for managing EFL classes, and for implementing instructional strategies. Pre- and post-tests using the TSES were given to the teacher candidates at the beginning and end of the semester.

## Findings

The average of the three TSES subscales was obtained for the pre-test (M:75.92; SD:16.075) and for the post-test (M: 89.92; SD: 9.349). A correlated samples t-test revealed that the post-test mean was significantly higher than that of the pre-test $(t_{(13)} = 3.364, p<.05)$. Findings indicated that the second language teaching methods course had a positive impact on the teacher efficacy of the teacher candidates. The pre-service language teachers improved their decision-making skills in selecting methods and materials for different levels of EFL classes and language learners. They became more aware of the characteristics of young and adult learners when designing lessons. They became familiar with various techniques and enhanced their understanding towards different implementations of a technique (e.g., role-playing, use of visual aids) in various language teaching methodologies.

The data show that the teacher candidates developed their self-confidence during peer teaching sessions. They reported that peer teaching sessions were the most effective and helpful part of the course, because they learned the theory and the practice underlying each method by demonstrating them to their peers. The peer teaching sessions also increased pre-service teachers' confidence to select methods based on the learners' age, interest, and proficiency levels. Furthermore, they found peer teaching effective in providing a context similar to real classrooms and in helping them to solve potential in-class problems.

## Conclusion

At the end of the course, the teacher candidates reached an understanding that there is no one best method and they need to be prepared for designing lessons based on their learners' abilities, interests, age, and proficiency levels. The pre-service language teachers increased their understanding of the theory and practice of different methods, and this helped them form their own teaching philosophies in teaching a second language.

Email: akcans@boun.edu.tr

## References

Tschannen-Moran, M., A. Woolfolk-Hoy and W.K.Hoy. 1998. 'Teacher efficacy: its meaning and measurement'. *Review of Educational Research* 68/2: 202–48.

Tschannen-Moran, M. and A. Woolfolk-Hoy. 2001. 'Teacher efficacy: capturing an elusive construct'. *Teaching and Teacher Education* 17/7: 783–805.

Wallace, M. J. 2001. *Training Foreign Language Teachers: A Reflective Approach*. Cambridge: Cambridge University Press.

## 3.3 Introducing the Certificate in Advanced Methodology

**Mike Cattlin** *International House World Organisation London, UK*

The Certificate in Advanced Methodology (CAM) is the new International House course aimed at two principal markets: those teachers looking for a high level of methodological input for reasons of personal self-development to enable them to become more informed and reflective practitioners, and those who are specifically aiming at a Diploma level qualification such as the Cambridge DELTA.

It achieves this dual purpose by offering a menu of 25 modules which range from CELTA-revision sessions to high level academic input. Each participant will have to complete 20 modules to be awarded the certificate, although anyone can, of course, cover more than this number.

### Course aims

The main aims are three-fold:

- to develop teachers' theoretical knowledge of teaching and so make them more informed practitioners;
- to develop teachers' practical teaching ability and develop their self-analytical skills to make them more reflective practitioners; and
- to raise teachers' awareness of what they can expect from a Diploma level course and explicitly prepare them to take the written component of the Cambridge DELTA.

Beyond these, there are many subsidiary aims, including developing the abilities initially fostered on CELTA/IHC/Trinity courses, developing participants' study skills and their ability to critically read articles and make appropriate selections from published works, encouraging their reflection on past and current practice, encouraging professional debate amongst teachers, providing participants with a historical perspective and encouraging more experimentation and eclecticism in the classroom.

### Participant requirements

Participants should be practising teachers with a CELTA, International House Certificate or similar qualification plus a minimum of one year's full-time experience

(600 clock hours) of teaching adults in a recognised environment (i.e. a school with in-house teacher development programmes). They will need access, during the course, to a range of General English adult classes at a variety of levels (two from elementary, intermediate and advanced)—this is to allow for the required classroom-based action research—along with access to both methodological books and classroom materials and also to a computer with good internet access; this last requirement is particularly relevant if, as envisaged, many participants take the course online. The course input demands a C1 (Advanced) level of English.

## Length of the course

Each participant will be required to complete 20 modules and each module involves pre-reading, a 90-minute input session (or online alternative) and a series of classroom-based action research/homework tasks. Input time will therefore be 30 hours with another 30–60 hours needed for reading and post-session tasks plus some additional time for two assessed lesson assignments. The experiential nature of the course demands classroom time between sessions so the optimum period for the course is 5–6 months part-time or online.

## Course components

In addition to the 20–25 sessions, pre-session reading, and post-session tasks mentioned above, there is observation of peers/academic managers in their schools, lesson planning and delivery with self-observation, peer observation or director-of-studies observation, materials design and in-class experimentation with them, reflections on the course and on their teaching in the form of an ongoing journal, a 1000-word assignment on an area of language skills and a lesson plan for a self-observed lesson. Finally there is either a full assignment involving research into an area of language or skills and an observed lesson which helps learners in the target area, or a reflective essay on what they have learned from the course and how their teaching has developed, plus an observed lesson.

## Course content

There are six strands on the course including CELTA-revision which quickly moves up a gear into Teaching and Learning, Study Skills, Language Skills, Language and Materials, and Theories of Learning and Teaching.

## Tutors

Online tutors are taken from the International House list of DELTA-qualified trainers who are also Certificate in Online Tutoring graduates but there will be opportunities for Academic Managers from across the International House network to get involved as trainers of face-to-face courses in their own school and region. Both online and face-to-face versions will be opened up to non-International House teachers over the coming months.

## Course availability

The first online course has already started (17 May 2008) and the face-to-face version will follow in September of this year.

Email: mike.cattlin@ihworld.co.uk

## 3.4 Making a virtue of 'public lessons'—supporting teachers for change

**Qiang Wang** *Beijing Normal University, Beijing, China*

China's eighth round of curriculum reform in basic education began in 2001. The newly issued English curriculum has reflected a clear shift of emphasis in goals from pure language teaching to whole-person education through language teaching. All teaching aims are described in terms of what students should be able to do with the language rather than what the teachers should teach. The new curriculum also stresses helping students to gradually take more responsibility for their own learning. The reform has followed a top-down process and posed tremendous challenges to teachers.

To support teachers for change, public demonstration lessons have been used as common practice for in-service teacher training at regional, provincial, and national levels to help disseminate new ideas, promote good teaching, and in particular, to help teachers see how new ideas can be put into classroom practice. However, public lessons have been criticised for their often 'artificial' contexts, staged performances, and competitive purposes. As little research has been conducted to investigate teachers' views on the kind of support needed, this paper reports on a survey study carried out in 2007 with 563 junior and senior high school teachers of English in four provinces using an open-ended questionnaire to find out teachers' attitudes towards change, their perceived difficulties, and their training needs. Then, an alternative model for using public lessons to promote change was proposed and applied. The main findings were as follows:

1.  48 per cent of junior and 35 per cent of senior high school English teachers held positive attitudes towards curriculum change while 34 per cent of junior and 50 per cent of senior teachers held mixed views - they recognised the need for change but felt difficult and worried. A small percentage of the teachers held negative views. See Figure 3.4.1 below.

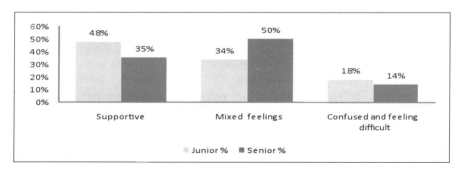

*Figure 3.4.1 Teachers' attitudes towards curriculum change*

2.  As regards difficulties, the one most often mentioned was the change to new textbooks which required new skills and demanded more preparation time. See Figure 3.4.2 below.

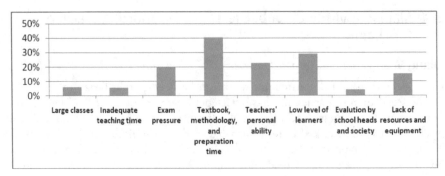

*Figure 3.4.2 Teachers' perceived difficulties*

**3.** When asked about training needs, many teachers in the survey called for fewer theory-oriented talks but more practical demonstrations. Figure 3.4.3 shows that observing and discussing demonstration lessons was the most often expressed training need (62 per cent).

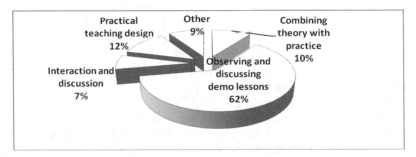

*Figure 3.4.3 Teachers' training needs*

The findings suggest that training that focuses on 'why' issues about curriculum change is not sufficient. It is the 'how' issue that needs more attention. Teachers need to understand curriculum ideas with reference to practice so that they can see how to teach within a context of large classes under exam pressures. Obviously, 'public lessons' as a bottom-up strategy has an important role to play in this respect. Moreover, nobody, in the process of change, including curriculum developers, teacher educators, teacher trainers, various levels of change agents, and classroom teachers, possesses all the expertise in terms of how to implement change. All parties involved need to collaborate to clarify meaning and seek out effective strategies.

To make a virtue of public lessons, an alternative model which integrates a top-down with a bottom-up process was proposed and applied. The model is characterised by using public lessons as a platform for team-building, leadership, collaboration, and negotiation among curriculum experts, materials developers, local change agents and classroom teachers. See Figure 3.4.4 below.

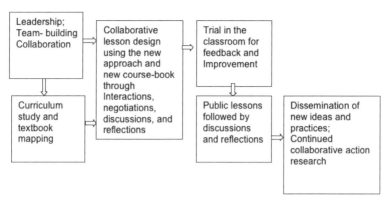

*Figure 3.4.4 An alternative model for using public lessons to support change*

Firstly a project team consisting of curriculum developers, textbook writers, local ELT supervisors and selected classroom teachers was formed. Curriculum study, textbook mapping, collaborative lesson design, and trial and feedback in classrooms followed by reflections and improvements was carried out. Lessons based on decisions taken during this process were then conducted publicly in natural classroom contexts to demonstrate good practice and disseminate new ideas. A forum was also created for teachers to share their views and discuss any issues arising from the lessons. In this way, public lessons helped increase collaboration instead of competitiveness, and promoted a community of practice and ownership rather than individual performance. Public lessons then function as a bridge as well as a scaffold to support teachers in transforming curriculum ideas into classroom practice. They create opportunities for collaborative learning, exploratory practice, and innovative teaching. The revised model for public lessons has received positive feedback from local educational authorities, from the teachers who offered the public lessons and from the teachers who participated in observations and discussions.

Email: wang_qiang99@yahoo.com

## 3.5 The role of online tutors in supporting teacher education

**Michael Bowles**  *British Council, Seoul, Republic of Korea*

### Overview

This presentation described a study that attempted to identify the online roles performed by course tutors through the messages they posted on the asynchronous, computer-mediated forums which are used as part of the Distance DELTA (Diploma in English Language Teaching to Adults) course and how these had the potential to contribute to the professional development of the course participants.

## Asynchronous computer-mediated communication (CMC) and in-service teacher education

A reflective and social constructivist approach was identified as the most suitable for the professional development of experienced teachers on an in-service teacher education course. In addition, asynchronous computer-mediated communication, through the use of online threaded forums, is seen as an ideal way to support this development when the course is conducted at a distance because its characteristics, such as the written medium and the time delay, have the potential to encourage such actions as critical reflection, knowledge construction and collaborative learning.

## The roles of online tutors and teacher education

The roles of online tutors using asynchronous threaded forums, as identified in the literature, were examined within Salmon's (2002, 2003) five-stage model of teaching and learning online and it would appear that there is a significant amount of congruence between these and the roles of teacher educators on face-to-face courses. In particular, the pedagogical roles of encouraging reflection and supporting knowledge construction as well as the social roles of encouraging dialogue are seen as vital in promoting and encouraging teacher learning.

## The learning context: the distance DELTA Course

This course aims to meet the needs of English language teachers who prefer to complete a DELTA course part-time by distance learning whilst remaining in their own teaching context. Course participants can access a dedicated website on which they can use asynchronous discussion forums. These are moderated by course tutors and it is the roles they perform through the messages that they posted on the forums that were described and analysed in this study to determine whether they had the potential for contributing to the teachers' professional development.

## The research design

This research employed two qualitative research tools, namely content analysis and semi-structured questionnaires, in order to gather and analyse data to help answer the two research questions. Aspects of reliability and validity were addressed at all stages of the research and a number of ethical considerations were also taken into account.

## Description and analysis of the results

There were three main findings: firstly, that the main roles performed by the course tutors were social in nature with few instances of pedagogical roles that had the potential to support the professional development of the course participants through a social constructivist approach to teacher education. Neither the course participants nor the course tutors considered the forums and the online contributions made by the course tutors particularly relevant to the professional development of the course participants. It was felt that they gained more from the feedback on draft assignments and through personal e-mail correspondence with course tutors.

Secondly, there was a gap between reality and the perceptions of course tutors. While the number of exchange acts in which a social role was performed was the highest, course tutors felt that the main role they performed was pedagogical.

Thirdly, that there was a wide difference in both the number and length of messages posted by different course tutors, as well as in the types of roles they performed, which suggests that some tutors were more committed to the use of the course participants' forums than others.

## Discussion, recommendations and postscript

Three recommendations were made to try and increase the commitment of both the course tutors and the course participants to using the forums.

Firstly, it is vital that all course tutors complete an online training course on online tutoring, so they gain an understanding of what it is like to learn online and the skills required by effective tutors. In particular, they need to be more aware of the how the theory of social constructivism underpins learning through asynchronous CMC. There are several courses currently available to learn about these roles, including:

* Consultants-E
  http://www.theconsultants-e.com/courses/em/index.asp
* University of Oxford
  http://cpd.conted.ox.ac.uk/personaldev/courses/effective_online_tutoring.asp

Secondly, there is a need to fully integrate the forums into the course, through online tasks (or e-tivities) which are assessed in some way.

Finally, the forums themselves need to be organised appropriately to facilitate discussion and online collaboration between participants. There could, for example, be several discussion areas on assignments, articles, general issues and an anonymous discussion area.

Email: Michael.Bowles@britishcouncil.or.kr

## References

Salmon, G. 2002. *E-tivities: the Key to Active Online Learning*. London: Kogan Page.

Salmon, G. 2003. *E-moderating: The Key to Teaching and Learning Online*. London and New York: Routledge Falmer.

# 3.6 What keeps teachers developing?

**Susan Barduhn** *SIT Graduate Institute, Brattleboro, USA*

## Introduction

What helps great teachers persevere—in spite of everything? My presentation looked at teachers who continue to be energised, fascinated and happily committed to teaching. These are the ones who keep going to conferences, keep reading new books on teaching, keep learning from other teachers and from their students. What keeps these teachers developing—in spite of everything? And what are the implications for teacher education?

## Why teachers go into teaching

It is possible to divide reasons for teachers entering the profession into three categories: practical or external reasons, personality type, and passion. Of particular interest in my study is the second of these. Maslach (2003) states that people who choose the helping professions tend to have high needs for approval, and heightened expectations of themselves. Nieto (2003) in her study of teachers who remain in the profession in spite of challenging contexts, found that the attraction is the opportunity to teach well and know it matters. Some describe it as a vocation, a calling.

## Why teachers drop out

Even under the best of circumstances, teaching is a demanding job, and most teachers do not work under the best of circumstances. The enthusiasm and idealism that caused them to choose teaching as a career dissipate quickly for many. Researchers have found that nearly half of all new teachers in urban public schools in the US quit within five years. Burnout and isolation are the main causes.

## Why teachers stay in the profession

In spite of the difficulties, many teachers persevere. I identified nine reasons for this: peer support, early rewards, student success, knowing that the subject matters, intellectual challenge, enjoying the life of a teacher, hope/optimism/faith, empowering experiences working within an educational system, variety and opportunities for risk taking.

There are other teachers, though, who not only stay in the profession, but are devoted to their own professional development.

## Why teachers not only stay in the profession, but actively keep developing

Perhaps one particularly important factor is persistence. I realised this when I was attending a talk about persistence in literacy students who keep working on their difficulties until they are successful. The talk wasn't about which techniques were most effective for achieving success, but about the students, and what it was in their personal make-up and experience that made them the ones who persisted.

All of the reasons for teachers remaining in teaching apply, and there are others:

• growing with colleagues,
• a commitment to and joy in lifelong learning,
• making opportunities for reflection,
• intellectual satisfaction,
• respect and belief in our students,
• congruence and presence.

A colleague who, like me, has been teaching for over 30 years, believes that for those of us who stay in the profession and continue to love it, an increasing source of fascination is presence, that is, being truly aware and mindful during teaching, connecting with the energy and dynamics of the actual learning that is taking place at each moment.

## Implications for teacher education

Awareness of burnout should be available at the workplace and as part of training. If trainees had more accurate expectations about the profession they are joining and what the future offers in that profession, there would be fewer reality shocks. Training should also include developing the special 'people skills' that will be required to deal with delicate problems such as telling students that they have failed, for example. The value of learning to use both objective detachment and sensitive concern could be explored before their emotions come under pressure.

Teacher education programmes need to emphasise that in the long run what energises and re-inspires teachers are lifelong opportunities to grow with colleagues, a commitment to and belief in the value and joy of lifelong learning, opportunities for reflection and intellectual satisfaction, belief in our students, and the power and fascination of being truly present during teaching.

Email: susan.barduhn@sit.edu

## References

Maslach, C. 2003. *Burnout: The Cost of Caring.* Cambridge, Mass.: Malor Books.

Nieto, S. 2003. *What Keeps Teachers Going?* New York: Teachers' College.

# 3.7 A class-centred framework for teacher professional development

**Rose M. Senior** *The University of Western Australia, Perth, Australia*

## Introduction

In his bravura *pecha kucha* performance at the end of the first day of the IATEFL 2008 Conference, Jeremy Harmer captivated his audience with the plethora of statements that he managed to cram into his allocated six-minute-40-second time-slot. One point that he made was the rushed nature of some introductory language teacher training courses. It is therefore hardly surprising that newly-trained teachers tend to be inward-looking, concentrating on themselves and their lesson delivery, rather than on the students and how well they are learning. It is only later that teachers come to view their classes holistically and to understand the importance of the relationships that they build with their classes—and of the well-being of their classes as wholes: the 'us' part of the equation.

## Classroom-based origins of class-centred teaching

In my presentation I focused on the notion of class-centred teaching (Senior 2002), a concept that emerged from an analysis and interpretation of the beliefs, motivations and classroom behaviour of 100 experienced language teachers (Senior 2006). Particularly in communicative classrooms (where interacting with peers in pair-work, small-group tasks or mingling activities is an integral part of classroom life) common sense suggests that the better that students get along with the teacher and with one another, the more willingly and enthusiastically they will participate in interactive tasks—and the more effectively they will learn. The classroom behaviour of experienced teachers reflects this common-sense assumption. Armed with an intuitive understanding of group-development principles (Dörnyei and Murphey 2003), experienced teachers behave in ways that encourage their classes to evolve into groups that demonstrate a spirit of cohesion.

## Definition of class-centred teaching

Class-centred teaching, then, means teaching and managing classes in such a way that each class has the best possible chance of developing into the kind of group that is a pleasure to teach: one in which the students are alert, responsive and respectful towards the teacher, and friendly, trusting and open-minded with one another. Such class groups have dynamic, vibrant atmospheres in which spontaneous events and behaviours serve to enhance (rather than to inhibit) the development of a sense of community within the class as a whole. Such classes are often characterised by spontaneous bursts of whole-class laughter that serve to affirm that a spirit of well-being prevails within the room. Laughter in such classes involves everyone (including the teacher) laughing briefly together before returning to the task at hand. It goes without saying that the kind of laughter that occurs in cohesive classes and that is valued by class-centred teachers is of the 'laughing with', as opposed to the 'laughing at', variety.

## Focus of the presentation

In my presentation I touched briefly on a number of aspects of class-centred teaching. I used the image of the double helix to emphasise how class-centred teachers understand that pedagogically- and socially-driven classroom behaviours cannot be teased apart—and behave in ways that are appropriate from *both* a teaching *and* a social perspective. I then used the image of the proverbial line in the sand—contrasted to an inclusive circle—to draw attention to the fact that class-centred teachers find appropriate ways of reducing the traditional 'me versus them' teacher/student divide—while at the same time maintaining their authority as teachers. I also made the point that class-centred teachers welcome diversity in their classes, regarding it as an asset rather than a hindrance. Such teachers recognise that acknowledging and valuing student difference can be a powerful way of building a spirit of community within their class groups.

Towards the end of the presentation I gave a list of the following dimensions of class-centred teaching: rapport, balance, control, alternation, imagination, flexibility, sensitivity, responsiveness, adjustment and goal-orientation. I concluded by suggesting that the notion of class-centred teaching may provide a useful framework for professional development programmes.

## Postscript

After the session I was approached by a high-school teacher of Welsh who expressed excitement at the notion of class-centred teaching, explaining that it not only closely reflected her personal beliefs and classroom practices, but also provided valuable affirmation of her intuitive approach towards teaching and class management. Feedback such as this suggests that the notion of class-centred teaching may resonate with teachers in a range of diverse language teaching situations.

Email: rsenior@iinet.net.au

## References

Dörnyei, Z. and T. Murphey. 2003. *Group Dynamics in the Language Classroom*. Cambridge: Cambridge University Press.

Senior, R. 2002. 'A class-centred approach to language teaching'. *ELT Journal* 56/4: 397–403.

Senior, R. 2006. *The Experience of Language Teaching*. Cambridge: Cambridge University Press.

## 3.8 Six circles—activities for teacher development

**Duncan Foord** *OxfordTEFL, Barcelona, Spain*

Here is what one teacher wrote when asked about his development as a teacher:

> I spend so much time just keeping up that I haven't developed as a teacher as I otherwise might have. You work so hard just to stay afloat that attending workshops and development programmes or reading books is the last thing on your mind when you have free time. You want to get away from work … not do more!

My workshop aimed to address this teacher's concerns by answering the question: How can busy teachers integrate teacher development into their daily working life?

The workshop included three main stages:

- I proposed and explained my *six circles* model for contextualising teacher development;
- I proposed four key principles for evaluating teacher development activities;
- participants worked in small groups and looked at a selection of teacher development activities designed by me and evaluated them according to whether they met the four key principles and whether they themselves would want to use the activities for their own development.

### The six circles model

We can think of the teacher development we engage in as falling into six categories. These can be represented in six concentric circles. In the inner circle are activities involving the teacher working alone. We can call this circle 'me'. Reading a book or reflecting on a class you have taught would be examples. The second circle we can call 'me and my students'. Development in this circle would include getting feedback from students about your teaching or trying out new material with them. The third circle is 'me and my colleagues'. Activities in this circle might include peer observation, team teaching and staffroom support. The fourth circle is 'me and my school'. This includes activities such as teachers' meetings, carrying out projects and interaction with management and other members of staff. The fifth circle is 'me and my profession'. Examples of activities in this circle include attending and presenting at conferences, membership of professional communities and writing for publication. The sixth circle is 'me and my world'. In this circle the teacher looks at the effect they can have outside their teaching, on their family and friends and in the community.

The model has three key features. First, it caters for diversity of teacher learning styles and teacher contexts in ELT by emphasising the fact that development can be individual as well as collaborative. Secondly, the concentric circles reflect increasing levels of challenge. As the community you work with broadens, the more you require interpersonal, leadership and time management skills to carry forward activities. Thirdly, the circles provide memorable categories for teachers to refer to when discussing their development.

### Four key principles for evaluating teacher development activities

The first principle is that development has the most impact (on the teacher and her students) when it involves doing something (action). Reflection on teaching behaviours can inform our choice of action, but such reflection without action is merely a shopping list. We need to then go shopping! The second principle is that developmental activities need to be time efficient. Teachers can gain a lot through activities which give a developmental twist to regular classroom teaching. The third is that for busy teachers, making things happen requires time management and leadership skills. (Some of the activities proposed included these areas.) The fourth is that development occurs not only through teachers' *proactive* choices, but also as a result of how they *react* to challenges that arise in their working life such as being observed by a director of studies or being asked to use a new syllabus.

### Evaluating activities for teacher development

Participants worked in small groups and looked at some examples of activities designed by the presenter. The aim of the activities was to be accessible, practical and time efficient. The activities were step-by-step guides which are designed to help teachers in areas such as videoing themselves, getting feedback from students, dealing with colleagues and school management, action research, self reflection, case studies of students, personal motivation and time management. Participants evaluated the activities in terms of the criteria proposed and also discussed which they would personally like to use in their own teaching situations. Workshop participants and readers of this summary are welcome to request copies of my activities.

Email: duncan@oxfordtefl.com

## 3.9 Storytelling our learning: a narrative approach to language teacher education

**Christine Savvidou** *University of Nicosia, Cyprus*

Stories and storytelling play an important role in our development as teachers. Throughout the course of our careers, we are exposed to countless numbers and types of stories: 'sacred' stories about theories of teaching and learning; 'cover' stories which project an idealised view of ourselves as teachers; and 'secret' stories revealed only to trusted friends and colleagues (Clandinin and Connelly 1996). Significantly, stories never stay the same; they are constantly being re-worked depending on where, when and to whom the story is told. On this premise, I decided to explore the role and function of storytelling in the construction of teachers' professional knowledge. In this study, 'story' is defined as a particular type of discourse in which the narrator 'relates the self ... to a significant set of personal experiences' (Denzin 1989: 38).

While many of us attend courses, workshops and conferences to enhance our skills and knowledge of language teaching, the scope of professional development (PD) extends beyond such conscious and formal learning activities. Day (1999) defines 'professional development' as 'all natural learning experiences and those conscious and planned activities which are intended to be of direct or indirect benefit to the individual, group or school' (p. 4). Therefore, as a 'natural learning experience', storytelling plays a significant role in the way teachers make sense of their professional experiences. When asked about our experiences of teaching EFL, we generally tell a story and, often, it is not until we tell our story that we know what we think about these experiences. In this way our understanding of teaching and learning is constructed narratively; in other words, experience is recounted and understood as story (Bruner 1991).

Moreover, as a form of professional development, storytelling has several positive attributes: it supports *reflection* on practice; it is *relevant*, relating to teachers' own experiences and context; it is *teacher-centred*, at a time when many PD activities focus on how language learners learn; it is *collegial* since storytellers need an empathetic audience in the form of other teachers; and, finally, it supports *critical thinking*, since our stories often reveal discrepancies between theory and practice.

Against this background, I decided to construct a digital storytelling space where EFL teachers could share their stories of professional development, and I could analyse the role and function of storytelling in the construction of teachers' professional knowledge. Eight teachers self-selected and told stories of significant learning experiences. Using *MS Producer 2003*, I helped teachers transform their oral stories into a digital format, which integrated video, text and audio. These digital stories included teachers' experiences of research, postgraduate study, teacher-exchange, the first year of teaching and the use of ICT in language teaching. Stories were then uploaded onto a password-secure website and made available to colleagues. After viewing the stories, another five teachers responded with their own digital stories.

In a narrative analysis of the initial and responding stories, I identified five social and cognitive processes teachers used to construct understanding of their professional learning:

1. Connecting: the story includes an explicit bridge to connect one's own story with another's;
2. echoing: the story echoes another's story through repetition of key words, synonyms and themes;
3. developing: the story develops and explores meaning by recalling, analysing, reflecting on main themes in the story;
4. questioning: the story questions, doubts, criticises established knowledge, meanings and understandings;

**5.** constructing: the story demonstrates meta-cognitive awareness of new meanings, understandings and knowledge of the experience.

As part of the reflective paradigm, storytelling is more than reflective monologue. This analysis confirmed that storytelling is a social and collaborative process in which stories act as 'significant others' (Vygotsky 1978) in teacher learning. When teachers tell their stories, new stories are triggered; moreover, when teachers hear the stories of others, they re-story their own experiences. The connections that teachers created between their own stories and the stories of others—connecting, echoing, developing, questioning and constructing—allowed them to construct and reconstruct new understandings and awareness of professional knowledge.

One of the implications of this study is that storytelling acts as a form of professional dialogue. By creating a formal space for storytelling, teachers engaged in dialogue about their professional practice and development in TEFL. In conclusion, this study shows how teachers' construction of professional knowledge is a complex, dynamic and narrative process. Suggestions for future research include plans to create a digital storytelling network across a range of educational contexts.

Email: savvidou.c@unic.ac.cy

### References

Clandinin D. J. and F. M. Connelly. 1996. 'Teachers' professional knowledge landscapes: teacher stories—stories of teachers—school stories—stories of schools'. *Educational Researcher* 25/ 3: 24–30.

Day, C. 1999. *Challenging Teachers: The Challenges of Lifelong Learning.* London: Falmer Press.

Vygotsky, L. S. 1978. *Mind in Society: The Development of Higher Psychological Processes.* Cambridge, Mass.: Harvard University Press.

## 3.10 Trainer training across borders: the perils and the pitfalls

**Anne Wiseman** *The British Council, Bahrain*

### Background

This talk focused on some of the issues which arise when planning generic projects. In this example a project was designed for countries in the Middle East region; specifically Bahrain, Iraq, Yemen, UAE, Kuwait, Qatar, Oman and Saudi Arabia.

There are a number of commonalities between the above countries, yet at the same time there is great diversity politically, historically, economically and socially. For example, in some of these countries women and men may not sit in the same room together, and women are heavily veiled; in others the genders mix freely. In some, state-of-the-art education resources are present; in others, classrooms barely have windows and blackboards.

After discussions with the Ministries of Education (MsoE) in these countries regarding their education reform programmes, a regional project was designed to support the current infrastructure in the MsoE. It had a number of 'strands', the main one of which was a professional development programme for teacher trainers in each country. The trainer development programme consisted of three main components:

- teacher training workshops: sessions which the trainers could take away and use in their own training rooms;
- trainer training workshops: sessions which focussed on the micro skills of training; and
- session design: during which the participants designed their own training sessions, to be observed and edited after the course.

## The best laid plans ...

Much of what initially didn't go to plan related to a mismatch between the project's planned expectations and the existing systems and cultures. Some examples of this are:

1. *Mismatch in the selection of participants* It was agreed that participants should already be teacher trainers. In some countries the participants sent were teachers who were unlikely to become teacher trainers.
2. *The staging and time allocation of the programme* This could not be synchronised as originally planned because countries varied considerably in size and systems—one country has two MsoE—and in Iraq the difficulties in attempting to run the programme were insurmountable.
3. *Follow-up process* Observation and trialling of the participant-designed sessions were planned to take place after the course. However, once the trainers were back within their own systems, contact was difficult. Thus, editing the participant-designed sessions was delayed, which then affected the timing of the follow-up programmes.
4. *Stakeholder engagement* Although representatives from the different MsoE took part in the initial planning stages, communication systems within the MsoE were not always effective, so the expected 'buy in' from other key MoE staff was sporadic or non-existent.

We may also possibly attribute the somewhat haphazard engagement from key stakeholders to an initially superficial concept of stakeholders and their roles, which stemmed from a desire to control behaviour rather than to become involved in a stakeholder-led project. This in turn may have led to what Holliday (1994) terms tissue rejection.

## Thinking regionally: acting locally

Bearing in mind the above difficulties, we followed the example of the corporate sector by adapting to the diverse cultures in the region and 'embedding ' more into their systems. By the end of the first year we were in closer touch with the MsoE and adapted the programme to suit the trainers' circumstances and needs. We did this by:

- re-structuring the programmes according to the different MsoE hours/systems,
- taking gender mixes more into account,
- developing new trainer sessions relating to particular needs, such as English for English teachers/teaching large classes,

- observing participants' own sessions and editing them *during* the course, and
- setting up email communities linked to the teachers' professional networks for post-course contact.

Since these adaptations we have had much firmer 'buy in', and as a result all participants sent by MsoE are appropriate for the course, and have continued with the post-course programme.

## Conclusion

In summary, I would suggest that both cultural and behavioural norms need to be taken into account at the outset of any project design, as well as existing systems and resources. Two other key factors are the 'what's in it for me?' and 'who are *you?*' questions—the answers to which will have a strong impact on the success or otherwise of the project.

Finally, when designing regional projects:

- don't take anything for granted, including time,
- assume the process will be untidy and messy,
- build in experimentation and learning,
- work with underlying (or deep)societal structures,
- avoid cascading toolkits without engaging understanding, and
- help educators find their own answers instead of /as well as spreading 'best practice'.

Email: Anne.wiseman@britishcouncil.org.bg

## Reference

Holliday, A. 1994. *Appropriate Methodology and Social Context.* Cambridge: Cambridge University Press.

## 3.11 Quality assurance in a multilingual teacher education programme

**Briony Beaven** *Freelance, Munich, Germany*

EUROLTA, the European Certificate in Language Teaching to Adults, is a qualification for language teachers. It is taught and validated regionally and recognised by members of the International Certificate Conference (ICC), a non-government organisation with participatory status at the Council of Europe which aims to promote quality in foreign language learning and teaching. The Certificate was introduced in Switzerland and Scandinavia in the 1990s and in 2001 in Bavaria, Germany, where I have been a member of the working party and a supervisor. In the early days of EUROLTA courses in Bavaria, quality and consistency of training could not be assured as there was neither content standardisation nor a system for grading written work. Furthermore, due to lack of expertise amongst the trainers there was no lesson observation.

## EUROLTA teacher trainers

EUROLTA teacher trainers are of different nationalities and first languages, with differing levels of mastery of the lingua franca used in training and meetings. They have followed a variety of routes to becoming language teachers and later, trainers. The trainers' priorities in language teacher education and their methodological preferences are diverse. They adhere to a disparate range of conceptions about teaching and learning and their professional discourse is 'non-convergent' (Jonkman 1996). Many speak different languages during meetings, assuming that others will understand, or conduct separate discourses with members of their language community while the main discourse of the meeting continues in the lingua franca, German. Their discourse is also non-convergent in that they do not share common understandings of terminology or concepts (e.g., 'reading skills lesson', 'presentation of new grammar item').

## Towards quality and consistency

### Training quality through systems

A working party was created to plan a syllabus, standardise marking and create a system for lesson observation. The working party was also charged with improving the quality of the training processes.

*Syllabus*

A new syllabus was devised but many trainers were resistant to change. Flexibility was essential if trainer loyalty was to be retained but trainers who rejected all standardisation had to leave EUROLTA.

*Dossiers*

Written work was put into the hands of specially appointed assessors. They were given standardisation training and help in writing positive, useful feedback whatever the standard of the dossier.

*Lesson observation*

Pre-lesson contacts, lesson plans, formal observation and feedback were introduced. Trainer training and trouble-shooting clinics were provided. However, both the training sessions and first observations were problematic owing to features of this multilingual teacher education certificate such as:

- the teacher trainers observe lessons in many languages;
- the observer may not know the target language well;
- the teacher being observed may or may not be teaching their native language;
- observation criteria are interpreted differently across languages and cultures.

Agreement on criteria for 'satisfactory' lessons has not yet been reached.

### Training quality through supervision

Teacher trainer development techniques such as self-monitoring and journal keeping were considered but rejected as unsuitable for the target group, some of whom would not have a robust mental model of 'good' teacher training. A supervision process was adopted as more likely to result in better quality EUROLTA training and to gain acceptance from the trainers.

Transparency was achieved through criteria for appointing supervisors and for their visits to training sessions. The observation form for trainer supervision mirrors the lesson observation forms used by the trainers to observe trainees and thus reinforces an understanding of the observation criteria amongst less experienced trainers. The 'mirror' observation form also encourages trainers to model in their training the teaching criteria they assess when observing lessons; lectures, for example, would not meet the criterion for varied interaction patterns.

### Preparation for supervision

In the train-the-supervisor sessions participants reported on their training experiences in order to bring to the surface the variety of training approaches and beliefs. Non-convergent discourse was encouraged in small group work in order to endorse the multicultural, multilingual nature of the trainer team. Plenary work established which content areas, techniques and methods fit into the EUROLTA Certificate.

### First results

Early supervisions indicated the need for trainer training in workshop organisation, in pre-supervision conferences and in more positive wording of teacher trainer evaluations. It is hoped that initial difficulties can be overcome since the supervision process offers benefits to both teacher trainers and supervisors. Supervision provides trainers with a chance to reflect on their training plans and activities and to articulate that reflection. Supervision is a source of new ideas and provides motivation to continue and develop successful training techniques. It reduces trainer isolation. The intercultural, multilingual context gives supervisors the opportunity to extend their concepts of teacher trainer competence. This context also allows them to improve their empathetic assessment skills and to become familiar with linear and circular training models.

Email: brionybeaven@t-online.de

### References

Jonkman, R. 1996. 'Non-convergent discourse in Friesland as a special type of codeswitching'. Paper presented at the Sociolinguistics Symposium 11, Cardiff, UK, 5–7 September 1996.

ICC—The European Language Network—What is EUROLTA? http://www.icc-languages.eu/what_is_eurolta.php

## 3.12 Student teachers' development as writers of poetry

**Mikaela Björklund** *Åbo Akademi University, Vasa, Finland*

This summary reports on an on-going course development with the aim of encouraging other teacher educators and language teachers to challenge their students to engage in writing poetry in EFL. For several years I have had the privilege of introducing English poetry to student teachers with English as a subsidiary subject. For many student teachers poetry is still felt to be unfamiliar, sometimes even boring and irrelevant. The two main challenges have been:

1. to help student teachers discover English poetry, while at the same time providing more advanced students with the necessary motivating challenges; and
2. to support student teachers' development as readers and writers of poetry in English, while covering the prescribed content within very limited time frames.

The approach developed during the course is based upon the following main rationales:

- students need to be gently pushed into exceeding their previous achievements (cf. Vygotsky);
- students need to discover the processes of writing 'from within' in order to understand poetry and learn to appreciate the beauty of poetical patterns and techniques;
- student teachers need to experience as learners what they intend to use as teachers in order to add authenticity and self-confidence to the process of teaching.

A written questionnaire was developed to gain an insight into the student teachers' cognitive and affective starting-points in relation to poetry as shown in the example answers below:

**Q:** *How would you describe your relationship to English poetry?*
**A:** '… not much of a relationship …English poets are beautiful to listen to and read, as far as I have experienced, but I'd say my experiences aren't that huge.'
**A:** 'I just haven't got in contact with it. Maybe I think the way poetry is written in a foreign language is too symbolic and far-fetched for me to fully understand.'
**A:** 'That relationship do not exist.'

English poetry is often experienced as unfamiliar, but after this 5–6 week course (eight contact sessions of two hours each) the students have read, analysed and written poems. The first tasks familiarise them with short, simple contemporary poems that they can readily relate to (by, for example, Wendy Cope and William Carlos Williams) and with different kinds of imagery. The poems introduced during the course then represent increasingly earlier periods. By the end of the course a historic span from the twentieth to the fourteenth century has been covered. The older poems introduce the students to some of the most well-known closed forms and the students are asked to write poems where they focus on typical elements of content and/or form of the sonnet and ballad.

The increase in complexity of task can be regarded as remarkable during this short course, but interestingly enough students at all proficiency levels have been able to manage the tasks at their own level and to develop as writers of poetry. The majority of the course participants start out as poor and insensitive writers of poetry, but reach a high standard regarding both by the time they try out the demanding sonnet and ballad forms. These poems show not only an awareness of the traditional elements of form and content, but also a dawning voice and the originality of the student poet.

Furthermore, the course evaluation shows that their relationship to English poetry has undergone a distinct change towards greater familiarity, in most cases a favourable attitude and even a readiness to use poetry as one written genre in their own teaching, as shown by the following comments:

'Better than before. Now I'm more familiar with different authors of poetry in different centuries. I also feel more confident in using poetry in my becoming classroom with children.'

'I still don't like poems with difficult words since they're above my level of understanding, but I'm still fond of poetry .... I've learned that I can write own really good poems in English.'

'My relationship to poetry has improved. The step into using poetry in my teaching seems smaller to take now.'

By providing an exploratory and open learning environment, providing the participants with authentic texts and tasks, moving from simple to more complex ones (including alternatives in terms of complexity), all the students have developed. They have developed a perception of themselves as readers and writers of poetry and at the same time they have started to understand and in most cases also to appreciate the intricacies of some poetical patterns. When evaluating the course most students express that, to their own surprise, they have exceeded what they thought were their own limits.

Email: Mikacla.Bjorklund@abo.fi

# 4 Reading, writing, literacy and coursebooks

## 4.1 Expansive reading: the text and beyond

**Robert Hill** *Black Cat Publishing, Rapallo, Italy*

### Expansive reading: a definition and an example

Over recent decades, the major debate about reading seems to have centred on the relative merits of extensive versus intensive reading, and within this debate it appears that a major issue has been whether to accompany texts with comprehension tasks and perhaps language practice. Supporters of extensive reading maintain that comprehension tasks interrupt reading for pleasure, are unrealistic, or indeed useless for purposes of understanding the text.

I find that the bipolar choice for material designers implied by the extensive–intensive debate—to have or not to have comprehension and language tasks— is restrictive. In what I call 'expansive reading' the focus and range of post-reading tasks lead beyond the text into areas which are stimulating and educational. In addition to the possibility—but not the necessity—of comprehension, interpretation, evaluation and meaningful language work, a text can lead us to explore any of the following:

- the biography of the author: her/his life and times,
- the historical-cultural background of the text,
- cross-curricular connections,
- project work (including using the Internet),
- intertextuality, and
- intercultural awareness.

As a first example, I showed posters of recent film versions of *Beowulf* and covers of comic versions (an example of intertextuality), all showing Beowulf brandishing a sword. It is both educational and linguistically productive to interrogate these images. What do we know about swords in Anglo-Saxon times? An informative text told us that the common weapon was the spear, while the sword was the weapon of noble warriors (an example of the historical and cultural background of the text). Beowulf's sword was called Hrunting: what other weapons of heroes could we think of, such as Excalibur? (An example of intertextuality, with possibilities of project work.) And why do comic-book superheroes, with sophisticated technology at their disposal, use no weapons at all, or at most a sword or something similar? (An example of intertextuality, with possibilities of intercultural awareness and project work, providing great motivation for oral production.)

### Background, cross-curricular connections, intertextuality and intercultural awareness

Is background information optional or necessary? Necessary, according to a recent survey review of graded readers:

> Not all titles need background information and certainly not simple originals at the lower levels. Classics and modern novels on the other hand cry out for information about the author and the setting of the story.
> (Hill 2008)

Hill goes on to claim that it is even more necessary when texts from one culture are read by members of another culture.

Background information necessarily involves cross-curricular connections: as any fictional text is set in time and place, background information will always involve history and geography, perhaps social studies too. Particular contents of certain texts will also suggest links to other subjects, such as art, music, science, etc.

The academic term intertextuality (Kristeva 1969) has come to be used in many ways. It can refer to an author's deliberate allusions to a previous text (as in T.S. Eliot's *The Waste Land*, or in the samplings of modern pop songs), or to the connection to other texts made by reader her/himself while reading the text in question. It is the second kind of intertextuality which is pertinent in the language classroom, as it provokes thought and discussion; the first is a question of factual knowledge.

In a parallel, practical development, connection-making has become standard in American reading comprehension methodology, for example in the work of Keene and Zimmermann (2007). Three kinds of connection are identified: text-to-self connection; text-to-text connection; text-to-world connection.

In addition, a further connection for a reader might involve intercultural awareness—how the text might relate to the reader's own culture.

## Further examples

The plot of E. Nesbit's children's classic *Five Children and It* (1902) hinges on a creature, the 'sand fairy', who grants a group of children their—often reckless—wishes. Young learners are invited to think of the circumstances in which people can wish in their cultures (intercultural awareness), what stories and films they know where wishes are involved, how many wishes can be made, how long they last and whether there is a 'catch' (intertextuality). Even young learners can research *Aladdin* and *Cinderella* on the Internet.

Finally, I showed how Chaucer's *The Franklin's Tale* has intertextual connections with so many pop songs (the pains of unrequited love) and the rash promises of so many folk tales, and how Chaucer's medieval *demandes d'amour* ('questions of love' at the end of a story: in this case, which man behaved most nobly?) are like medieval ranking activities, guaranteed to provoke discussion!

Email: robert.hill@blackcat-cideb.com

## References

Hill, D. R. 2008. 'Graded readers in English'. *ELT Journal* 62/2: 184–204.

Keene E. O. and S. Zimmermann. 2007. *Mosaic of Thought*. London: Heinemann.

Kristeva, J. 1969. *Semiotikè: recherches pour une sémanalyse*. Paris: Seuil.

## 4.2 Sentence Response Thumbprints

**Chris Roland** *The British Council, Barcelona, Spain*

How can you encourage a class of 15, 20 or 30 students to engage with a text? These Sentence Response Thumbprints (or SRT's) may help. Simply by inserting a pair of square brackets at the end of each sentence, we can give students the opportunity to record their responses, line by line, and to use these as a point of entry for general classroom discussion or analysis of the writing on various levels. If students have to *respond* to a text, we increase the chances that they will engage with it.

Try it yourself!

- Please check the 'Interest index' below.
- Read the three texts.
- Mark your responses at the end of each sentence.

---

Interest index

3 = A hugely interesting sentence and high point of the story.
2 = Very interesting. Made me want to read on.
1 = This sentence was interesting enough to make me want to read the next.
0 = Left me feeling indifferent.
−1 = Bored me. Made me yawn.
−2 = Made me want to stop reading.
−3 = Nearly made my head fall off with boredom.

---

*Text 1*

She waited [ ]. He said nothing [ ]. She began to go red [ ]. He began to smile [ ]. She went redder; he smiled more broadly [ ]. It was indeed as large as he'd claimed but without any kind of commentary, its size was probably working against him right now [ ].

*Text 2*

The branch manager recoiled in horror [ ]. The mere logic of the calculations on Pete's balance sheet was enough to bring out the veins at his temples [ ]. Pete put his head in his hands [ ]. He wanted to offer a glimmer of hope at least [ ].
"I could always Tipp-Ex over the third column." [ ]
It was probably at that point the manager stopped breathing [ ].

*Text 3*

She'd been pleased with the Chinese characters freshly tattooed onto her right shoulder but was now getting funny looks from the men, and women, on the beach [ ]. She'd meant to have painted some defiantly yelled Gibsonian proclamation of liberty [ ]. Of course, the context in which she'd conducted her research might have set alarm bells ringing [ ]. The Chinese waiter had obligingly written 'free' in kanji for her on a paper serviette [ ]. Under the circumstances it was all quite understandable [ ]. She was now parading up and down the shoreline with a bare shoulder labelled *FREE! (of charge)* [ ].

Students could transfer the data to graphs like those below. Please try this yourself.

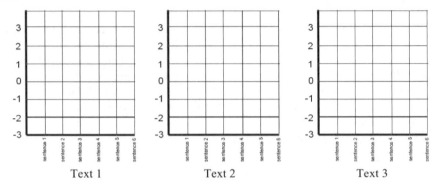

*Figure 4.2.1 Reading response text graphs*

What about the following questions?
1. Did you enjoy the activity?
2. Are your interest graphs different to your partner's? (for class work)
3. What do your graphs say about your own tastes as a reader?
4. What do they say about the texts themselves?
5. Look at the text you plotted the least impressive graph for. Is there anywhere in that text where you might be able to insert a more interesting sentence? What type of sentence would it be?
6. What would the graph of a really good story look like?
7. Which of the two stories below would you prefer to read?

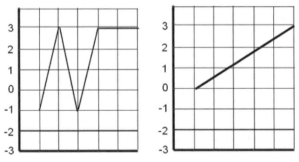

*Figure 4.2.2 Reading response text graphs: completed examples*

Students writing stories could be asked to insert empty sets of square brackets at the end of every sentence as they write. A classmate could then record *their* responses to the text before the work is handed in. This should encourage learners to think about writing for an audience.

If a text contains a lot of opinions or argument, we can change the index like this:

---

## Agreement index

  3 = I totally agree with this.
  2 = Agree.
  1 = Agree but not entirely.
50/50 = Neither agree nor disagree.
 −1 = Disagree but not entirely.
 −2 = Disagree.
 −3 = NO! NO! NO!

---

Or we can even use an 'Understanding index', like this:

---

## Understanding index

Wh?! = What?! I understand NOTHING NOTHING NOTHING!
?    = I'm not so sure about this sentence.
:-)   = I understand this sentence though there are some words that are new.
      *or* I understand all the words but I'm not so sure about the meaning.
100% = I understand this sentence completely.

---

Thumbprints could be lengthened to allow students to notice and record salient grammar patterns or repeating words, in keeping with an 'emergent' grammar approach such as Thornbury's (2001).

'Colour prints', are useful for primary classes or for poetry and literature. At the end of each sentence students select the colour they think would best represent the sentence as a whole and write, colour or thumbprint that colour with fresh paint into (an enlarged) set of brackets. Children could then choose their favourite sentence and paint a monochrome picture of it, using various shades of the base colour mixed with white. Literature classes could justify their choices in conversation.

Student response is something that is often overlooked in text books. There may be no room for the student to even record their answers to the questions that customarily follow a reading. If instead we make space for student responses by pre-printing texts with empty parentheses, the message is that personalised student responses form an integral part of class reading material.

Email: Chris.Roland@britishcouncil.es

## References

Thornbury, S. 2001. *Uncovering Grammar*. Oxford: Macmillan.

Schumann, J. 1999. 'A neurobiological perspective on affect and methodology in second language learning' in J. Arnold. *Affect in Language Learning*. Cambridge: Cambridge University Press.

Holme, R. 1991. *Talking Texts*. Harlow: Pilgrims Longman.

## 4.3 Teaching reading skills: mostly a waste of time?

**Catherine Walter** *Institute of Education, University of London, UK* and
**Michael Swan** *Freelance, Oxfordshire, UK*

The teaching of second-language reading typically involves instructing learners in the deployment of a battery of discrete 'reading skills': scanning, skimming, reading for gist, predicting, identifying main points, locating the source of anaphoric reference, etc. The underlying assumption, not usually made explicit, is that the learner effectively has a reading defect: s/he either does not possess these skills, or for one reason or another cannot 'transfer' them from the mother tongue. We challenge this metaphor of transfer: we believe that it is seriously misleading in principle, and that it serves in practice as the justification for a variety of relatively unproductive classroom activities. In its place, we propose a metaphor of access.

Work by Gernsbacher (1997) and others has shown that comprehension processes are independent of input mode. That is, comprehension involves the same processes whether the input is speech, written text, picture stories or moving images. Therefore, comprehension skill is not located 'in' the mother tongue, and cannot be transferred to the target language. Rather, when L1-literate learners become able to comprehend texts in L2, it is because they have reached the point where they can *access* their already-existing comprehension ability on the basis of L2 input. Earlier difficulty with L2 comprehension is best understood as resulting from overload: readers are fully occupied with decoding at the word and sentence level, and have little spare working memory capacity for higher-level processing. Two studies carried out by one of us (Walter) support this view.

Both studies involved two groups of French learners of English: lower-intermediate L2 learners, who had problems with comprehension of L2 texts which were linguistically at their level; and upper-intermediate learners, who could comprehend the same L2 texts. There was no difference between the two groups' comprehension of L1 texts.

The first study (Walter 2004) supported a prediction, based on Gernsbacher's framework, that the lower-intermediate learners were understanding the L2 texts sentence-by-sentence, but were not able to build reliable mental structures representing whole texts; while the upper-intermediate learners could do both. Thus, the lower-intermediates' problem was not related to proficiency in grammar or extent of vocabulary, since they were understanding each L2 sentence as they read it.

In the second study (Walter 2007), the same two groups were able to detect contradictions in L1 texts, and both groups detected contradictions of main points better than contradictions of subsidiary points. In L2 the upper-intermediate group performed only slightly less well than in L1. However, although the lower-intermediate group did not fail completely to detect contradictions in L2 texts, they performed spectacularly less well than in L1, and the 'main-ness' of the contradicted point was irrelevant. They could not access their comprehension skill.

There was a substantial difference between the L2-based verbal working memory (WM) scores of the two groups (and only a small difference between their L1-based scores). This corresponds to capacity problems being responsible for comprehension difficulty.

Therefore, it is not in our opinion useful to attempt to teach reading skills in a second language unless there is certainty: (1) that the learner does not already possess these skills, and (2) that s/he needs them. Recognising main points, for example, is an automatic result of normal comprehension processes, and need not be taught to most learners. It is also important to ensure that any skills one does set out to teach are in fact learnable and effective. This is not the case, for instance, for the alleged 'skill' of guessing unknown words from context. Research has shown, and it can easily be demonstrated practically, that unknown vocabulary can rarely be successfully processed in this way.

Students' L2 reading comprehension *can* however realistically be improved through training in dealing with the specific linguistic features that can make text hard to decode. These include rhetorical conventions that may be different from those in the L1, discourse markers whose function may not be apparent to learners, and difficulties caused by syntactic features such as embedding or the omission of relative pronouns. Fluency activities, for example extensive reading and paced reading with audiobooks, will also help to improve L2 comprehension.

Email: c.walter@ioe.ac.uk, swanmic@gmail.com

## References

Gernsbacher, M.A. 1997. 'Two decades of structure building'. *Discourse Processes* 23: 265–304.

Walter, C. 2004. 'Transfer of reading comprehension skills to L2 is linked to mental representations of text and to L2 working memory'. *Applied Linguistics* 25/3: 315–39.

Walter, C. 2007. 'First- to second-language reading comprehension: not transfer, but access'. *International Journal of Applied Linguistics* 17/1: 14–37.

## 4.4 Symposium on written texts across cultures

**Convenor: Tania Pattison** *Trent University, Canada* with
**Ahmad Al-Hassan** *University of Petra, Jordan*
**Siân Morgan** *University of Modena and Reggio Emilia, Italy* and
**Tina Wei** *University of Exeter, UK*

The topic of culture is one of the most fascinating aspects of second-language learning, but also one of the most controversial. Atkinson (1999), for example, states that 'except for *language, learning,* and *teaching,* there is perhaps no more important concept in the field of TESOL than *culture*' (p. 625). On the other hand, while culture is often cited as a contributing factor in the challenges faced by L2 learners, there is no clear consensus on exactly what culture is, or on the role it plays in the learning process.

Taking on a topic as contentious as culture as a research project requires a certain amount of courage; the three speakers in this symposium were brave enough to explore the cultural challenges faced by speakers of different languages when dealing with written texts in English, either as readers or as writers. Sharing the results of research carried out in Europe, the Middle East and Asia, they each took a very different approach to the topic. **Ahmad Al-Hassan** demonstrated how cultural constraints affect the understanding of written English text by speakers of Arabic; **Siân Morgan** reported on the cultural dimensions of one aspect of writing, that of hedging and boosting; and **Tina Wei** showed how cross-cultural email exchange leads not only to linguistic improvement but also to increased cultural understanding.

First to speak was **Ahmad Al-Hassan,** who reported on a study designed to analyse the effects of providing background information on Jordanian students' discourse relating to two short stories. The stories, *Before Their Time* and *The Lottery* were assigned at intermediate readability level to 40 undergraduate students, chosen at random and divided into four groups. Each group was exposed to two treatment conditions: (a) providing background information necessary for understanding the upcoming texts, and (b) a control condition in which no pre-reading instruction was provided.

Results of multiple-choice tests showed strong positive effects of providing background knowledge; in addition, students' responses to attitude questionnaires showed they generally responded positively to the provision of background information. The attitude questionnaire consisted of ten statements to which students responded on a five-point scale: strongly agree, agree, neutral, disagree and strongly disagree. A large percentage of students indicated that they appreciated explanations of difficult vocabulary, description of the characters of the stories, and some background information to better understand and enjoy the stories.

The syntactic, semantic and discoursal challenges identified by the forty students included grammatical affixes, tense, aspect, modality, grammatical and lexical cohesion, correlatives, and a range of technical and sub-technical vocabulary. As indicated in students' responses to the attitude questionnaire, students generally need assistance with difficult words. Because English vocabulary is likely to pose a problem for many EFL students, it is reasonable to spend class time pre-teaching vocabulary. Pre-reading activities that include vocabulary instruction should be particularly facilitative for difficult texts and with less competent and confident readers.

Cultural differences also presented a challenge. The presenter noted that cultural mores in Jordanian society may reasonably be presumed to be different from those in British or American society. In Jordanian culture, God's Word is an absolute; there is none of the liberalism demonstrated in western culture, where values are apparently more relative. Such differences may create misunderstanding of authentic reading discourse.

The implications of the findings should encourage EFL teachers to give some background information to assist students in reading. Teachers need to know their students and the sort of texts students are reading well, and then construct pre-reading activities that will work for their students.

Next to speak was **Siân Morgan**, who addressed the issue of how hedges and boosters—lexical items that express qualification and certainty—play a key role in native-speaker writing in that they allow writers to express modesty, show politeness and acknowledge potential alternative voices (Hyland 2005). This talk described how Italian undergraduate students use these linguistic items and suggested some consciousness-raising and writing activities to help learners expand their range of modal expressions.

The presenter described a study in which corpus analysis was used to explore discursive writing by upper-intermediate students at an Italian university. The findings were summarised as follows:

- Students overused the modals 'will', 'should', 'would' and 'could' to express probability, possibly a result of teaching or the large amount of attention devoted to modal verbs in textbooks. It may simply suggest that these items are more automatically retrievable for non-native speaker writers than other modal devices.
- Students made considerable use of a limited range of informal items, illustrated in this talk with a concordance line of 'really'. Again, several reasons may account for this kind of lexical poverty. Students may still be developing register awareness or may need to build up their lexical resources. Another possibility is that the complex demands of composing may cause them to default to lexis that is more automatically retrievable.
- Students preferred amplifiers to mitigators and expressed their views rather assertively: This practice leads to 'shutting down' rather than opening up a discursive space with the reader, and may be inappropriate for pragmatically sensitive writing events in future academic or professional contexts.

Next, some suggestions for teachers of writing were provided. Previous studies have suggested that modal devices often pass unnoticed by learners in their reading, so the following activities can raise awareness of their function and extend students' repertoire:

- Learners notice hedges and boosters in their reading, including lexical expressions and adverbials as well as modal verbs. The possible purpose of these is then discussed.
- Learners are given exposure to contextualised use through extensive reading of a variety of texts. This experiential approach helps them become familiar with grammatical and lexical fingerprinting which typically occurs in different writing events.
- Learners remove hedges from texts and discuss the resulting effect on the reader.
- Learners rewrite an academic essay (which uses hedges and boosters) into popular journalistic style (which doesn't), or vice versa (Hyland 2005).

The final symposium speaker was **Tina Wei**, who reported on an exploratory study of how Chinese university students perceived their experiences of exchanging emails with members of different cultures; this was done with the purpose of practising their English writing skills while simultaneously expanding their cultural understanding.

The participants were twenty-eight second-year English majors in China. They voluntarily wrote to their e-pals, who were a group of American high-school students and some American, British and Canadian adults, for at least two months. Data was collected from questionnaires, interviews, the participants' email texts, and a final report describing how they perceived what they had learned linguistically and culturally from the experience.

Data showed that the topics the participants were interested in writing about included their personal affairs, leisure activities, school life, festivals (Chinese and western), individualised questions for their e-pals, and some sharing (for example, of pictures, music, etc.).

Linguistically, some participants stated that they had learned English expressions, phrases, and conjunctions; some reported increases in the fluency and length of their emails. They also learned the informal and colloquial writing style from their e-pals. Above all, they all enjoyed the free writing experience.

Culturally, the Chinese students perceived that they had expanded their cultural understanding by learning about the following: holidays and festivals; western family structure; interpersonal relationships; western daily life; and the abundance of course options and extra-curricular activities. They also reported having learned about the freedom enjoyed by their high-school e-pals in the educational setting (for example, freedom to speak in their classrooms) and about the equality and respect between western teachers and students as well as between parents and children. The project also resulted in changing attitudes towards westerners and reconsideration of the stereotypes previously held. For example, some participants had previously believed that all Americans go to church on Sundays, or that American high-school students do not study hard.

While this was an exploratory study, initial results indicate that email writing may be considered an alternative way of teaching writing, particularly in the mainland Chinese context where English writing instruction is typically exam-oriented. The findings on students' preferred topics seemed to resonate with Warschauer's (2004) idea that students enjoy writing on 'issues of importance to students' lives' (6); in addition, the fact that the project resulted in changing attitudes towards westerners and reconsideration of stereotypes previously held suggests that intercultural understanding seems to have occurred.

Email: tpattison@trentu.ca, dral_hassan@hotmail.com, sianmorgan@katamail.com, tinatzou@yahoo.com

### References

Atkinson, D. 1999. 'TESOL and culture'. *TESOL Quarterly* 33: 625–54.

Hyland, K. 2005. *Metadiscourse: Exploring Interaction in Writing.* London and New York: Continuum.

Warschauer, M. 2004. 'Technology and writing' in C. Davison and J. Cummins. *Handbook of English Language Teaching.* Dordrecht, Netherlands: Kluwer.

## 4.5 Becoming a 'plagiarism-conscious' teacher: suggestions for good practice

**Nadezhda Yakovchuk** *University of Leicester, Leicester, UK*

The continuing salience of the student plagiarism problem within UK higher education provokes concerns that the current strategies for dealing with it have not been adequate. As the departmental and institutional plagiarism prevention guidelines tend to represent a public face of the current assumptions about plagiarism in academia, such guidelines can be a good indicator of potential problems in higher education. This paper briefly summarises recent research in the area and offers a critique of online student-oriented plagiarism prevention guidelines provided by British higher education institutions. It then outlines three guiding principles that need to underlie current pedagogic practice.

Recent theoretical discussion and empirical research into plagiarism point to four main requirements that need to be fulfilled in order to address the plagiarism problem effectively. The first one is departing from a simplistic view of plagiarism and recognising its complex nature. Pennycook (1996: 201) famously argued that plagiarism 'cannot be cast as a simple black-and-white issue, the prevention of which can be achieved via threats, warnings and admonitions, […] it needs to be understood in terms of complex relationships between text, memory and learning'. The second requirement is recognising the historical and socio-cultural situatedness of the concept of plagiarism, i.e. that the Western view of plagiarism is not universal, but is a result of the historical development of the concepts of authorship, textual ownership and intellectual property in this part of the world. As Scollon (1995: 23) pointed out, 'the concept of plagiarism is fully embedded within a social, political, and cultural matrix that cannot be meaningfully separated from its interpretation'. The third requirement is that, rather than equating plagiarism with cheating and taking a moralistic view that all plagiarism results from a deliberate attempt to deceive, teachers need to be aware of the multiplicity and complexity of students' reasons for plagiarism—failure to understand academic requirements, poor scholarship, language difficulties, inadequate study skills are just some of the many possible causes of student plagiarism. As Park (2003: 479) noted, 'the situation is often complex and multi-dimensional, with no simple cause-effect link'. And, fourthly, there has been a growing understanding among scholars and educational practitioners that plagiarism policing is not enough, and that there is a need for a holistic approach to solving the plagiarism problem, which would encompass improving research and practice in the areas of plagiarism detection and, most importantly, prevention.

These recent advances in the plagiarism debate point to the need for an informed *pedagogic*, rather than a traditional punitive, approach to dealing with student plagiarism. Recent institutional advice on plagiarism prevention, however, does not seem to have embraced these tendencies. My study of student-oriented plagiarism prevention guidelines at British universities has revealed that they tended to present plagiarism as a clear-cut and unproblematic issue, with very few explicit examples of what constitutes good and bad practice. Almost two thirds of the guidelines appeared to view plagiarism as a deliberate act, and the generally strict tone suggested that they were designed to perform a warning, rather than a supporting, function.

This discrepancy between current theory and practice with regard to student plagiarism highlights the importance of staff development in this area. I believe that three general principles that need to guide pedagogic attempts to solve the plagiarism problem are *awareness, neutrality* and *flexibility. Awareness* involves recognition and knowledge of various determinants and contexts of plagiarism, as well as of the variety of different forms plagiaristic practices can take. *Neutrality* implies departing from any judgmental attitudes to student 'plagiarists' and being ready to address the problem in light of the multiplicity of possible reasons for student involvement in plagiaristic practices. *Flexibility* implies freedom from accepted dogmas and readiness to constantly review one's own views and assumptions along with the continuous advances in research and theoretical discussion on plagiarism. This important set of basic beliefs should form the background of the mindset of a 'plagiarism-conscious' EAP teacher—a teacher who can deal with the plagiarism problem successfully.

Email: n.yakovchuk@hotmail.co.uk

### References

Park, C. 2003. 'In other (people's) words: plagiarism by university students—literature and lessons'. *Assessment & Evaluation in Higher Education* 28/5: 471–88.

Pennycook, A. 1996. 'Borrowing others' words: text, ownership, memory, and plagiarism'. *TESOL Quarterly* 30/2: 201–30.

Scollon, R. 1995. 'Plagiarism and ideology: identity in intercultural discourse'. *Language in Society* 24: 1–28.

## 4.6 Critical literacy—explore the possibilities

**Chris Lima** *Freelance. Porto Alegre, Brazil*

### 'What exactly is critical literacy?'

I have been asked this question a good number of times in the past three years and so have other people involved in the *Critical Literacy in ELT Project*. Thus, the first part of my talk in Exeter was devoted to giving participants a description or explanation of the basic principles of the critical literacy approach to education. The second part of the presentation was about the project itself, what we have achieved so far and our current activities.

### A brief introduction

Critical Literacy (CL) is an educational perspective that focuses on the relationship between languages and worldviews. It is an approach that sees language as a cultural construct and proposes the analysis of the relationships among texts, language, knowledge and society. It leads us to question texts—written, visual or oral—and to try to assess the assumptions, values and beliefs that make texts be written in a given way. The CL approach understands that language and reality construct each other since language does not simply communicate ideas and values but also generates them. What is more, it invites us to analyse our own readings of texts and realise that they are also influenced by contextual factors—our upbringing, education background, nationality, social status, place in history, etc. This perception of language brings profound repercussions for the way we work in ELT, since our main material is language. As we see it, one of the roles of the ELT educator is to try to help language learners to understand how meanings are created in language, how words and sentences create and influence our perception of reality and our readings of the world.

According to Jordão (2008):

Learning a language is learning ways to construct meanings; learning an additional language to one's native language would be a way to make contact with and construct other meanings, to relate to foreign cultures, and thus to enlarge interpretive procedures. By learning languages critically, [...] we learn to exist in a dynamic process that enables the production of multiple understandings about what makes it possible to elaborate certain points of view and about their implications to our lives on the planet.

The implications of such approach for the classroom practice are vast. Since any text can be the subject of a critical literacy reading—from newspaper articles to paintings, from ads to poems, from novels to informal conversations—what distinguishes the CL practice is the sort of reading tasks proposed to learners. Open-ended questions and classroom debate are techniques used to encourage students to question texts and their own readings and also to create a learning environment where both teachers and learners acknowledge the multiplicity of interpretations as valid in principle and avoid imposing their own textual interpretations.

Moreover, relationships in the ELT classroom are also deeply influenced by this approach to the teaching/learning process, as teachers start recognising that learners also possess some previous knowledge, experiences and perceptions about a series of issues and that this baggage has to be taken into consideration. It is the teacher's job to draw on learners' understanding and views, as well as using textbooks and other resources, questioning the models given and including different perspectives in order to promote awareness of knowledge construction.

## The project

The Critical Literacy in ELT Project was one of the outcomes of the Hornby Summer School Brazil 2006. Since then it has generated teacher development seminars in Brazil, Argentina and Peru, and two key documents entitled *A Brief Introduction to Critical Literacy in English Language Education,* published in October 2006, and *Collaborative Approaches to Critical Literacy in ELT,* published in March 2008. Currently, a team of forty-one volunteer ELT professionals is working on the translation of these documents into twenty-six different languages. Besides that, eight sets of teaching and teacher development materials were created by ELT professionals from Brazil and Peru and published online at the British Council Brazil ELT Community (http://www.britishcouncil.org.br/elt) where we also have a discussion forum open to all ELT professionals interested in the CL approach.

Our project counts on the support of the British Council Brazil, the Hornby Trust and ELTeCS (English Language Teaching Contacts Scheme), and it received the 2007 British Council/ELTeCS Innovation Awards in ELT.

Email: chrislima90@yahoo.co.uk

## References

Jordão, C.M. 2008. 'Reading the world as social practice: conceptual questioning as a tool for enhancing critical literacies' in *English Quarterly* 39/2–3. Canadian Council of Teachers of English Language Arts: Winnipeg, Canada.

## 4.7 Symposium on critical approaches to coursebooks

**Convenor: Richard Smith** *University of Warwick, UK* with
**John Kullman** *Canterbury Christ Church University, UK*
**John Gray** *University of East London, UK*
**Sue Wharton** *University of Warwick, UK*
**Denise Santos** *University of Reading, UK* and
**Discussant: Alastair Pennycook** *University of Technology, Sydney, Australia*

In a context of growing recognition of the status of English as an *international* language, and of needs for acknowledging diversity more generally, the cultural contents of teaching and learning materials have increasingly come to be seen as a matter for concern. Issues of representation and possible cultural imposition confront the authors and users of globally marketed UK-published coursebooks (henceforth, 'global coursebooks') and locally produced materials alike. Conventional approaches to materials evaluation have tended to bypass such issues, however, and how to identify and address the cultural messages explicitly and implicitly conveyed via coursebooks has not formed part of most teachers' training. This symposium therefore aimed to promote new, critical perspectives on the cultural contents of coursebooks, marrying insights from recent research to relevant practical considerations.

**John Kullman** ('Coursebooks, therapy, and learner identity') reported on research which demonstrates a gradual but marked change in global coursebooks for the young adult market since the 1970s. Learners' personalities, personal qualities, lifestyles, experiences, health, ambitions, views, preferences and emotions now comprise much of these coursebooks' 'content', and related tasks ask learners to focus on particular aspects of identity, pushing their contributions in particular directions.

This change can be understood in the light of commentaries on identity in contemporary Britain (and similar societies) which emphasise how individuals create meaning through constructing their own 'narratives' and by distinguishing themselves from others according to personal characteristics and lifestyle practices. In this model 'self-esteem' is a key motif. This contrasts with an earlier model in which stable structures and institutions helped determine the individual's 'life course'.

This contemporary British model of identity dominates global coursebooks and little account is taken of different understandings of the self. If we want coursebooks to allow for these different understandings, we need to think seriously about their topics, texts, tasks and images. Although there has been an increasing debate on the importance of culture and identity in language education, there is little evidence that publishers of global coursebooks have taken note. Until they do, coursebooks will continue to reflect and project a monolithic, culturally bound model of identity.

**John Gray** ('The imaging of English in contemporary British ELT coursebooks') began by arguing that the current literature on ELT materials evaluation tends to view textbooks as educational tools, focusing almost exclusively on micro-issues of task design and overall evaluation in terms of effectiveness in context. However, textbooks are also cultural artefacts and a more nuanced and cross-disciplinary understanding of their constructed nature is both useful and overdue. Drawing largely on the work of Stuart Hall, John Gray made the case for a cultural studies perspective on textbook analysis and he reported on the results of an analysis of ELT textbooks since the 1970s. Focusing largely on the evolving nature of the artwork in these materials, and using the tools of social semiotics, John Gray showed how artwork—far from being merely decorative as some critics have argued—plays a key role in the imaging of English and the construction of what ELT publishers refer to as 'aspirational content'. He concluded by arguing that in contemporary materials students are increasingly exposed to a cosmopolitan lifestyle which forms a fundamental part of the promotional promise of English, and that this promise is one in which a benign view of globalisation is repeatedly celebrated.

**Sue Wharton** ('Representations of local and "target" cultures in some EFL coursebooks') discussed three recent MA dissertation projects from Warwick University. All were situated within a critical discourse approach, acknowledging that texts construct as well as reflect realities, and that textual representations can influence the behaviour and attitudes of text users. This is particularly true for school texts, which can communicate not only their own message, but also an implied message of official approval.

Analysing materials published in Indonesia, Ika Lestari Damayanti (2006) explored the processes, relational attributes and circumstances associated with gender, as well as interaction patterns and visual representations. Her findings indicated a move away from traditional stereotypes and yet a considerable asymmetry in the representation of each gender's job behaviour, interaction patterns, speech content, and physical locations.

Mayumi Tanaka and Enrique Basabe (both 2005) investigated the portrayal of 'local' and 'target' cultures, and of intercultural communication scenarios, within Japan-published materials and an Argentinian version of a global coursebook, respectively. Both found that even in local or localised materials, 'Western' culture was portrayed as desirable. Tanaka also found that Japanese nationalism was promoted; however, in dialogues involving intercultural communication, there was a tendency to represent the learners' cultural group in an inferior position.

Sue Wharton concluded by highlighting how critical discourse analysis can uncover representations which are not immediately apparent. She recognised, however, that pedagogic impact is not predetermined, but depends on classroom treatment.

Taking up this theme of *treatment*, **Denise Santos** ('Textbooks as participants in the development of critical thinking') discussed classroom practices in a Brazilian language school undergoing change, and she contrasted reading practices involving the same textbook before and after the innovation. Specifically, from a more conventional approach to reading as vocabulary-decoding, students moved towards a critical engagement with the textbook.

In order to develop this latter approach, students were encouraged to use the textbook in a multi-stage reflection process which in turn involved (1) taking a stance towards naturalised assumptions about the social world; (2) problematising common-sensical generalisations; (3) reflecting about the process of developing generalisations and stereotypes; (4) associating ideas and broadening the initial reflections through group discussions; (5) doing some simple ethnographic work by observing instances of the issues in focus in their community; and (6) refining the reflections in collaboration with others in the class.

This process enabled the learners to challenge naturalised perceptions of gender and teacher-student roles in their community, and two implications were proposed: firstly, that what is considered problematic in a textbook can in fact trigger critical debate in the classroom; secondly, that a new research agenda is needed for textbook research—one that includes examinations of textbooks in use in and out of the classroom.

Finally, **Richard Smith** ('Approaching cultural contents critically: insights from teachers') argued for a more critical as well as realistic approach to coursebook evaluation within teacher education—one which incorporates considerations of actual use, takes account of teachers' own perspectives and incorporates critical 'on the page' analysis. Inappropriate cultural contents of published materials may be a major preoccupation of non-native speaker teachers, as revealed by a survey of MA students at Warwick University. Follow-up interviews revealed practical insights for coursebook use which can be usefully shared with other teachers. For example, a Cuban teacher reported that, although she uses US and Canadian materials, she always has students compare and contrast topics and situations with their own lives, in order to avoid 'assimilation'. Indeed, both in this study and in interviews carried out in Turkey by Derya Altınmaka for her (2005) MA dissertation, teachers often say they respond to the need to teach 'problematic' coursebook contents by engaging students in explicit comparison and contrast with their own lives and experiences.

These surveys lend support to the idea that it is appropriate to promote both critical reading and critical use of coursebooks within teacher education, and Richard Smith ended his presentation with an exemplar activity involving comparison of coursebook extracts from different decades followed by a task involving teachers in planning critical use.

**Alastair Pennycook**, in his concluding discussion of the papers, agreed that there is a strong need both for critical research into coursebooks and for improved teacher education in this area. He noted how both John Kullman and John Gray had identified a major focus on lifestyle in contemporary global coursebooks which ties English to aspirations learners may or may not be able to achieve. Research reported by Sue Wharton had shown that 'locally produced' coursebooks may have their own problems, and this highlighted the need to be critical of these, too.

Another overall point was the emerging need to look at classrooms, that is, not to be content with a critical discourse analysis of coursebooks but to engage in 'critical ethnography'. As Denise Santos' talk had shown, teachers and students are quite capable of doing critical work with books. A major practical issue, then, may be not only how to 'improve' the books, but, as Richard Smith had highlighted, how to enhance teachers' capacities for critical analysis and abilities to *use* coursebooks in a critical way.

Email: R.C.Smith@warwick.ac.uk,
john.kullman@canterbury.ac.uk, J.Gray@uel.ac.uk,
S.M.Wharton@warwick.ac.uk, denise@denisesantos.com,
Alastair.Pennycook@uts.edu.au

## 4.8  The IATEFL/Hornby Trust panel discussion: Teachers speak: ELT in Africa, Asia, Latin America and Russia

Convenor: **Rod Bolitho** *Norwich Institute for Language Education, Norwich, UK* with **The Hornby Scholars at IATEFL 2008**—Marcus Ferreira da Silva *Brazil;* Sudashana Moodliar *South Africa;* Setu Zahid Hossain *Bangladesh;* Yasna Ivonne Pereira Reyes *Chile;* Stephen Robert Bundala *Tanzania;* Antonio Oscar Pauline Portugal Mulima *Mozambique;* Islaura Tejeda Arencibia *Cuba;* Muhammad Gulubba Sirajo *Nigeria;* Iriz Anjelica Astillero *Philippines;* Rosa Maria Pelaez Carmona *Mexico;* Amanda Belarmina Zamuner *Argentina;* Consuelo Cedano Pineda *Colombia;* Vandana Lunyal *India;* Santee Moloye Dowlot *Mauritius;* Daniel Oginda Orina *Kenya;* Ludmila Sokolova *Russia*

As British government and British Council funding priorities have changed over the last decade or so, it has been more and more difficult for professionals from countries in transition to attend the IATEFL Conference, and a look around the delegates in each succeeding year heightens the impression that the conference is, increasingly, accessible only to those from countries whose strong economies make it possible for them to attend. In the face of this trend, it is really important that issues in ELT in these transitional countries are aired and discussed at the conference, and that the voices of the few teachers present who represent these countries are heard. Seen in these terms, this symposium, planned and led by Hornby scholars on Masters' courses in the UK was an invaluable opportunity. The scholars selected the four issues discussed at the symposium, conducted small scale research in their own countries to investigate the questions they came up with, and the summaries included here reflect the content of the presentations they gave so ably during the symposium.

### Class size and teaching approaches

The purpose of this study was to determine how class size affects English teachers' approaches in certain developing countries, namely, Bangladesh, the Philippines, Tanzania and Nigeria. Large classes are a common concern in these contexts. Some of the common problems associated with large classes are: less student participation, less individual attention by teachers, limited feedback on students' performance. In addition, class size can be a matter of perception.

As class size is a major concern in these countries, we wanted to find out how teachers were coping in their contexts. In particular, we looked into the effects of class size on matters such as a teacher's ability to give individual attention, and class management. We collected our data through an eight-item questionnaire. The survey produced mixed results. Overall, about 76 per cent of the respondents said their classes were large, the only exception being respondents from the Philippines. However, differences in perception about class size and their manageability were apparent. For example, some teachers said that a class of 45 was large and unmanageable, while others said it was not.

Around 50 per cent of respondents from Bangladesh said they were able to give their students individual attention though they thought their classes were large. The same observations were made by the teachers from Tanzania. When asked about teaching approaches, most of the respondents from Bangladesh said they used a Communicative Language Teaching approach, while a majority from the Philippines and Tanzania said they used an eclectic approach. Most respondents from Nigeria cited grammar translation and direct method as their teaching approach.

Thus we see here that except for the Nigerians, most respondents from the countries represented in our study do not limit themselves to traditional teacher-fronted approaches despite having large classes. Our conclusion is that class size is not the only factor in determining teaching approaches. Although a majority of our respondents admitted that large classes *are* a problem, it appears from their responses that they are responding to this challenge in creative and effective ways.

## ICT as a tool to enhance English language learning

The rapid development of technology and its diffusion into our everyday life opens new possibilities for communication. Consequently, the notion of communicative competence is changing: a competent language user should be aware of the pragmatics of online interaction, conventions for production and the interpretation of texts comprising or illustrated by multimedia. Warschauer (2002: 455) names four new electronic literacies:

- computer literacy (i.e. comfort and fluency in keyboard skills and using a computer),
- information literacy (i.e. the ability to find and critically evaluate online information),
- multimedia literacy (i.e. the ability to produce and interpret complex documents comprising texts, images and sounds), and
- computer-mediated communication literacy (i.e. the pragmatics of individual and group online interaction).

Acquiring these literacies requires reconsideration of the process of language education, taking into account one critical factor: local appropriateness, i.e. access to and attitudes to information and communication technology in different locations in our contexts. In our research we set out to find out more about the availability and perceived appropriateness of technology in ELT classrooms. The main data collection instrument was an open-ended electronic questionnaire administered to 27 teachers in primary and secondary schools in India, Kenya and Russia.

The following table summarises our findings:

| Questions | Most popular answer | Least popular answer | Comments |
|---|---|---|---|
| **1.** Technology used in English language classes | Audio recordings | None | ICT only in 3rd place |
| **2.** Computer skills mastered by the teachers | Finding and evaluating information online | None | Use the skills in English language class |
| **3.** The purposes of personal use of computers | Planning lessons | Preparing PPT, tests, chatting, | A teacher from Russia has own site but doesn't use it for teaching |
| **4.** Tasks requiring the use of computers given to students | To find specific information for lessons | Word processing | Respondents emphasised learner autonomy and access to resources |

*Figure 4.8.1 Availability and perceived appropriateness of technology in ELT classrooms*

All respondents consider the use of ICT to be challenging both for students and teachers. They support the idea of introducing ICT as a tool to enhance English language learning in schools, but stress the need for adequate teacher development programmes. As one of the respondents says, '... putting a computer and internet access in each school won't change the situation unless teachers have effective teaching tools and master modern teaching methods'.

## An investigation into teachers' views about culture and ELT materials

This investigation aimed at finding common perceptions in teachers about culture and its reflection in ELT materials.

Kramsch's view of culture as 'membership in a discourse community that shares a common social space and history, and a common system of standards for perceiving, believing, evaluating, and acting' (Kramsch 1998) proved suitable as a working definition to frame our study.

We decided we had to look at ELT textbooks and other related materials, such as learning materials, adaptations of coursebooks, authentic cultural material, and original teacher-produced material. This decision was also prompted by our experience of frequent over-reliance in our contexts on EFL textbooks produced in 'inner circle' countries (UK and USA), though in South Africa (the only L1 context in our study), learning materials normally do include local adaptations.

Nault's work on the teaching of culture raised questions we wanted to have answers to:

- Whose culture should be taught in ELT classrooms?
- What goals should guide culture teaching?
- How should culture-related course materials be designed and selected?
  (Nault 2006).

With these questions in mind, we designed an open-ended questionnaire. We had responses from EFL teachers in Brazil, Chile and Argentina.

- EFL teachers found largely American and British culture represented in their text-books, while L1 teachers commented on South African materials tailored to their cultural environment.
- The EFL teachers in our survey stated that the materials they used hardly reflected their national/local culture, with only some world famous people or geographical landmarks present, whereas South African teachers stated that their culture was amply represented, with not only famous Africans included but also key issues for the population (human rights, gender, HIV/AIDS, etc.).
- All the teachers consulted agreed that dealing with cultural issues in the ELT class-room fosters respect for all cultures and strengthens identity; it also unifies people and develops national pride and, perhaps most importantly for us as teachers, it promotes critical thinking among our students.

The main conclusions we draw are that a key challenge for teachers in our coun-tries is to design and/or adapt materials to suit their own context; that local content should be integrated into ELT materials; and that a holistic view of language teaching and learning, including cultural issues, should be fostered.

## Attitudes to teacher development

The Masters' programmes we are involved in and our personal interest in the area of professional development led us to carry out some small-scale research to find out about teacher development opportunities and their relevance to English teachers in our contexts. We administered an online questionnaire involving 53 teachers from universities in Colombia, Cuba and Mexico and the responses led us to the following significant findings:

- Teacher development courses and workshops focused on methodology and/or per-sonal language development, are considered the most important as they lead to improved teaching methods and to enhanced language skills and knowledge.
- Despite not having much involvement in decision-making about course content, planning and design, our respondents consider these development opportunities useful and are usually willing to take part in them, as long as they are affordable in terms of time and cost.

Current trends suggest that teachers should be involved in professional develop-ment not only for the acquisition of knowledge and teaching skills but also in order to heighten their understanding of their own practices, a perspective concerned primar-ily with professional and personal growth in terms of thinking, beliefs, experiences and attitudes (Jimenez Raya and Sercu 2007).

Our research findings suggest that in-university professional development provi-sion can be enhanced by:

- providing opportunities for teachers to participate as planners and decision makers of programmes and activities such as forums and discussion groups that facilitate professional interaction, and sharing;

- adopting approaches to teacher development programmes that allow participants to become aware of the need to improve by reflecting on their practices rather than focusing on the transmission of techniques; and
- providing teachers with opportunities to participate in action research projects as a way of promoting self-improvement through critical analysis and reflection on their practice.

These will be our own priorities when we return to our institutions after the year in the UK.

Email: rod@nile-elt.com

## References

Jimenez Raya, M. and L. Sercu (eds.). 2007. *Challenges in Teacher Development: Learner Autonomy and Intercultural Competence.* Frankfurt am Main: Peter Lang.

Kramsch, C. 1998. *Language and Culture*, Oxford: Oxford University Press.

Nault, D. 2006. 'Going global: rethinking culture teaching in ELT contexts'. *Language, Culture and Curriculum* 19/3: 314–28.

Warschauer, M. 2002. 'A developmental perspective on technology in language education'. *TESOL Quarterly* 36/3: 453–74.

# 5 Language policy

## 5.1 Plenary: Changing practices in global ELT

Alastair Pennycook  *University of Technology, Sydney, Australia*

### English and globalisation

*We cannot understand ELT without viewing the role of English in the context of globalisation.*

In this paper, I shall make ten points that I believe capture current issues and concerns about the global spread of English, our role as language educators in relation to this spread, and current thinking on language education. In a number of ways, all other concerns in this paper fall under this first, broad rubric of English and globalisation. We need to appreciate both the unevenness of the world we live in, and that globalisation is far more complex than economic disparity alone. New technologies and communications are enabling immense and complex flows of people, signs, sounds, im ages across multiple borders in multiple directions. And English and English language teaching are deeply bound up with this. We can never be 'just English teachers' on two counts: There is no such thing as 'just English'—it always comes amid cultural, political, and economic relations. And we can never be 'just teachers' since to teach is to organise people, knowledge and language according to certain moral, cultural and political principles. As English language teachers we cannot but participate in aspects of globalisation. Like it or not, when we teach English, we become actors in the processes of globalisation. Our challenge is to work out what that means.

### English as threat and desire

*English is deeply implicated in hegemonic global relations, yet it is also a language of hope, desire, and reappropriation.*

English, as Phillipson and Skutnabb-Kangas (1996: 447) make clear, 'can serve many useful purposes but will do so only if the linguistic human rights of speakers of other languages are respected'. We need therefore to confront questions of access and excess: how to balance the need to provide access to this key language of the 21st century without also filling schools worldwide with an excess of English studies at the expense of other languages, other subjects, other possibilities. For many of the world's poor, as Bruthiaux (2002: 292–3) points out, English language education is 'an outlandish irrelevance,' and 'talk of a role for English language education in facilitating the process of poverty reduction and a major allocation of public resources to that end is likely to prove misguided and wasteful'. According to Tollefson (2000: 8), 'At a time when English is widely seen as a key to the economic success of nations and the economic well-being of individuals, the spread of English also contributes to significant social, political, and economic inequalities'. And yet, we also need to understand how and why people desire English so strongly, and how this is far more than a pragmatic or economic question but also one of deeply ingrained desires.' Surrounded by the multiple discourses of English as a desirable and powerful language' (Piller and Takahashi 2006: 69), people's craving for English may be linked to a yearning for particular lifestyles, bodies, images, discourses and identities.

## English as a translocal language

*English has become a language of translocal use across the world, constantly changing and mixing with other languages and cultures.*

The global spread of English has also greatly affected the language itself. A world Englishes perspective that focuses on the 'implications of pluricentricity…, the new and emerging norms of performance, and the bilingual's creativity as a manifestation of the contextual and formal hybridity of Englishes' (Kachru 1997: 66) has opened up many new ways of thinking about different varieties of English around the world. We are now obliged to confront not only what were formerly seen as the only major varieties—those so-called native-speaker varieties in Britain and the US (and perhaps Australia, Canada and New Zealand)—but also those many emergent varieties in India, Singapore, the Philippines, Malaysia and so on. The goalposts have been moved when we consider what counts as correct, standard, or international English. Meanwhile, as James (2008: 98) observes, in an age of globalisation, of international mobility and communication,

a sociolinguistic consideration of New Englishes must accept such post-geographic Englishes as manifested in their lingua franca function, that is, as employed between/ among language users who choose to employ English as their verbal means of communication and who by convention are 'non-native speakers' of the language in traditional terms.

This emergent focus on English as a lingua franca, where 'English becomes the property of all' and is 'flexible enough to reflect the cultural norms of those who use it' (Kirkpatrick 2006: 79) suggests not just English as an international language, nor English in its many variants, but English as used translocally across domains, by users moving on different trajectories.

## Multicompetent language users

*English as a global language has no native speakers, only multicompetent language users.*

If we take this view of global Englishes seriously, we can see why Rajagopalan (2004: 112) argues that 'In its emerging role as a world language, English has no native speakers'. English as used globally is not the first language of any speakers, but rather the second language of many. Such a view is also part of the significant challenges that are being made to the very notion of the native speaker. As Canagarajah puts it,

unless the native speaker fallacy is effectively challenged and dismissed, we may not develop a formidable sense of professionalism in ELT that orientates to language learning and the language learner in a holistic sense.
(1999: 84).

There are two sides to this argument: On the one hand we may wish to challenge the very notion of the native speaker and suggest, particularly in relation to English, that it is simply an outmoded and inappropriate concept. Or, we may choose to leave the concept intact, but to argue nevertheless that it should not form the basis either for how we choose who should teach or for what models we adopt for our students. As Cook remarks, we need to 'convince students that they are successful multicompetent speakers, not failed native speakers' (1999: 204). If we still want to believe that the notion of the native speaker of English has any continuing meaning, we certainly don't want to make this a model for what our multilingual, multicultural and multicompetent students can achieve.

## English as a language always in translation

*ELT must be understood in relation to other languages: it is always in translation and we need to deal with translingual meanings.*

It is one of the great crimes of the global hegemony of communicative language teaching over the last few decades that it not only promoted a monolingual, native-speaker-norm-based and educationally shallow version of English (or other languages), but it eschewed the complexity and depth of understanding language education as a project of translation. With our ugly and simplistic labels of grammar-translation versus communicative language teaching we have dismissed a central aspect of language learning, and we have reduced English to a language used and taught only in its own presence. The role of the language teacher, suggests Kramsch (2006: 103) 'should be to diversify meanings, point to meanings not chosen, and bring to light other possible meanings that have been forgotten by history or covered up by politics'. Translation, argues Cronin (2003), plays a crucial role within globalisation, and there needs to be 'an *activist* dimension to translation which involves an engagement with the cultural politics of society at national and international levels' (p. 134). From this perspective, I would prefer to see ELT as a form of translingual activism. We need to oppose the long history of eschewing translation, where the use of languages other than English is denigrated as old-fashioned, as causing interlingual interference, as the strategy of the non-native teacher who knows no better, as indelibly tied to the chalk-and-talk methodologies that focus on grammar. This is to oppose the many interests and complicities that have supported the use of English and only English in classrooms. It is to reintroduce translation in all its complexity into English language teaching, to open up and explore the many possible meanings that can start to flow in and out of languages in relation to English. In its focus on activism, it is to see this as political action, as a way of confronting the possible threats to diversity posed by English (Pennycook 2008).

## Linguistic and semiotic landscapes

*We live in linguistic and semiotic landscapes that render language inseparable from the environment.*

In the global urban environments in which much language learning occurs, we are surrounded by complex semiotic landscapes. This suggests the need to rethink the ways in which we view texts and signs against the backdrop of the city.

> All of the signs and symbols take a major part of their meaning from how and where they are placed—at that street corner, at that time in the history of the world. Each of them indexes a larger discourse.
> (Scollon and Wong Scollon 2003: 2)

Graffiti too can be seen as 'integral parts of the City; they contribute to the definition of its exterior aspect, its size, as well as to the definition of its interior design, its soul' (Milon 2002: 87). This understanding of linguistic/semiotic landscapes suggests a need to include a dynamic account of space, text and interaction: Readers and writers are part of the fluid, urban semiotic space and produce meaning as they move, write, read and travel. The styles and locations of graffiti are about identity; they are statements of place, belonging, group membership and style. Landscapes are not mere backdrops on which texts and images are drawn but are spaces that are imagined and invented. Urban 'graffscapes' are animated by the movement and interactions of city dwellers. For many of us—teachers and students—the contexts through which we move in our daily lives—on the way to work, out on the town—are, therefore, complex semiotic and often multilingual environments that narrate particular stories about the world. Yet somehow, we do not seem to have a way for accounting for this in our static, suburban classroom narratives.

## Language as local practice

*Language is best understood as a practice; it is something we do rather than a system we draw on.*

Whereas once we tended to think of language teaching as the practice, or the work we got our students to do to improve their fluency and accuracy as classroom practice, while language was the object that we aimed to convey through these practices, a shift in the way we think about language suggests that now language itself is being seen as a practice. We talk of literacy practices, discursive practices, language practices. What this means is that language is being reconceived not as a system that we draw on in order to communicate but rather as a social activity, one of whose outcomes may be communication. Practices are habitual activities that occur in social and cultural spaces. As Baynham remarks,

> investigating literacy as practice involves investigating literacy as 'concrete human activity', not just what people do with literacy, but also what they make of what they do, the values they place on it and the ideologies that surround it. Practice provides a way of linking the cognitive with the social, opening up the possibility of an integrated approach to the study of literacy in use.
> (1995: 1)

To look at language not as a system but as a practice brings our attention down to the local, to 'discursive activity in opposition to structuralist, semiotic, and poststructuralist conceptions of it as structure, system, or abstract discourse' (Schatzki 2001:1). This also allows us to think of language knowledge

> not in terms of abstract system components but as communicative repertoires—conventionalized constellations of semiotic resources for taking action—that are shaped by the particular practices in which individuals engage
> (Hall *et al.* 2006: 232).

## Local practices and third way pedagogies

> Instead of seeking context-free teaching methods, teaching practices need to engage with local cultural and linguistic practices.

We need to 'shift the research focus from the pursuit of universal, context-free knowledge about the most effective technology to teach English' in order to develop 'a deeper understanding of diverse local pedagogical practices and beliefs in their sociocultural situatedness' (Lin *et al.* 2005: 218). For too long in the field of ELT we have tried to establish a notion of teaching methodology as if this existed outside social and cultural contexts. Yet teaching is always a deeply embedded activity, happening here, in this space, at this time, with these students. To overcome the attempts to establish context-free pedagogies and to engage with local practices and knowledge is not to return to what may be less than effective traditional practices but rather to encourage and focus on what emerges when different pedagogies encounter each other. As Phan Le Ha puts it in the context of Vietnam, teachers 'make full use of their cultural resources to enrich their language competence. This way of doing things demonstrates a harmonious combination of global and local pedagogies' (2004: 52). This is to open up the possibility for 'third way' pedagogies, ways of teaching that are neither new nor old, neither global nor local, neither grammar-translation nor communicative language teaching. Thus teachers can develop 'pedagogies and material that are socially and culturally more relevant for their students' and they can

> feel more comfortable about using language teaching to negotiate the sociopolitical realities of their communities through a more critical and transformative pedagogy. The English language and its discourses will themselves undergo considerable changes. English will be nativized more constructively and consciously to complement the local needs and aspirations.
> (Canagarajah 1999: 90).

## Digital literacies and metroethnicities

> Digital literacies and increased mobilities allow greater options for both learning and identity claims.

In the fast-changing digital world in which many of us now operate, it is important that we link what we do in our classrooms to the shifting, and sometimes virtual environment in which our students live. As Gee has remarked with respect to video games, their power

resides not just in their present instantiations, but in the promises the technologies by which they are made hold out for the future. Game designers can make worlds where people can have meaningful new experiences, experiences that their places in life would never allow them to have or even experiences no human being has ever had before. These experiences have the potential to make people smarter and more thoughtful.
(Gee 2005: 6).

This does not by any means suggest that we should all be playing video games in our language classrooms, but it does mean that we need to understand the possible worlds in which our students may dwell. At the same time, the changing cultural and linguistic worlds in which they live also pose challenges for how we conceive of culture, ethnicity and language. As Maher describes it in the context of Japan, students are rejecting fixed ascriptions of cultural identity and instead playing with notions of metroethnicity:

Cultural essentialism and ethnic orthodoxy are out. In Japan, Metroethnicity is in. Cool rules. Metroethnicity is a reconstruction of ethnicity: a hybridised 'street' ethnicity deployed by a cross-section of people with ethnic or mainstream backgrounds who are oriented towards cultural hybridity, cultural/ethnic tolerance and a multicultural lifestyle in friendships, music, the arts, eating and dress. Both Japanese and persons with minority backgrounds 'play' with ethnicity (not necessarily their own) for aesthetic effect. Metroethnicity is skeptical of heroic ethnicity and bored with sentimentalism about ethnic language.
(Maher 2005: 83).

As language learners move around the world in search of English or other desirable languages, or stay at home but tune in to new digital worlds through screens, mobiles and headphones, the possibilities of being something not yet culturally imagined mobilises new possibilities of identity.

## Popular transcultural flows

ELT cannot be isolated from transcultural flows of culture, language, music and text.

In this world of transcultural flows, it is forms of popular culture that our students are typically tuned in to. Hip-hop, for example, constitutes

a global urban subculture that has entered people's lives and become a universal practice among youth the world over …. From a local fad among black youth in the Bronx, it has gone on to become a global, postindustrial signifying practice, giving new parameters of meaning to otherwise locally or nationally diverse identities.
(Levy 2001: 134)

And in these popular transcultural flows, languages, cultures and identities are frequently mixed. Code-mixing, sampling of sounds, genres, languages and cultures is the norm. And again we need to tune into this. According to Preisler, 'the social forces of the subcultural environment are … generally speaking, more successful than the classroom at ensuring the learning of active functional variation in English' (1999: 260). This does not necessarily imply that we should all be doing hip-hop, or whatever cultural forms our students are into, in our English classes, but it does suggest that unless we stay tuned to where our students are at, our assumptions about language, pedagogy, culture and identity may be deeply at odds with our students' worlds. Global Englishes are changing, mixing shifting; so too are cultures; so too must our pedagogies (Pennycook 2007).

Email: alastair.pennycook@uts.edu.au

## References

Baynham, M. 1995. *Literacy Practices: Investigating Literacy in Social Contexts.* London: Longman.

Bruthiaux, P. 2002. 'Hold your courses: language education, language choice, and economic development'. *TESOL Quarterly* 36/3: 275–96.

Canagarajah, A.S. 1999. 'Interrogating the "native speaker" fallacy: non-linguistic roots, non-pedagogical results' in G Braine. *Non-native Educators in English Language Teaching.* Mahwah, N.J.: Lawrence Erlbaum.

Cook, V. 1999. 'Going beyond the native speaker in language teaching'. *TESOL Quarterly* 33/2: 185–209.

Cronin, M. 2003. *Translation and Globalization.* London: Routledge.

Gee, J. P. 2005. 'Learning by design: good video games as learning machines'. *E–Learning* 2/1: 5–16.

Hall, J. K., A. Cheng and M. Carlson. 2006. 'Reconceptualizing multicompetence as a theory of language knowledge'. *Applied Linguistics,* 27/2: 220–40.

James, A. 2008. 'New Englishes as post-geographic Englishes in lingua franca use: genre, inter-discursivity and late modernity'. *European Journal of English Studies* 12/1: 97–112.

Kachru, B. 1997. 'World Englishes and English-using communities'. *Annual Review of Applied Linguistics* 17: 66–87.

Kirkpatrick, A. 2006. 'Which model of English: native-speaker, nativized or lingua franca?' in R Rubdy and M Saraceni (eds.). *English in the World: Global Rules, Global Roles.* London: Continuum.

Kramsch, C. 2006. 'The traffic in meaning'. *Asia Pacific Journal of Education* 26/1: 99–104.

Le Ha, P. 2004. 'University classrooms in Vietnam: Contesting the stereotypes'. *ELT Journal* 58/1: 50–7

Levy, C. 2001. 'Rap in Bulgaria: between fashion and reality' in T. Mitchell (ed.). *Global Noise: Rap and Hip-Hop Outside the USA.* Middletown, Connecticut: Wesleyan University Press.

Lin, A, W. Wang, N. Akamatsu and M. Riazi. 2005. 'International TESOL professionals and teaching English for glocalized communication (TEGCOM)' in S. Canagarajah (ed.). *Reclaiming the Local in Language Policy and Practice.* Mahwah, N.J.: Lawrence Erlbaum.

Maher, J. 2005. 'Metroethnicity, language, and the principle of cool'. *International Journal of the Sociology of Language.* 175/176: 83–102.

Milon, A. 2002. 'Tags and murals in France: a city's face or a natural landscape?' in A-P. Durand (ed.). *Black, Blanc, Beur: Rap Music and Hip-hop Culture in the Francophone World.* Lanham, Maryland: The Scarecrow Press.

Pennycook, A. 2007. *Global Englishes and Transcultural Flows.* London: Routledge

Pennycook, A. 2008. 'English as a language always in translation'. *European Journal of English Studies.* 12/1: 33–47.

Phillipson, R. and T. Skutnabb-Kangas. 1996. 'English only worldwide or language ecology?'. *TESOL Quarterly* 30/3: 429–52.

Piller, I and K. Takahashi. 2006. 'A passion for English: desire and the language market' in A. Pavlenko (ed.). *Bilingual Minds: Emotional Experience, Expression and Representation*, Clevedon: Multilingual Matters.

Preisler, B. 1999. 'Functions and forms of English in a European EFL country' in T. Bex and R. Watts (eds.). *Standard English: The Widening Debate.* London: Routledge.

Rajagopalan, K. 2004. 'The concept of 'World English' and its implications for ELT'. *ELT Journal* 58/2: 111–17.

Schatzki, T. 2001. 'Introduction: practice theory' in T. Schatzki, K. Knorr Cetina and E. von Savigny (eds.). *The Practice Turn in Contemporary Theory.* London, Routledge.

Scollon, R. and S. Wong Scollon. 2003. *Discourses in Place: Language in the Material World.* London: Routledge.

Tollefson, J. 2000. 'Policy and ideology in the spread of English' in J. K. Hall and W. Eggington (eds.). *The Sociopolitics of English Language Teaching.* Clevedon: Multilingual Matters.

## 5.2  What do teachers think about English today?

**Hsuan-Yau Tony Lai** *Centre for Applied Linguistics, University of Warwick, UK*

The concept of English as an international language has been discussed extensively in the ELT field for many years. Theoretically the concept promotes the idea that English is no longer a possession of any particular English-speaking country and that there are many different varieties of Englishes; however, in reality what are teachers' perceptions of it?

In recent years, most universities in Taiwan have placed their emphasis on developing the students' skills and ability to face the rapidly changing and competitive global village. English plays an important role in connecting Taiwanese university students to today's world. However, when I was teaching English to both English majors and non-majors at two universities in Taiwan, I perceived that my students' perceptions towards the language were varied. Some believed that English was an international language and could help them to broaden their views. Nevertheless, some (especially English majors) had a strong desire to study or work in an English-speaking country and experience the culture after they graduated. These phenomena inspired me to conduct my study.

Since teachers play an important role in the classroom, my study investigated Taiwanese university teachers' perceptions of the role of English today. A focus group interview was conducted aiming to explore five experienced Taiwanese university teachers' thoughts on issues of the ownership of English and acquiring target language culture knowledge in the English classroom. The findings indicate that the teachers have different thoughts on the issues and face a dilemma as to whether they should follow theory or reality when teaching English in the EFL classroom. Some teachers agree that English is an international language and it is important not to limit the view on the ownership of English. Some insist that there should be a *standard* model for students to follow in the English classroom.

These findings suggest that although Taiwanese university teachers may think that English has become an international language today, they still would like to follow ENL (English as a native language) varieties or models in the English classroom. As Chien (2007: 5) argues, in Taiwan

Non-native English teachers, too, tend to invest heavily in reaching near-native English competence. Although the majority may agree that conveying meaning is more important than perfect conformity with a native-speaker standard, they are still generally inclined to keep the native norm as a teaching model.

My suggestion is that *local* ELT professionals follow the most *appropriate* model based on the students' needs and wants. Presumably, since the local ELT professionals have more knowledge about the local context, they should try to listen to their students and understand their needs and wants. Together, both sides can find the most appropriate model to follow in the English classroom. Meanwhile, it is also crucial to raise the students' awareness of varieties of Englishes including English as a lingua franca today so that they can appreciate the differences. To extend these suggestions even further, I think Canagarajah's (2006) claim provides us with a new perspective. As he says, 'we have to focus on strategies and processes of language negotiation' in order to equip users with a 'repertoire of language competence' which will enable them to 'transfer their knowledge and competence in the underlying deep structure of their variety to the other varieties they will confront (including standard American and British English)' (Canagarajah 2006 citied in Prodromou 2007: 10).

Email: tony823@ms17.hinet.net

## References

Canagarajah, S. 2006. 'An interview with Suresh Canagarajah' in R. Rubdy and M. Saraceni (eds.). *English in the World: Global Rules, Global Roles.* London: Continuum.

Chien, S.-C. 2007. 'English as a lingua franca: emerging awareness in Taiwan'. *IATEFL Voices* 199: 5.

Prodromou, L. 2007. 'ELF models and "linguistic capital"'. *IATEFL Voices* 199: 9–10.

## 5.3 English versus Arabic: languages for science and academia

**Salah Troudi** *School of Education and Lifelong Learning, University of Exeter, UK*

My presentation reported on an on-going research project investigating tertiary students' views on the use of English as a medium of instruction and the possibility of using Arabic to teach scientific and other academic subjects in the United Arab Emirates (UAE). The study was informed by an interpretive and a critical perspective to research and was situated within the main tenets of critical applied linguistics and mother-tongue education.

The phenomenal spread of English as a global or international language and its effect on minor, indigenous and endangered languages are two main themes that have undergone much analysis, scrutiny and criticism in the last decade (for example, Phillipson 1992; Pennycook 2006) but the effect of English on some major languages is still not being addressed by educationalists and language policy specialists alike. In a recent volume on language policy Ricento (2006) positions language policy studies within the broader area of sociolinguistics and states that language policy debate includes elements of political, social and economic theory. While there is a recognition and even a warning that mother-tongue education and multiligualism are driving the moral framework for language policy debates (Pennycook 2006), the underlying assumption is that it is minor languages that are affected and which need to be protected through more equitable governmental and educational policies. Major languages like Arabic are not seen to be under any threat. The presentation highlighted the fact that minor and major were terms used to describe the usership of a particular language and not its importance. In this case Arabic is a seen as a major language because of the number of its speakers and the number of countries where it is considered as the first language.

Arabic, the first and official language in all the Arab countries, is currently being pushed into a minor role in post-secondary education. Many universities in the Middle East and the Gulf, for instance, use English as a medium of instruction (EMI) for all natural science and even some human science subjects. The status of Arabic as a medium of instruction (AMI) in primary and secondary schools is also threatened as there is a growing trend to introduce English at a very early stage and to maximise classroom contact hours while gradually replacing Arabic, especially in the private sector.

Twenty male students in their twenties were interviewed about their experiences of studying scientific subjects through the medium of English. They were also asked if Arabic could be used to teach the sciences. It was found that the participants associated English mainly with technology, sciences, business, international trade, employment and travel. The findings confirmed the results of other studies on students' views of English. English was seen as the normal thing to do in a competitive world as the participants were aware of the limitation of their employability if they did not have an English medium qualification in an increasingly competitive market that requires a high command of English. EMI comes with its academic and learning challenges; and some participants mentioned the difficulty of understanding the scientific register and lexis of a number of subjects. The specialist discourses of chemistry or medicine are not familiar to students who studied their sciences in Arabic in their secondary education. One of the effects of an EMI policy on the learning experience of the student is that English becomes a challenge and sometimes a burden or an obstacle instead of a medium. In addition to dealing with the academic demands of a given area of scientific study the Arab student has to grapple with specific linguistic structures and the semantic challenges of the linguistic vehicle. These last two challenges, I argued, could be avoided if the mother tongue was used instead of English.

Arabic was found to be associated with linguistic, cultural and religious heritage. All participants recognised the importance of Arabic but very few saw it as a possible language of science even though they all did mathematics, biology, chemistry and physics through Arabic in secondary education. It was clear that the spread of English and its association with power and modernity had a strong effect on the Emirati male student. There were two sides to the participants' linguistic identity: the cultural, maintained through Arabic, and the scientific, which is maintained through English.

The audience raised a number of points during and after the presentation and these were mainly about the possibility of translating modern sciences to Arabic, and the effect of AMI on employability.

Email: S.Troudi@exeter.ac.uk

## References

Pennycook, A. 2006 'Postmodernism in language policy' in T. Ricento (ed.). *An Introduction to Language Policy: Theory and Method.* Malden, Mass.: Blackwell.

Phillipson, R. 1992. *Linguistic Imperialism.* Oxford: Oxford University Press.

Ricento, T. (ed.). 2006. *An Introduction to Language Policy: Theory and Method.* Malden, Mass.: Blackwell.

## 5.4 The status of English language in Saudi Arabia: a critical analysis

**Manssour Habbash** *TESOL Department, University of Exeter, Exeter, UK*

The era in which we live nowadays witnesses an unavoidable flow of global and international communications in all aspects of life. Education is no exception and the need to cope with the rapid speed of developments in technologies, economies and sciences has raised the need for rethinking current educational policies in many countries. This international/global convergence has increased the need for English language education in many Arab states, particularly in the Gulf Countries where English, unquestionably, brings advantages to the millions who learn it. In Saudi Arabia, English language has gained a higher status in many domains. This stems from the fact that it is a crucial component in public and higher education, academia, international communications, job market, and all other domains related to science and technology. As a result a large-scale curricular reform has been launched, including changes to considerable parts of English language syllabuses as well as the introduction of English as a compulsory subject to be taught from the sixth grade of the elementary school rather than from the intermediate school onwards. There seems also to be a trend to lower the level of compulsory English to start from Grade 4 as well as to teach scientific subjects through the medium of English so that students will have already become familiar with the language when they start their higher education. In fact, this is already happening in a number of local private schools where English is taught as an independent subject from the first grade of the elementary stage. Coupled with official and public discontent with poor English language proficiency among students at pre-university level, such increased reliance on English in the absence of empirical research will not best serve the future of Saudi English language learners nor will it safeguard their Islamic values and cultural heritage. Equally important is the fact that such decisions do not take into account the fact that global English might be seen as unilateral in vision (Zughoul 2003) and thus create a potential threat to Arabic.

With such concerns in mind I focused on global English in my presentation and its role in shaping English language policy in Public Education in Saudi Arabia. I briefed my audience on key aspects relating to the phenomenon of global English as well as a number of scholarly perspectives that have arisen from this area of critical applied linguistics and language policy. Such perspectives included came both from those who view the universally acknowledged importance of English with great alarm (Pennycook 2001; Canagarajah 1999) and those who view it positively as a potential means for growing world unity and peace (Crystal 1997). They also included other perspectives, particularly those which take a more critical stance and refer to the phenomenon of global English as 'linguistic imperialism' (Phillipson 1992 and Skutnabb-Kangas 2000). In addition, I pointed out to the audience that a salient feature these opposing views have in common is that they approach the issue of global English from a macro-level of analysis or as Graddol and Meinhof (1999:1) succinctly put it: 'the issues raised by global English go beyond concerns about teaching methodology, or the linguistic analysis of varieties'.

Drawing on a postmodernism conceptualisation of critical theory, I then intro-duced my ongoing research as an attempt to examine critically the significance of English language teaching and its role in shaping language education policy in Saudi Arabia as well as to investigate whether global English forms a potential threat to Arabic as a medium of instruction. I followed this with a reflection on key aspects of data collected so far. I indicated three themes that have emerged from interviews with Saudi ELT students and teachers. Those were: (1) the unchallenged realities of global English, (2) Arabic as a language of science and (3) the threat to Arabic.

I indicated that the findings show some examples of the simplistic view of global English in which English is glorified and is associated with modernity, high quality life, technology, science, career, success, etc. I also explained that while some of the participants view negatively the role of Arabic as a language for science and depict it as a language for localism and religion, others express concerns about the potential threat that English may pose to Arabic as the language of instruction. Finally, the session concluded with a follow-up discussion in which the audience raised some interesting issues related to my work. Such discussion was invaluable and will definitely inform the steps that I will take in the next stage of this research.

Email: mmrh201@googlemail.com

## References

Canagarajah, S. 1999. *Resisting Linguistic Imperialism in English Teaching.* Oxford: Oxford University Press.

Pennycook, A. 2001. *Critical Applied Linguistics: A critical Introduction.* Mahwah, N.J.: Lawrence Erlbaum.

Phillipson, R. 1992. *Linguistic Imperialism.* Oxford: Oxford University Press.

## 5.5 The continuing use of English in Nigerian schools: undergraduates' perceptions

**Adejoke V. Jibowo** *Olabisi Onabanjo University, Ago-Iwoye, Nigeria*

### Introduction

English continues to be the official language and medium of instruction in Nigerian schools. Textbooks, learning materials and examinations are written in the language. English is everywhere; at home, markets, offices, technical workshops, business centres, hospitals, etc. Some people even see it as a lingua franca. Meanwhile, there are about 400 indigenous languages spoken, but only three—Hausa, Igbo and Yoruba—are recognised as national languages. Mother-tongue advocates such as Awoniyi, Bamgbose, Banjo and Fafunwa are of the view that it is high time Nigeria began educating her citizens through the use of indigenous languages. Fafunwa (2005) asserts that when a child is properly grounded in the mother tongue, he/she stands a better chance of understanding concepts taught. The debate about which language is desirable for instruction in the nation's educational institutions continues. There are arguments for and against the continuing use of English as the medium of instruction in schools. The study on which I reported in my presentation sought to find out through a survey the perceptions of university undergraduates on the matter.

### Research questions

Two questions guided the study:

1. How would undergraduates see the continuing use of English as language of instruction in schools?
2. Would the undergraduates' demographic characteristics—gender, type of institution, specialisation, level of study, mode of entry and socio-economic status—have any significant influence on their perceptions?

### Methodology

Three hundred undergraduates from federal, state and private universities in Ogun and Lagos states were randomly selected. The instrument was a ten-item-scale questionnaire on which subjects indicated their degree of agreement or disagreement. The survey included subjects' perceptions on the necessity of the continuing use of English in schools, the importance of English to global, scientific and technological interactions, problems of the multilingual nature of the country and the need for Nigeria to be in tune with a global academic lingua franca. Subjects' responses were collected and analysed using descriptive and inferential statistics.

### Results

1. Descriptive analysis revealed 51.7 per cent for and 0.7 per cent against the continuing use of the English language in schools;
2. Subjects' level of study, specialisation, socio-economic background and type of institution had no significant influence on their perceptions.
3. Also, gender and mode of entry did not significantly affect subjects' perceptions.

## Discussion

The undergraduates selected for this study perceived the continuing use of English for instruction in Nigerian schools as being necessary, even in the twenty-first century although many students often wished this was not the case, simply because of the difficulty they encounter in learning English language in schools. They affirmed, through high positive ratings, the idea that English enhances students' understanding of scientific and technological concepts, and gives them opportunity for useful linguistic interactions, English, being a global academic lingua franca ought to be used and taught in Nigerian schools. Also, the undergraduates noted the facts that Nigeria was yet to evolve a national language that could effectively replace English and that because of the multilingual nature of the nation, English was serving as a unifying factor among the peoples of Nigeria.

## Conclusion

This study reveals that the Nigerian undergraduates sampled had a positive perception about the continuing use of English for instruction in schools. They value the continuing use of the language because of its importance in the global linguistic, scientific and technological development. The study also indicates that the teaching of language, materials and personnel are the areas that need more attention.

## References

Ayodele, S. O. 1988. 'The problem of language for educating Nigerian learners'. 4th Faculty of Education Lecture, University of Ibadan.

Fafunwa, A.B., J. I. McCauley and J. A. Sokoya. 1989. *Education in Mother Tongue—The Ife Primary Research Project (1970–1978)*. Ibadan: University Press Limited.

# 5.6 Teachers' roles in team-teaching in upper secondary schools in Japan

**Akiko Nambu** *Tohoku University, Japan*

## Introduction

Ever since team-teaching was first introduced into English language teaching in Japanese secondary schools in 1987, the role of native-speaking assistant language teachers (ALTs) has been regarded as a key part of English language education in Japan. According to Andrewes (1999), team-teaching between native-speaker teachers (NSTs) and non-native speaker teachers (NNSTs) supplies learners with the best of both worlds, a natural authenticity and the expertise of the non-native. Medgyes (1992) points out that NNSTs never stop being learners of English as they meet the same sort of difficulties as their students. My presentation attempted to explore how Japanese teachers of English (JTEs) can promote students' learning by maintaining a good balance of classroom roles with ALTs' in the team-teaching of English as a foreign language in Japan.

## Study findings

My research involved interviews with seven JTEs and three ALTs. All the participants have been given pseudonyms. The research was conducted in two different public upper secondary schools in Japan in 2004. The interview data showed that the roles of JTEs are:

- to function as a bridge between ALTs and students, and
- to anticipate language difficulties.

Suzuki (JTE) encourages students to do their activities while providing an example for emulation: 'I ask the ALTs a question first, and then students speak to the ALTs with my questions as a starting point'.

However, the observation data revealed that, generally, the JTEs did not show much empathy with the students. Also the JTE did not achieve their stated role of a bridge between the ALT and students. Only the ALTs seemed to attempt to check how well students could understand the class. In one class, when students attempted to create expressions for apologising, they tended to write 'I am sorry, I cannot', and they did not explain the reasons why they could not. When Richard (ALT) noticed this, he immediately started to explain to the class why it is necessary to express their reasons for not being able to complete the task. Owen (ALT) also added his opinions to those of Richard. Richard and Owen did not seem to have planned this before the class; however, these explanations helped the students to produce more creative expressions. Tanaka (JTE) did not join the ALTs. He was simply watching the class. In another group, Aoki (JTE) seemed to conduct the class precisely according to his lesson plan. One student pointed out of the words 'hot chocolate' on a menu written in the course book, and said to the class loudly in Japanese, 'Hot chocolate sounds strange! Is that melting chocolate?' Nobody answered her question. Richard did not understand her Japanese. Aoki could have answered the question; however, he frequently checked his watch, and tended to concentrate on adhering to the textbook rather than responding to questions. Possible reasons for this relate to the JTEs as NNSTs, who tend to avoid unpredictable situations, and favour safer forms of classwork (Medgyes 1999). JTEs still find it difficult or puzzling to handle team teaching effectively during the class.

## Discussion and implications

In team-teaching classrooms involving JTEs and ALTs, JTEs will sometimes encounter situations in which only the JTEs can find out what difficulties students feel in their learning process and why, from the point of view of Japanese speakers. The role as the bridge between students and the ALT is closely connected with the students' difficulties and questions. In the one class, if the JTE (Aoki) had listened to and answered the student's question about the words 'hot chocolate', and also explained why it seemed odd in a Japanese context to the student and to the ALT at the same time, they could all have benefited and learned something. In the other class, when students did not attempt to express their reasons when apologising, if the JTE Tanaka had asked the ALTs, 'I'd like to accept his or her offer or invitation, but I cannot. How can I express my feelings?', the discussion would have helped students understand how coursebook expressions can be used in real-life situations. The biggest challenge for JTEs is to cope with unpredictable situations flexibly in team-teaching classrooms.

However, if the JTEs can grasp the opportunity of using the students' questions to discover their difficulties during class, the JTEs as NNSTs can fulfill insightful roles (Medgyes 1999) similar to the ALTs as NSTs.

Email: akikonanbu@hotmai.com

## References

Andrewes, S. 1999. 'Team teaching'. *English Teaching Professional* 11: 39.
Medgyes, P. 1992. 'Native or non-native: who's worth more?'. *ELT Journal* 46/4: 340–9.
Medgyes, P. 1999. *The Non-native Teacher*. Ismaning: Max Hueber Verlag.

## 5.7 Codeswitching in teacher talk of primary English teachers in China

**Xiaofang Qian** *Beijing Normal University, Beijing, China*

## Introduction

Codeswitching (CS) is a common phenomenon of language contact in bilingual, multilingual and even monolingual societies. It is generally understood as 'the alternative use by bilinguals (or multilinguals) of two or more languages in the same conversation' (Milroy and Li 1995: 7). Many classroom researchers investigate bilingual classroom CS of various types, while a few study CS in foreign language classrooms where the foreign language is both the means and ends of learning and teaching.

## Research methods

I presented my research, a case study of CS between Chinese and English occurring in primary English classrooms, which analysed CS of two teachers participating in the Primary English Curriculum Innovation (PECI) project in Beijing, China. This adopts a holistic approach to the innovation and implementation of curriculum. This research addressed three questions:

1. What types of CS can be found in the primary English classroom?
2. Is there any change in the quantity of teachers' CS as students' move to a higher level?
3. What functions does teachers' CS serve in classroom interaction?

Data consisted of transcripts of twenty videoed lessons given by the two primary English teachers (ten lessons each), covering lessons from grade 1 to grade 4. An estimate of the distribution of the two languages via word count was conducted. The units of analysis—a turn of speaking in teacher–student interaction—were identified and assigned to a category, namely, whole target language (TL) units, L1 units and mixed units. A functional language alteration analysis framework following Kim and Elder (2005) was applied to identify the functions. When coding, I took into account where in a sequence of actions the switch occurred. Patterns of the teachers' CS over the four years were compared to see if there were any changes.

## Findings

My findings comprised syntactical identification of the switches between English and Chinese and the pedagogical and social functions these switches served. They were (1) there is far more inter-sentential CS (switching at sentence level) in both teachers' language than tag (i.e. insertion of discourse markers) or intra-sentential switching (i.e. switching at word, phrase or clause boundaries); (2) the quantity of CS decreases drastically as the students move from year 1 to year 4; (3) it was found that teachers used CS as both a methodological and social strategy in classroom interaction.

The methodological functions identified were (a) for translation, (b) for clarification, (c) for highlighting and (d) for efficiency. The social functions included CS (a) for praise, (b) for encouragement and (c) for disapproval. It was also found that many examples overlapped in the description. Teachers integrated both methodological and social motivations in one single switch. They wanted either to remind pupils kindly or encourage them, and to make the pupils aware of the problems or their dissatisfaction.

## Conclusion

The following conclusions were drawn:

1. CS is a readily available and frequently applied strategy for teachers in classroom interaction and classroom management.
2. It is obvious that teachers' CS does not impede the learning of young learners. Appropriate use of it helps cultivate and reinforce good habits of learning for students (especially for lower levels) and fosters a healthy and close relationship between students and teachers.
3. It can be inferred that the teachers had the ability to instruct the lesson mostly in the target language or in the mixed form, switching into and out of the instructional language. Only when efficient instruction is essential in their classrooms or when they want to maintain a favourable social relationship with students do they turn to L1 to communicate the message to students.
4. The drastic decrease of CS in both teachers is also strong evidence of the success and impact of the PECI Project. It improves the pupils' English to the extent that teachers can dispense with CS and L1 in classroom instruction in year 3 and year 4. It also proves that the holistic approach to curriculum innovation has been effective in the fulfillment of the educational objectives laid down at the time of curriculum change.

Email: amandaqxf@sina.com

## References

Milroy, L. and W. Li. 1995. 'A social network approach to code-switching: the example of a bilingual community in Britain' in L. Milroy and P. Muysken (eds.). *One Speaker, Two Languages: Cross-disciplinary Perspectives on Code-switching*. New York: Cambridge University Press.

Kim, S. H. O. and C. Elder. 2005. 'Language choices and pedagogic functions in the foreign language classroom: a cross-linguistic functional analysis of teacher talk'. *Language Teaching Research* 9/4: 355–80.

## 5.8 *ELT Journal*/IATEFL debate: North, south, east or west, good language teaching is always the best

**Anthony Bruton** *Universidad de Sevilla, Sevilla, Spain* and
**Adrian Holliday** *Canterbury Christ Church University, Canterbury, UK*

### Anthony Bruton

The point of the motion is whether good foreign language (FL) teaching is contextually specific or not, and whether it is methodological or contextual considerations that should be prioritised. My view in defence of the motion is that we have to characterise the common requirements of good FL teaching before taking account of context. It may seem obvious, but it is good teaching, not good teachers, that is under consideration.

### Major issues

It is commonly recognised that there are two major reasons for including FLs on most secondary state education curricula. One is to encourage more intercultural understanding and tolerance, and the second is to develop the ability to communicate with other peoples. These goals of compulsory FL learning are not really controversial, though there remain a few voices questioning communicative FL learning goals in certain contexts. The main area of contention in ELT is the oral medium in communicative language teaching (CLT), especially in relation to the following:

- ability in the oral medium as a goal;
- the FL as the oral language medium in the classroom; and
- peer-to-peer work as a necessary organisational feature of FL classrooms, since both teacher-fronted and student–student interaction patterns seem to be accepted.

### Arguments against

The case against all three of the above points tends to be couched in either cultural (Bax 2003) or institutional terms (Holliday 1994). The argument is that they reflect so-called western viewpoints and are impositions, which are insensitive to local cultural norms and/or to institutional constraints. In both cases, there is a political slant defending those local practices which do not include oral or peer FL interaction.

### Counter arguments

This view is to be refuted. To begin with, empirical evidence shows that students of EFL in state secondary and tertiary educational systems generally rate the need to be able to speak over the other skills. If spoken ability is a significant target goal, there seem to be good reasons for it to be developed in secondary classrooms. A logical extension of this would be that the FL should be the medium of most, or at least some, of the classroom discourse. In turn, for most students to have the opportunity to speak in the FL, the justification for some peer work seems self-evident. Furthermore, presumably the students are accustomed to speaking, and hopefully in class, and to relating to each other in groups, hopefully also in class. So, the issue is whether they do these things in the FL or not, not whether such practices are imports. A very good example of the possibilities of bringing communicative oral activity into the state secondary EFL classroom was given by Yanghee Han from Korea in her excellent presentation at the Exeter IATEFL conference.

Instead of defending the cultural and institutional reasons for not adopting a communicative classroom approach to FL teaching, or for adopting a non-communicative approach, it would be more productive to attempt to understand why the communicative approach does not reach most state educational classrooms across the world, including those in places such as the US, the UK and Australia for example, in the way it reaches private language school classrooms. I would suggest that there are a number of common contributing factors, but they are not just or even necessarily cultural. If we do not make greater efforts to understand why so many FL students in compulsory education fail to develop the capacities many of them want and believe they need, we are perpetuating injustices by denying these very students what other more economically privileged ones can generally obtain elsewhere on the open market (Bruton 2005).

## Back to the motion

Returning to the motion, the position defended here is that good FL teaching has to be seen in relation to FL learning goals. Therefore good FL teaching means good communicative FL teaching, not good non-communicative FL teaching. So, although there might be teachers who are considered good in different cultural contexts, if they are not good communicative teachers, that is not good enough for me.

## Adrian Holliday

I would like to argue that good teaching *is* universal, but that it should look very different in different scenarios, and that it needs to be a lot more adaptable than the packaged style of teaching that has originated in the private sector of the English-speaking West.

At the 'standard' end, this packaged form is a 'communicative method' which corresponds to what I have referred to in the past as a 'learning group ideal'—where teacher-imagined 'learners' are expected to conform to a very particular oral régime, have to be 'learner trained' to conform to it and, hence, culturally changed. At the liberal end there has been a preference for the notion that 'communicative' must mean 'oral'; and classroom research has been restricted to what 'learners' and teachers say to each other, ignoring the social and political aspect of the classroom.

In contrast to this packaged form, I offer four examples of good universal teaching from four scenarios. I wish to emphasise that I am not presenting these examples as representing 'national contexts'. National context implies a simple and entirely homogenous set of circumstances. If I cannot say 'my context' easily in my own complex country, no-one should be encouraged to say 'my context' about their country.

### Scenario 1

A small class of ten Iranian students in a UK university studying English for engineering. The teacher is very skilfully employing communicative activities. The students quickly break the stereotype of wanting grammar and learn the values of a communicative approach—so much so that they feel that the teacher is not going far enough.

The students rebel and ask the teacher to give them activities on paper and then to sit back and wait to be consulted. When this happens the students' grades improve.

*Scenario 2*

A very large grammar class of three hundred Egyptian university students. The teacher writes grammar tasks on the blackboard, and asks the students to form their own groups to produce oral outcomes. They use their own books, read and produce English, while the teacher monitors from a distance because it would be inappropriate for him to get close and there is no room anyway.

*Scenario 3*

Following Canagarajah's theme of 'private sites of learning' Sri Lankan secondary school students scribble their own lesson scripts and cultural agendas into their American textbooks, converting the characters in the textbook situations into Tamil film stars.

*Scenario 4*

Hong Kong Chinese students in the UK will only talk outside the U-shape classroom which they consider to be a repressive régime of teacher surveillance.

All these scenarios show students in very different types of locations practising high degrees of autonomy, communicative competence and intelligence, sometimes *despite* the way in which they are being taught, and always against common expectation. These are qualities which the students bring with them, but which they will hide from their teachers if they are not acknowledged. Good teaching seeks out these qualities in students and allows them space, and in so doing needs to get to grips with the deeper realities of scenarios within which teaching takes place. This is very different from a 'standard' communicative method, which tries to construct its own classroom scenario within which students must fit. However, in a very different manner, a broad communicative *educational approach* does adapt to the students and scenarios it finds. Hence the second two communicative principles: (2) communicating with what the students bring to the classroom and (3) communicating with the exigencies of the classroom. These principles need, however, to be interpreted broadly. The first principle—(1) treat language as communication—does not necessarily imply oral group-work tasks. At a very basic level, a teacher can lecture for an extended period, and this can be communicative provided that the intelligence and communicative competence of the students is being actively engaged, through listening and working out what is going on, and that what is being said is something meaningful (and therefore authentic) to the students' lives.

## References

Bax, S. 2003. 'The end of CLT: A context approach to language teaching'. *ELT Journal* 57: 278–87.

Bruton, A. 2005. 'Power to the people?'. *IATEFL Voices* 185: 11–12.

Holliday, A. 1994. *Appropriate Methodology and Social Context*. Cambridge: Cambridge University Press.

## 5.9 Plenary: Empowering EFL students through teaching World Englishes

**Rosa Jinyoung Shim** *Seoul Digital University, Seoul, Korea*

### Introduction

The 17th President of Korea, Lee Myung-bak (MB), was inaugurated on the 25 February 2008. The new administration subscribes to a hard-core conservative political line which is a definite change from the rather liberal and anti-authoritative administration that was led by president Noh for the past five years.

On Thursday, 31 January 2008, a morning radio programme on a national broadcasting network (SBS) in Korea began a two-hour 'English immersion broadcast'. Listeners' reactions to the broadcast were diverse but mostly negative. Some even accused the station of attempting to curry favour with the new administration. Later, that day, the producers of the programme announced that they won't be doing it again, and that they were simply trying to bring the issue of English immersion education to the public's attention and obtain an estimate of the proficiency level of listeners who were confident enough to participate in an all-English radio programme.

The problem was that throughout the two-hour broadcast, the strongest message conveyed to the listeners was that 'Koreans needed to learn English so as to communicate with Americans'. Thus this radio broadcast effectively demonstrated that one of the most coveted 'symbolic capitals' in Korean society today is 'English.' Moreover, it was made clear that we were to aim for one specific brand of English, that is, American English. In other words, 'symbolic power' was vested in American English. By promoting this 'symbolic power', 'symbolic violence' was exercised against all others who dared to advocate the concept of world Englishes (WE) or even that of British English (cf., Bourdieu 1991).

### The plan to achieve perfection for public education in English

As the producer of the radio programme asserted, the idea for this special broadcast was sparked by the presidential transition team's proposal to 'strengthen' public school English education. What exactly are the specifics of the proposal? It pledges two main objectives and several specific actions to realise the objectives:

### Objectives

All high school graduates
1. will be able to communicate in everyday practical English,
2. can go to college without private spending on English education.

### Specific actions

The government will:
1. Spend 1.7 billion dollars to hire 23,000 new English teachers who are qualified to practice TEE (Teaching English in English).
2. Spend 480 million dollars to provide in-service training for 3,000 current teachers each year for five years so that current teachers may become proficient enough to practice TEE.

3. Provide financial aid to national teacher training colleges when they hire 'native-speaker' lecturers. Specific amount not announced.

4. Spend 340 million dollars to provide schools in farming and fishing communities with teacher helpers who will be hired from college students, housewives, local residents and overseas residents that are competent in English. And spend 230 million dollars to hire, train and deploy 'native-speaker' teacher helpers in schools located in farming and fishing communities.

5. Increase English classroom hours for 3rd and 4th graders from one hour to three hours a week and teachers will practise TEE in all English classes by 2010. By 2011, 5th and 6th graders will also receive three hours of English lessons instead of two hours a week, and TEE will be practised in all English classes.

6. Implement TEE for 9th and 10th graders in 2010. By 2012, middle and high schools will practice TEE for all conversation focus classes (70 per cent for middle school, 50 per cent for high school—the rest will stay the same as now—regular English classes without TEE).

7. Grant complete autonomy to the provincial governments or the municipal offices of education in authorising textbooks to be used in schools that fall under their jurisdiction. Restrictions placed on books published by foreign publishers will be lifted.

8. Develop and adopt a national English proficiency examination that concentrates on practical English. This exam will be executed multiple times throughout the year so that students will have the chance to improve their scores until they achieve their goals.

This proposal is now in the hands of the Ministry of Education, Science and Technology waiting to be implemented. No doubt, it has initiated a myriad of reactions. One must remember, however, that the proposal did not appear out of thin air. It was fuelled by the social discourse surrounding 'English' that propelled an insatiable thirst for 'English' in Korean society. Foucault (1980) explains this process as the circulation of 'truth' through the reproduction and exertion of power/knowledge.

## The 'fact/truth': 'English as the life-line'

In Korea today, it is simply a fact or truth that English is the life-line. The key concept that was employed in this discourse was that of the 'English divide', which was derived from the term 'digital divide'. The term 'digital divide' became popular when former President Bill Clinton and his Vice President Al Gore used it in a speech in Knoxville, in 1996. It originally referred to gaps in ownership of computers between groups in society. A few years later the concept of 'English divide' was also born through an article printed in *Business Week Online* (2001), which describes in detail:

- how the ability to speak English divides the wealthy and the poor in Europe,
- how crucial it is for anyone looking for a good job to speak English, and
- how the power to take control can shift from the parents to the children in a family because of the ability to speak English.

A few months later in Korea, an op-ed contributor for the widely read *DongA Daily* (Kim 2002) claimed that English proficiency is the determining factor of 'social caste' in Korea. She writes quite persuasively that people without the ability to speak English fluently will eventually sink and drown. She also quotes the work of Lakoff (2000) and says that language defines reality and has the power to change it, and goes on to claim that this power now resides with English. Henceforth dozens of articles in Korean newspapers reinforce the idea that English is not only critical to the survival of a nation in the international market, but that it provides a way to pass on a respectable social caste to our children. In 2002, the fierce debate on adopting English as *an* official language, or *the* official language began in Korea.

Last year, as the MB presidential campaign sought to criticise the Noh administration for failure in education policies, major/popular newspapers began printing whole series of articles on the importance of English, and how the Noh administration had turned its back on the people by not delivering a strong public education policy for English. Some of the evidence presented was:

- Eight out of the ten countries ranked for national competitiveness (Singapore, Hong Kong, Luxembourg, Denmark, Switzerland, Iceland, the Netherlands, and Sweden) are small but strong, and the common factor in these countries is that they emphasise English education for their people.
- All of the successful European countries have adopted English as an official language and the people speak it fluently.
- In France, the bilingual literacy rate is 45 per cent, much lower than the other successful European countries. As a result, their national competitiveness was ranked 28th, just one step ahead of Korea, nowhere near the top ten.
- Early English education must be introduced as soon as possible so as to become as competitive as the successful small-but-strong European and Asian countries.
- More than 300,000 Indians living in India are employed by American and multinational companies because of their ability to speak English.

## Reactions to MB's proposal for public English education

### Negative reactions

Even among English education professionals, people don't necessarily see eye to eye on every aspect of this debate. The first set of arguments is as follows:

1. The 23,000 new English teachers who will be hired must be graduates of teacher training colleges who are already qualified to practise TEE and they should be hired as regular teachers rather than as temporary teachers with fixed-term contracts.
2. The teacher helpers should be hired from college students enrolled in teacher training colleges.
3. The practice of TEE should begin in primary schools and middle school lower grades rather than high school.
4. The national English proficiency examination should be administered separately from the college entrance examination, or rather, the evaluation of English should be removed from the college entrance selection process altogether.

As one may notice, this first set of concerns represents the voice that wishes to uphold the rights of new teachers and preserve respect for current teachers. The concerns could not be considered opinions against the goals of the proposal.

Then, there is a second set of reactions that focuses on four major issues:

5. The economic issue: the contention is that the proposal will result in a waste of national resources, i.e. it is too expensive and not cost-effective. Reasons for everyone studying English are questioned since only a handful of people need it.
6. The educational/developmental issue: the increase in English classes will be detrimental to the balanced development of children's intellect and psychology.
7. The national identity issue: too much emphasis on English will destroy national identity. Korean culture, literature and language will suffer.
8. The social conflict issue: private spending for English education will increase and conflict between social classes will escalate.

## Positive reactions

With such strong negative reactions, one might wonder why the proposal continues to stoke heated debate, both pro and con. That is because the 'truth' surrounding the 'need' for English that had permeated our society still stands strong. Not surprisingly, the people who support the proposal are aware of the problems pointed out by those that are opposed to it. They admit that there are problems. In fact, more than 70 per cent of the respondents in a recent survey said that they expect private spending in English education to increase. Nevertheless, 51 per cent of the same respondents were in favor of the proposal. They are willing to pay the price.

The arguments for positive reactions can be summarised as follows:

1. The economic issue: the globalisation of the world market does not allow a nation to take a laid-back position. We do not live in a state where the majority of the nation's industry is based on manufacturing plants (28.7 per cent in 2004). Thus we cannot assume a specific working class who don't need English to survive. The service industry (67.2 per cent in 2004) upon which our economy heavily depends today is controlled by information that can be accessed only with English. This explains the phenomenon of discrimination against non-English speakers in highly sought-after occupations such as the law, medicine, academia and upper-level business. All of the small but strong economies are supported by an English-speaking citizenry. Therefore, everyone in the nation must speak English if we want to become citizens of a wealthy country.
2. The educational/developmental issue: the general perception is that there are enough success stories that show success is achievable by any child. So, people are not worried. The changing demography of our society—the birth-rate in 2004 was 1.08, increasing to 1.25 in 2007—is such that the majority of families have only one child, on whom the parents and grandparents are willing to concentrate all of the family resources (cf., 'little emperors' in China). Parents will do anything to provide the English competitive edge for their children. If possible, English education will be provided to foetuses in the womb. And since it is in a family's best interest to ensure the well-being of their child, the educational issues shouldn't be a problem. It's the 'I know what's best for my child' attitude.
3. The national identity issue: national identity in the post-modern society/market is not uniform. It is complex, fluid, and at times contradictory (cf., Graddol 2006). Many successful small but strong countries are multilingual. They don't seem to have problems with national identity.

**4.** The social conflict issue: the rich already have access to English education with private education or overseas training. 7000 students left the country to study English in 2005 from Seoul alone. The majority of foreign students in language schools in North America, Singapore, Shanghai, Manila, Hong Kong, and Johannesburg are Korean. People who cannot afford to go overseas need to be provided with a free service through public education. So parents are voluntarily asking for more and more public school English education

Both sides of the argument seem to present persuasive and logical reasons to support their positions. But in the end, even those that are opposed will reluctantly agree if promised that their concerns will be taken care of. Then, is that the end of the debate? Not quite. There are critical issues that both sides of the argument have overlooked.

## Critical issues overlooked

### The perfectionist attitude issue (the native-speaker myth)

The government promises financial aid to national teacher training colleges when they hire 'native-speaker' lecturers. Why is this necessary when there are already many competent bilingual lecturers? In addition, the new proposal says that native-speaking teacher helpers will be placed in schools? Again, why is this an issue when there are thousands of qualified bilingual teacher trainees ready to be deployed? Moreover, will qualified NABAN (North America, Britain, Australia, and New Zealand) teachers come for non-regular jobs with low pay?

The proposal also calls for a lift of restrictions placed on books published by foreign publishers. This attitude stems from the belief that these books are better than what we already have. The unspoken view here is that whatever is American standard is global standard. Pretty soon, we can start teaching students to measure in yards and pounds instead of metres and kilos!

The problem here is that this perfectionist attitude will make students feel insecure about their abilities to speak English no matter how high their proficiency.

### The pronunciation issue

There is a strong sentiment that native-like pronunciation is the most important factor in proficiency. Examples of social discourse that promotes this attitude are:

**1.** In India, a columnist (Dutt 2006) prints a confessional article describing how not all Englishes are treated equally in India. Certain brands have more prestige. Elite society is hypocritical and dishonest because its members seem to join in the celebration of the rise of the middle class but are still finding excuses to exclude and sneer at others who lack Westernised sophistication and speak with local Indian accents.

**2.** Also, in the Philippines, 'Arroyism' characterised by 'Englished Tagalog' expressions are considered a humorous style of Filipino English while 'Carabao English' characterised by 'Tagalogised English' spoken by the working class is considered a variety of Filipino and is deemed unintelligible by English speakers. In reality, both types are unintelligible to someone who does not speak Tagalog. Arroyism may contain English expressions but they cannot be understood outside the circle of Tagalog speakers because it borrows from idiomatic expressions in Tagalog (Tan 2007).

## The America-as-the-supreme-power issue

In the past, there was a time when China was the centre of the universe: The elite (Yangban) class had to learn Chinese in order to get ahead in society. None of the commoners (Sangmin) class could learn Chinese because it was the language of the elite.

In the West, French used to have the same status that English now enjoys. Then we went through a time when Japanese was the tool for success: rich people sent their children to Japan to learn the 'new knowledge'. There were people who said with conviction that the only way for Koreans to survive was to speak Japanese and become a true citizen of Japan. Very similar to what the current administration is doing … except now it's America that we are looking to.

The question is 'How certain are we that America will prevail?' The proportion of trade relations is twice that for non-English-speaking countries as compared with English-speaking countries: US 12.3 per cent, Britain 1.8 per cent, Germany 3.1 per cent, China 22.1 per cent, Taiwan 3.5 per cent, Hong Kong 5.0 per cent. For travel the figures are: as many as 50 per cent go to China and Japan while only 7.2 per cent go to the US. Of tourists coming into Korea those from China and Taiwan make up 21 per cent of the total, from Japan 35 per cent and from the US 9 per cent.

## The TEE issue

480 million dollars have been promised to provide in-service training for 3,000 current teachers each year so that current teachers may become proficient enough to practise TEE. By 2010, 3rd and 4th graders will get three hours of English classes a week in TEE. By 2011, 5th and 6th grades will also receive three hours of English classes in TEE. Seoul Metropolitan Office of Education announces the policy of three-strikes out for teachers that cannot pass the evaluation for TEE.

It seems that all of the difficulties in English learning are caused by lack of input in the classroom, and therefore they would all be solved if teachers give students more input in the classroom by speaking English.

However, English is already accessible to everyone through the internet. Tens of thousands of children and adults are already enjoying non-stop American broadcasting. TEE is not going to be the magic potion that will deliver English proficiency to students learning English in the classroom. Motivation and interest are the catalysts that will make it happen. Confidence building of both teachers and students must precede anything else.

## The spread of 'materialistic values' issue

The focus behind the new proposal is most definitely centred on 'progress' and 'materialism' which are the most salient characterisations of the MB administration. The extent of the urgency for money to provide education to children and the extent of disintegration of morality in favour of materialism has resulted in housewives taking on jobs in extreme conditions (both morally and physically). These women would most probably not have resorted to such employment if they hadn't been driven to provide a better education for their children.

## The private schools issue

Another important aspect of the MB administration's education policy is the lifting of restrictions on the establishment and management of private schools.

According to de la Croix and Deopke (2007) 'states with higher inequality have a larger share of private schooling and less overall spending on public schooling'. For example, in the US, rich parents send their children to private school and thus they don't stand to gain from high-quality public education. That is why they vote for lower taxes and less spending on public schools.

The reason this has not happened in Korea is because private schools were restricted by government policy. Autonomous private schools must be authorised by the government and the process is very difficult. Also the selection process of new students in the few available private schools used to be strictly monitored and based on objective academic criteria. Thus the limited number of spaces in private schools is not controlled by wealth other than the process of rich kids getting more chance to get private tutoring in preparation for entrance exams.

When these restrictions are lifted, as the new administration promises, people who can afford private schools will simply send their children to these private schools and soon they will lose interest in public education policy.

## The human rights issue

Teachers considered incompetent in TEE will be labelled as incompetent teachers. Students who do not show interest or progress will be labelled as lazy or inferior. Advocates of WE might be considered 'crazy.' Social marginalisation of people who do not agree is imminent. So how do we prevent such social marginalisation and promote human rights in the English education field? We need to become empowered as professionals and help our students to empower themselves.

## Empowering the student

In order to empower our students, we need to practise critical pedagogy: a teaching approach that attempts to help students question and challenge domination, and the beliefs and practices that dominate. In other words, it is the theory and practice of helping students achieve critical consciousness.

The first step for critical pedagogy in English education is accepting a non-native speaker variety as the goal of English education. Then we can go on to discuss the choice of the most suitable non-native speaker variety for our situation.

## Non-native speaker varieties of English

### The lingua franca core perspective

One set of perspectives is based on a lingua franca core where the target model is 'not a native speaker but a fluent bilingual speaker who retains a national identity in terms of accent and who also has the special skills required to negotiate understanding with another non-native speaker' (Graddol 2006: 87). In effect, this is a call for 'world standard English' and it should not be confused with the English as a lingua franca (ELF) perspective of Jenkins (2007). Some examples from this school are:

- The world English perspective (Brutt-Griffler 2002)
- The international English perspective (McKay 2002; Melchers and Shaw 2003)

- The global English perspective (Graddol 2006)
- Globish (Nerrière 2004).

In this framework, English is no longer a foreign language learned for purposes of communication between native and non-native speakers. Rather English is used principally as a lingua franca among its non-native speakers. However, research is just unfolding in the search for a lingua franca core. There is still a long way to go before any practical outcomes can be reaped. The list of 1,500 words suggested through Globish is certainly not the end of the journey in search of the 'core.' One should also note that all of the examples in this school of thought refer to English in the singular form.

The fallacy in the 'lingua franca core' perspective is that the concept of a 'fluent bilingual' is just as invalid as the concept of a 'native speaker'. It is not possible to get to a uniform lingua franca core grammar that is shared by fluent bilinguals with different L1 backgrounds because the grammar of a 'fluent bilingual' is just as intangible and non-existent as the grammar of a 'native speaker'.

## The local linguistic standard perspective

Another perspective that employs the concept of 'standard' is that of the local linguistic standard (Holliday 2005). A 'local linguistic standard' in this framework is a variety that is accepted as professional, cultured and prestigious. This perspective rejects the notion of Globish since Globish is a simplified form that will not be used in professional circles, will not acquire a desirable culture and therefore will never become prestigious.

The problem with the 'local linguistic standard' perspective is that such local linguistic standards cannot be achieved in reality because the native speaker variety (North American for Korea) is already widely accepted as standard and this variety is highly sought after by everyone, especially government officials and policy makers. Thus there is absolutely no need to develop a different standard derived from local varieties.

## The world Englishes perspective

The world Englishes perspective avoids taking sides and includes the discussion of linguistic features of new Englishes, the future of English as a world language, and the possibility of an English 'family' of languages. For example:

- The world Englishes perspective (Kachru *et al.* 2006; Kirkpatrick 2007)
- English as a global language perspective (Crystal 2003)
- English as the lingua franca perspective (Jenkins 2007)

## Teaching world Englishes

The problem is accessibility. American English is everywhere. It dominates cyberspace. Students are trapped in this world. School education plays only a small part in the overall language input of students. Nowadays language input cannot be controlled in the systematic way that may have been possible in the past. The question is how we let the students know that there are other varieties of English in the world.

My proposal is to adopt a paradigm of teaching world Englishes, the main characteristics of which are:

- create materials with world Englishes,
- emphasise the function of world Englishes as the lingua franca, i.e. the tool of communication among non-native speakers of English, and
- de-emphasise the importance of pronunciation, i.e. train students to practise communicative pragmatics (shift from language as a system to language as social practice).

## Conclusion

The rights of students learning English will only be observed—i.e. true empowerment is only possible—when they are free to choose what they want (without fear of being penalised) on the basis of accurate and comprehensive information on the status of English use in the world today.

Email: edufuture@primenet.co.kr

## References

Bourdieu, P. 1991. *Language and Symbolic Power*. Cambridge, Mass.: Harvard University Press.

Brutt-Griffler, J. 2002. *World English: A Study of Its Development*. Clevedon: Multilingual Matters.

*Business Weekly Online* (2001-08-13). 'The Great English Divide'. http://www.businessweek.com/magazine/content/01_33/b3745009.htm (Retrieved 3 February 2008.)

Crystal, D. 2003. *English as a Global Language*, Second edition. Cambridge: Cambridge University Press.

de la Croix, D. and M. Deopke. 2007. 'Politics and the structure of education funding'. *VOX*. http://www.voxeu.org/index.php?q=node/559 (Retrieved 3 February 2008.)

Dutt, B. 2006. 'The English divide'. http://www.ndtv.com/columns/showcolumns.asp?id=1043 (Retrieved 3 February 2008.)

Foucault, M .1980. *Power/Knowledge: Selected Interviews and Other Writings*, 1972-1977. New York: Pantheon Books.

Graddol, D. 2006. *English Next*. London: British Council.

Holliday, A. 2005. *The Struggle to Teach English as an International Language*. Oxford: Oxford University Press.

Jenkins, J, 2007. *English as a Lingua Franca: Attitude and Identity*. Oxford: Oxford University Press.

Kachru, B. B, Y. Kachru, and C. L. Nelson (eds.). 2006. *The Handbook of World Englishes*. Oxford: Blackwell Publishing.

Kim, S. 2002. ['English determines caste']. *DongA Daily*. (dongA.com. 2002-09-16.)

Kirkpatrick, A. 2007. *World Englishes: Implications for International Communication and English Language Teaching*. Cambridge: Cambridge Universtity Press.

Lakoff, R. 2000. *The Language War*. Berkeley, Calif: University of California Press.

McKay, S. L. 2002. *Teaching English as an International Language*. Oxford: Oxford University Press.

Melchers, G. and P. Shaw. 2003. *World Englishes: An Introduction*. London: Arnold.

Nerrière, J. P. 2004. *Don't Speak English, Parlez Globish*. Paris: Eyrolles.

Tan, M. 2007. 'Pinoy Kasi: The English divide'. http://services.inquirere.net/print/print.php?article_id=85260 (Retrieved 3 February 2008.)

# 6 Young learners

## 6.1 Investigating MEC Worlds: blended learning resources for young learners

**Susan Holden** *Swan Communication, Callander, Scotland*

My session discussed the stages in development of a new range of blended learning materials for young learners (10–14-year-old age range) to be published by Macmillan English Campus (MEC) in late summer 2008. It focused on the discussions and decisions taken at various points in the project: at the start, in preparation for piloting, and as a result of that pilot. Such 'steps' on the route towards a final version may be useful for other similar projects, highlighting the need for a mixture of clear objectives, analysis of feedback, flexibility, timescales and—at the end—clarity of objectives again.

### The starting point

At IATEFL 2006 (Harrogate), we discussed devising a range of interactive topic-based material which would make use of the existing MEC framework, but would be content- rather than language-driven. Given the growing interest in CLIL-type learning materials, and the increasing use of interactive whiteboards (IWBs) in many classrooms, it seemed sensible to bear these two factors in mind while planning the material, as well as an awareness of likely IT and educational developments.

### Questions

Several basic decisions had to be made before finalising the material. These included:

- web-based or on CD-ROM?
- for use on IWB or in a media centre?
- a bank of material, or several 'packages'?

Beside these unanswered questions, we decided at the outset that the material would:

- be content-based and flexible,
- be teacher-centred and encouraging blended learning applications,
- exploit both IWB capabilities and restrictions ,e.g. no scrolling and
- minimal keying-in,
- encourage the development of project work and learning skills.

It was also important that the material was open to future developments and local variations in education, technology and teaching and learning styles.

### Users and topic(s)

Initially we decided to use the topic of 'the animal world' as a framework for a range of interconnected materials to explore different aspects of this world, including the environment, animal/animal and animal/human relationships, and animals in art and literature. From a CLIL viewpoint, these lend themselves to subjects such a science, geography, history, art, literature and music. The users were envisaged as being in the 8–14 age range, with a receptive language level in the elementary–intermediate range, and an elementary to pre-intermediate productive level. It was thought that teachers would select specific aspects of the material suited to their groups of learners.

## Piloting (mid-2007)

A selection of material representing the above was prepared for piloting in mid-2007. The pilot groups came from a number of IH schools in Europe and the Cultura Inglesa in São Paulo, Brazil. The materials were made available online, and accompanied by downloadable Teacher's Notes and a Questionnaire focusing on method of use (mostly media centres), age groups (mostly 10+) and reactions from students (very positive) and teachers (pleasantly surprised at the student's enthusiasm, but unsure how to handle such a large bank of resource material within limited teaching hours).

## Feedback: selected comments

'The students were very engaged—much more than expected.' CISP

'The students found it very interesting, enjoyed looking at it and liked sharing information with each other. They learned about the animals themselves, although they already knew something about most of them.' IH Prague

'The students enjoyed the fact that they weren't purely tasks with language aims.' IH Braga

'They did enjoy it and wanted to go back for more.' IH Cordoba

## Decisions (late 2007)

Using this feedback, and further discussions among the planning team, we made decisions about the final material. It was decided that this would be:

- web-based for flexibility of delivery and updating,
- designed primarily for use in class by the teacher on an IWB or with a
- projector,
- divided into several 'mini-worlds' for ease of use.

Each mini-world would contain five or six different 'zones' and be suitable for learners in the 10–14 age range, although flexible enough for use by both younger or older users at the teacher's discretion. It was also decided to retain the language range of 'elementary to pre-intermediate' or 'pre-intermediate to intermediate', with a distinction between receptive and productive language levels.

## Results (mid-2008)

The first three *MEC Interactive Worlds* are:

- *Animal World* (elementary–pre-intermediate),
- *Human and Animal Worlds* (elementary–pre-intermediate),
- *Natural World* (pre-intermediate–intermediate).

Each contains a range of input, including images (photos, artwork, video), text (a variety of styles), serious content to explore and learn from, and fun and challenging activities—a variety of resource material for the teacher to use in a blended learning context.

The material is content-driven, with CLIL relevance, and includes project work to be done both in and out of the classroom and through websearches. There is an emphasis on the interaction between the learners' own world and that presented through the material.

The zones for exploration within each world are:

- The Animal World
  - Animals and tourism
  - Caring for pets
  - Safari park
  - Survival strategies
  - The elephant story
- The Human and Animal Worlds
  - Adopt an animal
  - Animal expressions, proverbs and similes
  - Animal fables
  - Animal jokes
  - Fantastic animals
  - The Chinese calendar
- The Natural World
  - Animal types
  - Animals communicating
  - Climate change
  - Food chains
  - Horror story
  - Migration

## Accessing the *Interactive Worlds*

There are three types of access:
1. via the OnestopEnglish CLIL site (for subscribers),
2. for MEC users, and
3. via a link to users' own portals.

## Future worlds

The pilot feedback and general discussions have thrown up ideas for future worlds … find out more from the MEC website.

Email: sh@easynet.co.uk

## References

Macmillan English Campus: www.MEC.com

onestopenglish: www.onestopenglish.com

## 6.2 English inside and outside the classroom: an empirical perspective

**Maike Grau** *Justus-Liebig Universität, Gießen, Germany*

The research project 'English inside and outside the classroom' explores the relationship between out-of-school language contacts and institutionalised language learning as two aspects of the presence of English in the lives of German teenagers. The study's twofold objective seeks to expand knowledge about teenagers' contacts with English in their free time (cf., Berns *et al.* 2007) and to investigate the relevance of these language contacts to their language learning at school. Following a mixed-method approach, the project combines a questionnaire study with qualitative focus-group interviews. 957 questionnaires from 15-year-old secondary school students and English teachers were analysed and then used to stimulate discussion in focus groups.

While the teacher and student data in the first part of the questionnaires indicating students' frequent out-of-school exposure to English are fairly similar, there is a noticeable difference in the figures given for the intensive overall contact with English—see Figure 6.2.1 below. While the first six items refer to different types of exposure to English, the last item asked the students to consider again carefully how much time per week they spend in intensive contact with English, excluding mere channel surfing, browsing, or scanning of texts. The wording in the teachers' questionnaire is similar. Teachers seemed to be willing to admit that students spend a considerable time listening to music, watching TV and browsing the internet. Their estimate of the time students spend in *intensive* contact with English texts, however, is much lower than the students'. The teachers' data thus seem to suggest that students are passive consumers rather than active listeners or readers of the English brought to them through the mass media. This is an issue that repeatedly came up in the focus group interviews, in which students frequently emphasised their wish to understand the lyrics of pop songs or other English texts they encountered in their free time, whereas many teachers expressed a more sceptical view.

| | Students (girls) | Students (boys) | Students (total) | Teachers' estimates of students' contact with English (total) |
|---|---|---|---|---|
| Music: general | 3.92 | 3.78 | 3.85 | 3.74 |
| Music: focus on lyrics | 1.40 | 1.19 | 1.30 | 1.10 |
| TV/films | 2.55 | 1.81 | 2.19 | 1.41 |
| Internet communication (chat, email) | 0.42 | 0.57 | 0.50 | 1.33 |
| WWW texts | 0.54 | 1.01 | 0.78 | 0.45 |
| Computer games | 0.50 | 2.17 | 1.33 | 1.61 |
| **Total exposure** | **1.67** | **1.56** | **1.62** | **0.74** |

*Figure 6.2.1 Out-of-school exposure to English in episodes per week[1]*

Given the students' considerable contact with English indicated in the first part of the study, the results for the second research question are surprising. In the eyes of both students and teachers, out-of-school exposure to English does not influence the classroom in a noticeable way. See Figure 6.2.2 for selected questionnaire items.

| | (very) frequently (%) | sometimes (%) | rarely or never (%) |
|---|---|---|---|
| I use words or phrases from music, film, or the Web in class. | 29.8 | 32.9 | 37.3 |
| I ask my teacher about the meaning of words I have heard (read) on the Web or in songs. | 22.9 | 26.8 | 50.3 |
| I talk about (English) films or TV programmes I have seen | 5.3 | 11.1 | 83.6 |

*Figure 6.2.2 Influence of out-of-school language contact on EFL in class (data from students' questionnaire)*

Apart from concerns about the content of out-of-class texts, the issue of the language used inside and outside of class came up repeatedly in the focus-group interviews. Some students seemed to be unsure about the kind of language they learn at school, compared to the English in the 'real' world. A number of students showed that they were aware of their problems understanding colloquial language, given that the English they use in school is slower and different in terms of word choice. Teachers also often expressed concern about the kind of English used in the media.

In conclusion, many teachers and students perceive a distinction between 'school English' and the English used outside of school. Reasons include lack of time for authentic materials in class, a generation gap between students and teachers, and an incompatibility of language and topics. Nevertheless, a majority of the students and some of the teachers also indicate their wish for closer links between these contexts of language use. A dialogue between teachers and students about the English displayed in the media could lead to a discussion of standards and appropriate language use. Additionally, it could inform teachers about their students' potential problems in listening and reading comprehension. Efficient comprehension strategies could be developed in class to support out-of-class language contacts. Data from this study suggest that this is something many students miss in their English classes and which would make learning English in school more meaningful to them.

Email: Maike.Grau@anglistik.uni-giessen.de

## Reference

Berns, M., K. de Bot and U. Hasebrink. 2007. *In the Presence of English. Media and European Youth.* New York: Springer.

[1] To allow for a direct comparison of results, the answers in the student and teacher questionnaires were transformed into 'episodes per week', ranging between 4 and 0.1. (e.g. 'I/My average student play/s English language computer games several times a week equals 4, once a week equals 1, rarely or never equals 0.1 etc.').

## 6.3 TEYL—Challenges of today's classrooms

**Samuel Lefever** *Iceland University of Education, Reykjavík, Iceland*

My presentation discussed the findings of a national survey of English language teachers in Icelandic primary schools (grades 5–7) carried out in spring 2007. The objectives of the study were to gather information about English teaching at the beginning level.

In Iceland English instruction currently begins at age 9 but schools have the option of introducing English in younger grades. The amount of English instruction ranges from two lessons (40 minutes) per week in grades 4–7 to 3–4 lessons in grades 8–10. The National Curriculum guidelines emphasise Communicative Language Teaching principles and recommend that teachers use a variety of methods that take into account diverse learning needs and use the target language as much as possible during instruction.

Teachers from a representative sample of primary schools completed a written questionnaire consisting of questions regarding background and education, teaching methods and areas of emphasis, use of teaching materials, target language use, and assessment methods. Teachers were also surveyed about their attitudes towards National Curriculum objectives, learners' needs and abilities, teaching policy, in-service training, and areas for improvement.

### Results

The findings of the survey shed light on a number of issues which are challenging English teachers in today's classrooms. A growing number of schools are beginning to teach English at ever younger ages, but in most cases the teachers have no training or experience in teaching English. In this survey over 60 per cent of the English teachers were general subject teachers. Only about 25 per cent of the teachers had some form of special training in English or language teaching methodology and even fewer had any training specially geared to teaching English to young learners.

The teachers were asked what they emphasised most in their teaching. Most ranked vocabulary and reading highest followed by listening and speaking. Traditional teaching methods were most commonly used, according to the teachers, such as reading and listening to English materials and doing workbook activities. Teaching methods such as theme work, role play, video and computer activities received very little emphasis according to the teachers' responses. A majority of the teachers used materials designated by the State Materials Commission consisting of coursebooks, graded readers, and grammar booklets. Many teachers said the materials were lacking in reading texts so they used supplementary materials for additional reading and grammar exercises. Only a few teachers said they used supplementary materials for listening, videos, songs and games—materials that children enjoy!

The National Curriculum recommends informal, ongoing assessment methods for grades 5–7 and introducing pupils to self-assessment, for example by using the European Language Portfolio. However, the majority of the teachers said they used written tests to assess the pupils. Many teachers used a combination of assessment approaches and continuous assessment. Few teachers said they used portfolio or self assessment methods.

The teachers were very clear about what they wanted to change in their teaching. They would like to use:

- more diverse teaching methods, for example, pairwork, role play, speaking activities,
- more active teaching methods, for example, songs and games,
- more theme teaching and use of own materials,
- more English in teaching and encourage pupils to use more English,
- less emphasis on tests.

The teachers were also asked what kind of training would help them to be better English teachers. They most frequently mentioned training in language teaching methods and the use of teaching materials, information about supplementary materials, and training to improve their own English skills.

## Conclusions

The results of the study highlight several challenges faced by English teachers. They find it difficult to incorporate diverse teaching methods and materials into their lessons, especially methods that activate students in creative and authentic language use. They often feel as if they don't have time to try out new approaches in the classroom and feel bound by the curriculum or the book. They also find it difficult to adopt new assessment methods and to teach groups of students with diverse needs and varying skills levels. Finally, many teachers lack the necessary language skills in order to feel confident enough to use English in the classroom.

Teachers need more opportunities for in-service training in language teaching methodology and for improving their English skills. In addition, more attention needs to be given to programme development and new developments in language teaching. It is essential that teachers are well-trained in language teaching methodology, have access to suitable materials, and feel confident about using English in the classroom. In this way teachers will be better equipped to meet the challenges of today's classrooms.

Email: samuel@khi.is

## 6.4 English as a second language in Irish post-primary schools: responding to a new challenge

**Rachael Fionda** *Trinity College, Dublin, Ireland*

Ireland, traditionally a country of emigration, is presently experiencing a vast increase in immigration. The impact of immigration on the post-primary school system should not be underestimated. Some of the issues faced by teachers include sudden high numbers of ESOL students, arriving at varying stages of the school system, during various stages of the school year with varying educational experience and with varying levels of English. Trinity College's Trinity Immigration Initiative (TII) comprises six projects researching diversity and immigration; this paper presents the project strand entitled English Language Support Programme for Post-Primary Schools.

## Project background

Previously, support for ES(O)L students has been provided by Integrate Ireland Language and Training (IILT), which has successfully started to offer in-service seminars and a range of materials, guidelines and assessments. Since 2000 Integrate Ireland Language and Training, a not-for-profit campus company of Trinity College, has been funded by the Department of Education and Science to support the teaching of English as a second language in primary and post-primary schools.

The post-primary school context is more complicated than the primary because there the curriculum is delivered by many subject-specialist teachers, and so TII's English Language Support Programme research project has taken up the post-primary challenge.

## New challenges for schools

An estimated 17,000 non-national students enrolled in post-primary schools in 2006/07 (Ryan 2007) and 60 per cent have a mother tongue other than English. All children of school age have the right to enter education, and the Department of Education and Science (DES) offer the following provision and guidelines:

> Post-primary schools with an enrolment of fourteen or more non-national students with English language deficits are entitled to an additional teacher to address the needs of these students. An individual student is entitled to a maximum of two years language support.
>
> (DES 2003)

TII's English Language Support project carried out a survey of ten schools in Dublin in spring 2008 and discovered prominent issues which teachers identify as urgent needs. Issues highlighted include: lack of materials and resources, definition of English language support, timetabling complications, limited teacher training, exam results pressure, segregation from mainstream teachers, students arriving at different times during the year, and addressing multi-level classes.

Researchers on the project have undertaken first steps in addressing these needs, including the development of subject specific materials, and enhanced versions of the European Language Portfolio and English Language Proficiency Benchmarks. These tools have all been created on the foundation of a corpus specific to the Irish post-primary curriculum, developed by the project.

## Key deliverables

The global aims of the English Language Support project are to work with teachers in a number of post-primary schools to develop approaches to English language support that can be generalised throughout the sector, to support this activity by empirical research that identifies dominant patterns of language acquisition and recurrent problems for language pedagogy and to investigate at a more general level the linguistic challenges that surround the longer-term integration of non-English-speaking students in mainstream Irish education (TII website).

By 2010 the project plans to pull all strands of the research together to distribute the following key deliverables:

- a description, analysis and evaluation of English language support system in Ireland,
- a handbook of good practice,
- CEFR linked English Language Proficiency Benchmarks and European Language Portfolio,
- materials, and
- assessment tools and procedures.

Further development of the survey, corpus and resources follow from 2008 until 2010.

## Conclusion

Recent immigration to Ireland provides new challenges for Irish schools and increasing numbers of ES(O)L teachers. TII's English Language Support Programme research project has carried out an exploratory survey of schools in the Dublin area, and identified many key issues. Addressing the key issues by developing corresponding key deliverables includes a comprehensive analysis of the Irish curriculum mainstream subjects, developing corpus-informed materials, assessment tools and resources, and by maintaining links with the ES(O)L teacher and classroom.

## References

Ryan, P. 2007. *The Educational Needs of Newcomer Children.* DES: Dublin.

DES. 2003. *Summary of All Initiatives Funded By the Department to help Alleviate Educational Disadvantage.* DES: Dublin.

TII website: www.tcd.ie/immigration.

# 6.5 ADHD learners in the communicative classroom

**Dorota Nowacka** *Adam Micackiewicz University, Poznan, Poland*

According to The American Academy of Pediatrics Attention Deficit Hyperactivity Disorder (ADHD) affects between 4 per cent and 12 per cent of school-aged children in the USA. These figures were confirmed by a study conducted in Poland (Nowacka 2004–2006). The most commonly cited research (Barkley 1998) says ADHD affects approximately 2–9.5 per cent of school-aged children worldwide; thus it is perceived as the most common behavioural disorder diagnosed in children and teenagers. It is not defined or described as a learning disability. Nevertheless, its interference with attention and concentration strongly affects the child's learning and communication processes.

## Symptoms of ADHD

ADHD refers to a group of symptoms which can be observed in childhood but can continue into adulthood if not recognised and treated.

Symptoms of *inattention* include inability to pay attention to details or to focus on one activity for a longer period of time. Furthermore, the child is unable to sustain attention in conversations, play activities and any tasks that require mental effort. The ADHD learner also has difficulty with understanding teacher talk (for example, with following the teacher's instructions, chronological sequences of a class session, etc.)

Symptoms of *hyperactivity/impulsivity* include difficulties with controlling body movements and impulses. ADHD learners find it difficult to remain seated during a lesson and always act before thinking.

However, the line between the two categories is often blurred; the behavioural patterns from both of the subtypes tend to co-occur and/or be combined. Furthermore, ADHD has been observed to accompany other learning disorders (for example, dyslexia). Therefore, the diagnosis of ADHD is time-consuming and requires professional assistance of teachers, psychologists and medical doctors.

## Communicating with ADHD learners

ADHD children have difficulty with mastering *conversational skills* and *strategies*. They may initiate conversations at awkward moments; they often interject unconnected ideas in their speech production; they tend to interrupt their communication partners and switch topics of conversations abruptly. Turn-taking also poses problems for ADHD learners; they find it difficult to wait for their turn, they often miss their conversational turns and consequently abandon their communicative goal. Furthermore, features of classroom communication and context, task demands and the presence of numerous incentives make it impossible for ADHD learners to monitor and evaluate their performance, and hence, to succeed in foreign language learning.

Thus, teaching a foreign language for communication may seem to add another difficulty, since the children have not mastered communicative competence in their first language. However, preliminary research (Nowacka 2006) has revealed that incorporating foreign language training in ADHD children education may facilitate their overall school work and performance.

## Planning a communicative lesson

While planning a communicative lesson for ADHD learners, *class management* is of paramount importance. The teacher should make sure that interior décor does not disturb the child; it is, for example, better not to make frequent replacements of classroom posters, decorations, etc. and thus to limit the number of distractions. The teacher is encouraged to provide play areas that are *less stimulating* and place the child near the teacher to allow him/her to read from the teacher's lips and prevent the child from bothering his/her classmates. *Background music* may also prove effective while dealing with an ADHD learner, since it helps to calm the child down and prevents him/her from getting distracted by other school noises.

Furthermore, the teacher's approach to *activity design* should highlight the importance and versatility of *short, varied, situation-orientated language activities*. By using *multisensory* stimulation, the teacher clarifies his/her message and facilitates the overall learning and communication process. Clear, straightforward instructions, constant repetition may enhance what the teacher is saying. What is more, activities involving varied performance may help sustain the learners' attention in classroom tasks. That is why language-orientated classroom activities designed for ADHD learners are often accompanied by drawing, painting, modelling, cutting out, etc. The activities often include *new, surprising, unusual* elements in order to capture the learners' attention.

As has been suggested throughout this summary, ADHD can interfere strongly with learning and interpersonal communication. The importance of training ADHD learners in conversational skills and communication strategies consists in the fact that they help the children remain in a conversation, regardless of numerous limitations they may encounter. What is more, it has been observed that foreign language learning may enhance the children's *self-esteem*. The children are vulnerable to periodic experiences of anger, communicative frustration and anxiety, disappointment and consequently depression. Thus, frequent encouraging feedback on their foreign language performance can help them identify with a sense of competence and may be extremely motivating for ADHD learners.

## References

Nowacka, D. 2006. 'Attention Deficit Hyperactivity Disorder and the learner's communicative competence' in J. Fisiak (ed.). *English Language, Literature, Culture.* Poznań: Adam Mickiewicz University.

Barkley, R. A. 1998. 'Dzieci nadpobudliwe i roztargnione'. *Swiat Nauki* 11: 50–5.

## 6.6 Who do YLs consider an ideal language teacher?

**Mandana Arfa Kaboodvand** *Azad University, Tehran, Iran*

### Introduction

The number of young learners who need, like or are supposed to learn English, is on the rise. This increase could be a reason for at least some language teachers to be receiving training in ways of teaching and treating children and adolescents. Also from the twentieth century up to now the attention of language teaching/learning has shifted to the needs, desires and interests of the learners so as to make language learning a more pleasant and effective experience.

When there is so much attention paid to the learners, young and adult, then their views and perceptions should be sought and as much as possible included in the teaching programmes. Teachers who are in daily and direct contact with these learners should be informed of these views and helped to take this information into account to be able to build *rapport* with the learners and to add that ability to their knowledge of language and teaching to make their classes more successful.

My study, which is taking place in Iran, is to determine the characteristics of EFL teachers that Iranian adolescents believe to be desirable. The next steps will be discovering the views of the teachers, parents and school authorities and comparing and contrasting them.

## The survey

Language teaching in Iran officially begins at 7th grade when the students are almost 12 years of age and ends at 12th grade when the students are almost 18. The curricular structure, including the timetable, syllabus and books for all the school subjects is stipulated by the Ministry of Education and therefore, throughout the country the students study exactly the same books and follow the same kind of syllabus. Normally, the teachers are also recruited by the same Ministry. During school year 2006–2007 there were 14,450,214 boys and girls studying at schools, 8,069,431 of them in middle and high schools.

In order to determine the kind of characteristics a sample of Iranian students found favourable, a pilot study was done, the findings of which along with the information gathered from other relevant resources and personal experience, were incorporated into a closed- questionnaire to systematically investigate the ideas of Iranian teenagers on the kind of language teacher they liked to teach them. The questionnaire was in Farsi, so that everyone regardless of their level of language proficiency would be able to answer. In most parts of the questionnaire a Likert scale was used to collect responses.

So far the questionnaires have been distributed among 48 boys and girls who have not really been selected randomly. They mainly live in the well-off neighborhood of Tehran, the capital city. Many of them have language learning experience in the private language institutions out of their schools. This selection of participants was chosen in order to seek the ideas of those who had (1) experience of a teacher they had chosen to study with, out of school time as a part of their extra-curricular activity and (2) of a teacher who was chosen for them by school authorities without being given any option. The findings based on the completed questionnaires offer some clues as to what else can and should be done to implement the research at a bigger scale and collect the required information.

## General findings

The majority of the pupils:

1. believed that language teachers in general should at least in some aspects be different from the teachers of other school subjects. For example, the pupils expected them to be more patient, friendlier and more creative than other teachers,
2. favoured a teacher with a good accent,
3. preferred the classes to be held mainly in English, but 22 mentioned that sometimes Farsi should be used by the teacher,
4. believed that teachers should use teaching aids,
5. liked their teacher to look smart, and
6. preferred their teacher to use their first names, rather than family names.

## Conclusion

Iranian educational organisations, in particular, the Ministry of Education, the college for language teacher training, the schools both private and public, the language institutions and last but not least language teachers can use the findings of this research. The same kind of research can be repeated in different regions inside Iran, or with different age groups and/or be done in other countries. Seeking the views of the language teachers, parents and school authorities could complement this study.

Email: m_arfa@yahoo.com

# 7 Quality in English teaching

## 7.1 Quality in the classroom

**Justin Kernot** *British Council, Madinat Sultan Qaboos, Oman*

Quality in teaching is something that all institutions and organisations offering English language courses should be advocating and delivering.

Research carried out in British Council teaching centres identified students perceived the organisation positively in relation to:

- mother tongue speakers,
- reputation,
- qualified teaching staff,
- quality of facilities,
- teaching style,
- provision of recognised qualification, and
- convenience of location.

Potential and existing students identified the factors they consider when *selecting* an English language school. Again, mother-tongue and qualified teachers and teaching style ranked in the top ten, as did the location of the school. A preference for small class sizes and relevance of course content also featured in their considerations.

The research highlighted three main reasons for students wanting to study English:

- important for career,
- English is important for socialising and building confidence, and
- English is about developing yourself and fulfilling your expectations.

It was found that the courses being delivered were only partially meeting students' expectations:

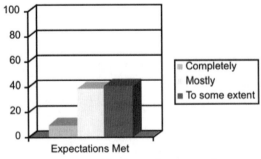

*Figure 7.1.1 Meeting student expectations*

Reasons for this shortfall included lack of opportunity to practise conversation in class, lack of progress and lack of attention from the teacher.

These results indicated that the communicative aspect to teaching and learning had diminished somewhat and students were no longer receiving the kind of language tuition they expected.

The Bangkok centre set up a project to address the main trends in the research results. The Quality in the Classroom (QC) project was born. The aims of the project were:

- to ensure the courses and how they were delivered meet the customers' expectations,
- to enhance the professional support for teachers and maintain the standards of teaching expected by the organisation and its customers, and
- to build positive perceptions of the quality of teacher training and development to facilitate and encourage recruitment and retention of qualified and quality teachers.

## The project

The stages of the project began by developing student and teacher personas. Through conducting anecdotal focus groups, this meant the creation of student 'types' and 'ideal' teachers drawing on the main trends and characteristics coming out of the anecdote circles. This would provide an opportunity to see whether the student styles and types matched the preferred teacher type and teaching style.

The next stage was to develop teaching skills and competencies set to try to measure aspects of lesson delivery and teacher's approach and techniques to teaching language.

A training plan was designed for the academic year. It was important to encourage teachers to develop the plan to make sure that they were driving the project forward for their own professional development. This training plan was set to address the areas of teaching that needed work to meet students' expectations from the courses. It also provided teachers with the opportunity to relate their own teaching style more directly to the local market and deliver in a way that appealed to and worked for those signing up for lessons.

Focus group meetings and questionnaires were carried out—mid-year and at the end of the process—to gauge how the project was progressing and explore any changes learners felt the courses were meeting their expectations.

The teacher personas project proved enlightening for teachers who were often unaware of what their students expected and desired from them as tutors. The results can be summarised thus:

- Teacher shouldn't be too strict. They should promote a relaxed atmosphere    50%
- Teacher should give more counselling on students' strengths and weaknesses    39%
- Teacher should include variety of tasks    28%
- Teacher should provide clear explanations    13%
- Teacher should communicate 1 on 1 with students    13%
- Teacher should spend time with students outside class    13%

The implications for the results above and the student personas consolidated previous research and led to the following considerations for the English language classroom at the British Council in Bangkok:

- Lowering the affective filter is particularly vital in Thai classrooms and is seen as the teacher's responsibility.
- Students want more individual feedback.
- Variety is the spice of Thai classrooms.
- Accessibility to resources and teachers outside the classroom is extremely important.

As students have become more discerning and aware of what different English language programmes can offer, institutes and language schools need to be more tuned in to what and how they are delivering their courses.

This project is ongoing. It will continue to make every effort to meet the changing demands and expectations of students. It will strive to deliver the consistency in quality of teaching to give the customers what they want and not be driven by what the institute or the teacher believes they want.

Email: justin.kernot@om.britishcouncil.org

## 7.2 Maintaining consistent standards across a world-wide TEFL network

**Simon Buckland** *Wall Street Institute International, Baltimore, Md., USA*

### Introduction to Wall Street Institute

Wall Street Institute is a global provider of English language teaching to adults, with almost 400 learning centres in 28 countries. We use our own 'blended learning' method, which integrates computer- and print-based guided self-instruction with face-to-face small group classes led by teachers. The Wall Street curriculum, which was originally introduced in the 1980s, and which has been updated five times since then, is based on the Council of Europe 'Threshold Level'—a precursor of today's Common European Framework of Reference (CEFR).

### From assessment to alignment

Like the instruction system, the Wall Street assessment system is also blended: students can measure their own progress through computer-based self-assessment, while the teachers provide a systematic progress check at each end-of-unit class. This combination of micro- and macro- level testing is designed to ensure continuous and accurate placement of Wall Street students across the 17 levels (from zero Beginner to just below CAE equivalent) which constitute the Wall Street progression ladder.

### The alignment study and its motivation

In 2006 Wall Street Institute decided to carry out a large-scale statistical study to verify the accuracy of our internal assessment procedures, and to discover and demonstrate the systematic alignment of our progression levels with the CEFR.

Our principal reasons for carrying out this study were:

1. to verify the linkage between the Wall Street Institute curriculum and the Threshold Level/CEFR,
2. to demonstrate recognised and accredited learning outcomes to current and potential students,
3. to provide systematic benchmarking of Wall Street Institute course for the benefit of students' actual and potential employers, and
4. to comply with the requirements of governments and other regulatory bodies.

We were lucky enough to enjoy the support of Cambridge ESOL throughout our study: as well as providing the benchmarking examination, they advised us on methodology, and endorsed the overall study as methodologically sound.

## The alignment study and its two parts

The alignment study was in two parts:

1. 5500 Wall Street students in six different countries, at all levels apart from Beginner, took the Cambridge BULATS examination (the computer-based version). Their scores were then statistically correlated with their Wall Street Institute levels, using Rasch calibration to reduce distortions caused by variance in teachers' or centres' assessment of students (i.e. systematically more or less 'strict' than average).
2. We selected 120 key can-do statements from the CEFR and divided them randomly into six groups of 20. A panel of 72 experienced Wall Street Institute teachers was divided into six subgroups, and each teacher was required to match one of the groups of can-do statements against the corresponding Wall Street Institute assessment level—i.e. to identify at what level students would achieve the competence described in the can-do statement. The results were statistically analysed and 'smoothed' using Rasch calibration, and the most poorly correlated can-do statements were 'discarded'.

## Conclusions from the alignment study and support from Cambridge ESOL

1. The alignment study demonstrates that Wall Street's internal progression ladder levels have international reference and relevance.
2. Thanks to the alignment against CEFR can-do statements, Wall Street students now know explicitly what they can do with their English at each stage of their courses.

In conclusion, we would like to thank Cambridge ESOL for their support and guidance throughout the project. They not only gave advice in planning the study, but also reviewed the methodology employed, and the reports generated.

It is also noteworthy that the Wall Street Institute learning system is the first major English language programme ever to be objectively and statistically aligned with an internationally recognised standard. This fact was also acknowledged by Cambridge ESOL, in the public statement which they issued: '[This is] the first such study from an English language school with a global presence of which University of Cambridge ESOL Examinations is aware'.

Email: s.buckland@wallstreetinstitute.com

# 7.3 What do adult learners of general English really need today?

**Ian Lebeau** *London Metropolitan University, London, UK*

My aim in this talk was to show how integrating elements of Business English and EAP into an adult general English course can provide students with the key skills they need to participate successfully in 21st century society.

## Who are these adult learners of general English and what do they want?

In terms of both the institutions where they are studying and their ages, this group comprises a very wide range of people, all over the world. Because of this diversity, one might think that they do not have much in common. As teachers, we might be tempted to assume that these general English students do not have very specific wants or needs. However, my own experience and that of colleagues suggests that these students share a commonality of aspiration. They want to be 21st century, international citizens and participate actively in modern, globalised society.

## What do they need?

To achieve their aims requires a diverse set of skills. First, these students need transferable skills: critical thinking, problem-solving and teamworking skills. Good communication skills are also essential for them, in order to handle complex global communication. Writing skills are becoming increasingly important, as these modern learners want to communicate across national borders, often by use of the internet. They need to acquire or improve learning strategies as well, so they can learn fast in a time-poor society.

## To what extent are their needs currently being met?

By and large, it seems, general English coursebooks are not satisfying their needs—or at least not in a very systematic way. Even a brief analysis of several of the most popular general English coursebooks will reveal a number of problems. Many of these coursebooks are very lifestyle-based and tend to feel quite young. Overall, there is scant reference to the learner's study experience—instead, social experience dominates. In addition, the range of skills work is limited. For example, there is little focus on improving reading skills and little analysis of models of writing. Longer listening passages are infrequent, as are extended speaking activities.

## Where can they find what they really need?

Many of the things they need, I argued in my presentation, are to be found on Business English and EAP courses, and in the materials developed for those courses.

Business English students get frequent opportunities to take part in meetings, and many general English students are—or will be—involved in meetings, both in and out of the work environment. Anyone who is involved in running a sports club, or who wants to organise a fund-raising event, will benefit from strong meeting skills.

Business English students also do a lot of work on negotiations. It is important, however, to recognise how big a part negotiations play in all our lives, whether it is asking the boss for a pay rise, or trying to reach a compromise with some noisy neighbours.

Presentation skills are another key area of Business English (as well as of EAP). For all of us, presenting is becoming more and more important for actually getting a job, as presentations become a routine part of job interviews.

These business skills are often developed through case studies which provide extended speaking practice in real-life situations. Students have to manage information, meet and have in-depth discussions, practise teamwork, solve problems and come to a final decision. There is usually a follow-up writing task, such as producing a report.

The general English student can also benefit from EAP, particularly in the areas of study and writing skills. Study skills that help students to be better learners are central to EAP courses. The same is true for writing skills; they are not tacked on, put at the back of the coursebook, or in the workbook, as frequently happens in more general English materials. In EAP, there is a focus on the writing process and writing sub-skills are crucial.

## Conclusion

My argument was (and is!) that these skills (negotiating, presenting, study and writing skills, etc.) need to lose their specialist labels—whether it is Business English or EAP— and become central to the mainstream English language classroom. A learning programme that integrates these elements with the more traditional components of language study, such as the learning of grammar, is, I believe, the answer to the needs of the twenty-first century adult learner of general English.

Email: i.lebeau@londonmet.ac.uk

## 7.4 Age effects upon second language learning: implications for adult learners

**Rebecca Hooker** *University of Exeter, UK*

### Introduction

Much research in the second language learning field has been devoted to the teaching and learning experiences of younger learners. Whereas my research does not draw a comparison between younger and older learners, it examines the background to the 'younger is better' claim and explores whether this has any resonance amongst older adult ESOL learners. With his controversial critical period hypothesis, Lenneberg (1967) proposes that after puberty: automatic acquisition disappears, foreign accents remain and that 'conscious and labored effort' is needed.

As many previous 'age' studies have investigated attainment as a measure of language learning success, the rationale for this study was to research the learning in the social context of the adult ESOL classroom, from the learners' own perspective. This study set out to report learners' perceptions of the kind of teaching: 'active instruction', or informed help outside the class: 'deliberate intervention', which they find to be helpful and useful in achieving 'fit for purpose' English for their lives in England.

## Methodology

The research questions framing this enquiry were:

1. How do adult second language learners feel about their age?
2. To what extent do older learners value 'mediation' in their learning: with 'active instruction' in the classroom, and 'deliberate intervention' outside?
3. What kind of instruction is helpful and should it be explicit?

In order to answer these questions, I interviewed and observed nineteen adult ESOL learners, from six different classes, in South Devon, England. In my presentation I reported on ten learners with seven different mother tongues, reflecting the heterogeneous mix of these immigrants living in England. The average age of participants was forty years old with the average starting age for learning English being twenty years old.

Determined to give the learners a voice about their views of their teaching and of any outside help with their English, I did not rely upon more accessible participants with a greater command of English. This methodological choice caused controversy with some of my IATEFL audience, who felt that interviews in participants' L2: English, did not give a true representation. However, even the students at a very elementary level were very committed to voicing their opinions and contributing to knowledge about their learning. The interviews and field notes from the observations were then transcribed and categorised according to some of the key constructs from the literature.

## Summary of the findings

### Beliefs about their age

Although it was clear from the interviews that learners did not have a 'near-native' proficiency in English, they were all positive about learning English later in life:

'No problem.' Zena, 63;

'If you are really interesting, you will pick it up, if not, it doesn't matter which age.' Wilda, 52;

'The age is not important. You can learn at any age.' Somchai, 40.

They quoted, too, some advantages of learning English as an adult, such as the greater relevance of English and a greater opportunity to practise English, with the reverse having been true for them as children learning in their native countries.

Participants stated that they needed to 'work' hard on their English. Mei, 56, also describes the everyday concerns and distractions that plague her learning, which was not so when she was a child.

### Beliefs about the value of 'mediation'

*All* the interviewees considered formal language classes pivotal for success, with the teacher being vital. They gave metaphors of the teacher as a 'window' or a 'guide'.

Furthermore they all valued the 'deliberate intervention' they receive in their daily lives, given by well-meaning host families, customers, English friends or work colleagues, even going as far as to actively seek it out.

## Beliefs about explicit instruction

The fact that adults consider explicit explanations of the grammar, the rules and focusing on form important is reflected in the learners' comments. Added to which, learners believe that the teacher/native speaker should be explicit about corrections, giving negative evidence (Ioup 1995) and writing corrections down. They appear not to value peer corrections.

## Conclusion

This study reveals that older SL learners are not inferior learners, only 'different' learners who value 'active instruction' in a social context, as well as 'deliberate intervention' outside the classroom. As Doughty (Doughty and Long 2003) points out, for adults, 'instruction is necessary to compensate for cognitive disadvantages' caused by chronological aging. As teachers we can do nothing to alter a student's age, but we can endeavour to deliver the type of instruction appropriate to the learner's strategies, motivation and environment.

Email: rebeccahooker@ yahoo.co.uk

## References

Doughty, C. and Long, M. H (eds.). 2003. *The Handbook of Second Language Acquisition.* Oxford: Blackwell.

Ioup, G. 1995. 'Evaluating the need for input enhancement in post-critical period language acquisition' in D. Singleton and Z. Lengyei (eds.). *The Age Factor in Second Language Acquisition.* Clevedon: Multilingual Matters.

Lenneberg, E. 1967. *Biological Foundations of Language.* New York: John Wiley.

# 7.5 Sociocultural teacher education

**Gary Motteram** *University of Manchester, Manchester, UK*

There is an increasing interest in what has been called the 'sociocultural turn' in teacher education (Johnson 2006: 237) as well as in language learning (Lantolf and Thorne 2006). This viewpoint sees learning not as a purely cognitive activity inside the head of a willing recipient, but as a process that occurs through mediation with cultural artefacts which may include: language, objects (books, DVDs, computers) and tasks, and with the support of other people: family, friends, peers and teachers.

There are several theoretical strands to this sociocultural turn, but this short summary will focus on looking at the way that what is called Cultural Historical Activity Theory (CHAT) has helped me to understand the role that Enquiry-Based Learning (EBL) is having in raising the awareness of our University of Manchester MA students of their identity as teachers.

CHAT has its 20th century origins in the work of Vygotsky (1978, 1986), but has been brought to prominence in the west by scholars like Engeström (2001). Below is a diagrammatic representation of the theory:

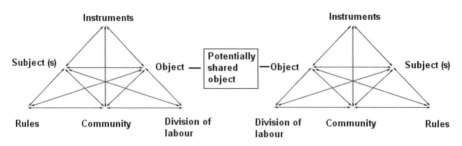

*Figure 7.5.1 Conceptualisation of Cultural Historical Activity Theory (based on Engeström 2001)*

In brief it proposes that someone trying to achieve their goal, in this case gaining a Master's degree, comes from a particular community (triangle on the right) where there are certain ideas (Rules) about how people learn and how learning is organised (Division of Labour). Various artefacts also govern activity, so in our participants' community there may be limited technology, but on the course at Manchester a lot of technology is used to deliver the programme. In the left-hand triangle we find the MA tutor as subject who is also embedded within his/her community where academic study is seen to occur in certain ways, some of which are governed by university rules and the community of practitioners who teach on MA programmes. Some also stem from tutors' own sociocultural development.

Course participants thus arrive with a certain cultural history, a way of viewing the world. The tutors on the MA also have a view of the world that is informed by their life experiences and their scholarship. What we work on together is a 'Potentially Shared Object' where our differing views come together and over time new identities are forged. What we offer our course participants is a process through which they can explore their practice as teachers in a variety of different ways. This enables them to re-examine it, to reflect on their identity as practitioners. MA tutors' views of the world also change over time, too.

This recreation of new shared objects is achieved on the course by making use of a number of different approaches to teaching and learning, two examples of which are: Enquiry Based Learning (EBL) (Savin-Barden 2000) and Co-operative Development (Edge 2002). Course participants will have experienced higher education in their own contexts in a variety of ways, mostly through undergraduate courses where teaching and learning is still often conducted through: lectures, handouts, coursebooks and exams. Teachers are supposed to teach and learners learn:

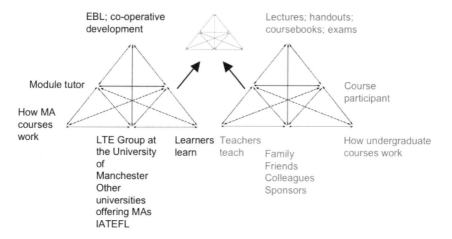

*Figure 7.5.2 Different experiences of higher education: changed identities?*

The tutors on the MA, supported by their community see learning as the learner's responsibility and make use of the tools of EBL and Co-operative Development to present this viewpoint. The course participants engage in certain activities that ask them to see the world of learning differently. Having explored this for themselves they are then asked to consider whether such approaches have value within their own context. This is partly a process of orientation to the ways of study on the MA and the way that we see learning as taking place, but it is also saying to the participants: this is another view of these processes, does it have any relevance to you as practitioners? On the module that we call 'Psychology of Language Learning', instead of the 'input' being presented as a series of weekly lectures followed by seminars, we present an overview of the field that we are going to explore and then ask the participants to explore a puzzle from their own context, look for ideas in the existing literature, attempt to apply this to their own context and then present their ideas to the class for a critical review. They reflect on their journey via a diary. By the end of the process they have perhaps begun to better understand the MA they are studying and are beginning to modify their identity as teachers to take on board in a critical way new ideas about ways of learning:

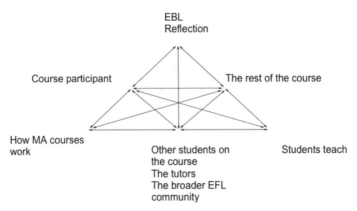

*Figure 7.5.3  Learning on the University of Manchester MA: changed identities?*

Email: gary.motteram@manchester.ac.uk

## References

Edge, J. 2002. *Continuing Cooperative Development: A Discourse Framework for Individuals as Colleagues.* Ann Arbor: Michigan University Press.

Engeström, Y. 2001. 'Expansive learning at work: toward an activity theoretical reconceptualization'. *Journal of Education and Work* 14/1: 133–56.

Johnson, K. E. 2006. 'The sociocultural turn and its challenges for second language teacher education'. *TESOL Quarterly* 40/1: 235–57.

# 8 Developments in technology for ELT

## 8.1 Making virtual learning environments work for us as teachers

**Jody Skinner** *Universität in Koblenz, Koblenz, Germany*

While most of us have been using computers for years now, only recently has advanced technology for organising courses, creating exams, monitoring grades electronically, and increasing student participation been made available. This technology has many names with many—at times confusing—abbreviations like LMS (learning management systems) or LP (learning platform) or LCMS (learning content management system) or VLE for virtual learning environment; this last is now one of the most commonly used, also at former IATEFL conferences. While many of these technological advances are intended to help educational administrators, I focused in my swapshop on one commercial platform geared towards helping teachers and students at universities, Blackboard Learning System CE 6, which I've been using in advanced writing and Anglo-American Studies courses for the past few years.

The commercial product Blackboard, which has been generously funded by the German state where I teach, provides my students and me with three main advantages: freeing us from the restrictions of space and time, helping me to organise courses and track student progress, and increasing student participation and autonomy. Advantages for all my students include increased practice in writing, reading, and critical thinking. Many of my students are digital natives and thus expect the computer to be used intensively as part of their courses. I can use a VLE for doing management work and for easily generating databanks of student writing. For most of my students and for me using a VLE is a lot of fun too!

But my students and I have of course experienced problems in using a VLE in the classroom. Initially, I spent a lot of time setting up the platform and there are always possible problems with computer down-time and slow-time. I sometimes wonder if blindly adopting new technology could increase mere busy work, and I'm sometimes worried about a shift from speaking skills to a possible overemphasis on writing. For commercial products a big hurdle is the cost to institutions, and as with all computer technology the question of accessibility to all people remains an issue.

We found in the swapshop that experience with VLEs varied around the world. Some participants were provided with training in Moodle (a free, open-source virtual course management system), others were faced with a deadline to implement, others again with fully 'voluntary' participation. One participant shared her experience of creatively using much cheaper ways to encourage student participation and e-learning by using student-owned mobile phones and digital cameras to create blogs for primary and secondary school students. These gave rise to some of the same results in increased student participation as is the case with expensive commercial products. A publishing representative explained one use of the student tracking tool, which many of us had been somewhat uncomfortable using. No one wants to play a Big Brother teacher with the power to know exactly who logged on to which pages when. The publisher considered it important to learn which resources are actually being used by students so that future platforms can be improved. And someone was able to answer my question about the etymology of the name 'Blackboard', which for me is a very strange name for something that seems as far from the old-fashioned blackboard as a keyboard is from chalk. The name comes supposedly from the attempt to reassure 'older' teachers that the platform would become as easy to use and as essential to teaching and learning as the chalk blackboard.

Participants in the swapshop especially appreciated how easily VLEs provide accessible databanks of student writing, improve the possibility for student scaffolding, encourage group solidarity, and foster learner independence. We also realised that students doing teaching degrees are attracted to courses that feature VLEs. Even though not all teachers or institutions can afford some of the expensive commercial products currently flooding the market, we all agreed that VLEs in general could make our working lives more efficient and help us in doing what we love most—teaching.

Email: jody@uni-koblenz.de

## Website sources of some of the more common VLEs

Blackboard http://www.blackboard.com
*Moodle http://moodle.org/
Angel Learning http://www.angellearning.com
ANGeL http://www.afghanequalityalliances.net/
*ATutor http://www.atutor.ca/
Claroline http://www.claroline.net/
CyberExtension http://rightreasontech.com/
Managed_Learning_Environment/CyberExtension.php
Desire2Learn http://www.desire2learn.com
Digication, A New Concept in Educational Software
*Dokeos http://www.dokeos.com/
eCollege http://www.ecollege.com
First Class http://www.firstclass.com/
FrogTeacher http://www.frogteacher.com
Fronter http://www.fronter.com
*Ilias http://www.ilias.de/
Jenzabar http://www.jenzabar.com
*KEWL.NextGen http://avoir.uwc.ac.za/
Meridian KSI http://www.meridianksi.com
Plateau http://www.plateau.com
*Sakai http://www.sakaiproject.org/
Scholar360 http://www.scholar360.com/
Studywiz http://www.studywiz.com

* Open Source software

Helpful discussion showing the complexity of the names of the many kinds of terminology used: http://en.wikipedia.org/wiki/Talk:Virtual_learning_environment.

## 8.2 Power2learn

**Johanna Stirling** *Freelance, Norwich, UK*

Does technology solve your classroom problems or does it just cause you more head-aches? In this workshop we explored which problems technology can really help us with and which it cannot.

### Less is more?

There seems to be a common evolution in the use of technology. We tend to start with an 'I *can*, therefore I will' approach. All those settings on your digital camera? You try them out when you first get the camera but you soon find yourself using just the few most useful (or maybe just the auto setting). This is because we've matured towards an 'I *need*, therefore I will' state.

I illustrated my workshop with the new Classware from Cambridge University Press (a component of the adult general English coursebook *face2face*) which can be used with an interactive whiteboard, or a computer and projector or even, with a very small group, just a computer. I believe it heralds a new generation of class-room presentation software which has itself matured into something that is simpler and therefore more user friendly, flexible and affordable than many other interactive whiteboard packages available.

### Help me!

We started the workshop by each writing three challenges we experience in teaching. Mine were:

1. Getting some learners to speak enough.
2. Helping some learners to understand.
3. Helping all learners to remember.

We then explored how technology could help with these problems.

So how can technology get my students speaking more? One advantage of the internet is that it provides a huge potential audience for our students' English. There are people all over the world wanting to get into conversations with other people … in English. Now that's motivating!

And how could classroom presentation software help my students to speak? As they can see each page from the book on the screen, at normal size or zoomed, they have their heads up and are all focused on the same point. Have you ever noticed the change that comes over many learners when you ask them to open their book on page 33 or give them a worksheet? Their heads go down and learning becomes a more private activity. However, for language learning we want them to communicate and collaborate, so if their heads are up they may well be relating to each other, not to a piece of paper. Also the teacher does not have to keep turning his or her back to write on the board because all the language is available onscreen. Pre-prepared files and 'sticky notes' can be opened which feed in useful language for speaking activities. There may also be also teacher's tips on many other ways to maximise the effectiveness of the software.

My next problem was that learners sometimes just cannot understand—language or instructions—especially when all teaching is done in L2. Multi-media helps us to make learning visual. A picture not only tells a thousand words but it does so in a universal language. And the multi-sensory approach it offers taps into different ways that different people learn at different times—so if we have the option of playing the audio with a synchronised recording script visible, or we can choose to play video with or without subtitles, we can aid understanding where necessary.

Lastly, how can we stop students forgetting what they have been learning? In fact does all this technology not exacerbate this problem? So much information is available at the click of a mouse that there is much more competition for a bit of memory space. Yes, but technology also provides us with solutions to the problems it creates! It allows us to use colour easily to indicate distinctions and salient points, and thanks to digital storage we can return to material previously studied whenever needed. This means we can exploit a piece of learning material in several different ways. For example, if you have studied a text in one lesson, you could display it on the classroom presentation software in a subsequent lesson, and use the 'pen' tool to hide selected words. The students work in pairs to reconstruct the text. It is an engaging and useful revision activity.

### Good, but not *too* good

Workshop participants then shared the problems they had identified from their own teaching and discussed which could and could not be solved by technology. The conclusion we reached was that technology could help with many issues such as motivation, clarity, recycling, variety, mixed ability classes and the need for accuracy. However, when it comes to the 'warm' skills, as one participant put it, teachers will never be replaced!

Email: johanna.stirling@googlemail.com

## 8.3 Designing a 'portable' virtual learning environment virtually cost-free

**Manuela Reguzzoni** *LEND (Lingua e Nuova Didattica), Genoa, Italy*

### Introduction

Creating an inexpensive but effective virtual learning environment (VLE) is easier than most people think. In fact, writing HTML pages and using free facilities is all you basically need to do.

### Using free tools to produce electronic materials

If you cannot write HTML pages, WinWord can help you produce them and add hyper-textual links. Free 'applets' (a computer programme written in the Java programming language) to enliven your pages, and Javascripts (scripting language that controls a software application) to create tests and provide built-in support can be downloaded from the Web together with free programmes to design interactive language activities (for example, Hotpotatoes, TexToys, Crossword Compiler, Quandary, Flashspeller, Gerry's Vocabulary Teacher, etc.), mark homework (for example, Markin) and verify the word frequency and the level of difficulty of a text (for example, Word Classifier).

Free programmes usually have restricted functionality but using different tools provides a variety of content and appearance thus contributing to the maintainance of impact.

## Adding external links

Once you have created a core of teaching/learning materials, adding a well devised set of links allows your learners to easily access selected online resources to exploit the support provided by the Web, listen to, view and read authentic materials, without breaching any copyright rules, and practise their skills. To the ready-to-use opportunities already existing you can add your own, cost-free facilities. Setting up a platform (for example, at Nicenet), a group or even a site (at Yahoo, Quia, etc.) can give you free online spaces to post materials and messages and discuss topics, thus extending tuition time beyond the class and making dealing with your learners' queries and homework easier and more effective.

## Creating a 'portable' VLE

By saving your materials and links on CD-ROMs you can create a kind of VLE which just needs an internet connection to become fully functional—a VLE structured along three main axes (Bertin 2001):

- a 'didactic axis' constituted by the sequence of screen pages (containing 'core' readings and a wide selection of related activities);
- a 'heuristic axis' created by the 'escape' links leading to selected online resources (further reading materials, sound and video clips, podcasts, interactive activities, games, tests, WebQuests, blogs, chats, moos, wikis, the teacher's own platform, group/s, website/s, email account, etc.);
- a 'referential axis' providing help and support (feed-back, prompts, notes, translations, links to dictionaries and encyclopaedias, etc.).

## Developing a new way of thinking

Your VLE may be designed on the cheap but making it effective is not a straightforward process. You have to move from a linear to a multi-dimensional perspective, envisage synchronous and asynchronous opportunities and realise that you are not only a materials designer but also an editor, a 'stage director' (Laurel 1993) and a guide on a voyage of discovery. You have to consider the setting/location, its visual layout and impact, the places you wish your actors/explorers to visit, the different routes they may take, the things you would like them to do or the ones they may decide to do ignoring your prompts, the roles and games you want them to play, the moments in time and space when your virtual world will be explored. You may propose a 'default route', 'the route that you deem optimal' (Laurillard 1996), but you should also leave your explorers free to pursue their own paths thus catering for different learning styles and fostering learner autonomy.

## Designing an effective VLE

Well-targeted, interesting contents, challenging activities, variety of presentation, clarity of design and ease of use are essential. The materials should not only meet the learners' target needs but also their wants and have face validity while being enjoyable, stimulating and motivating. The activities/tasks should be of different types (pedagogic and authentic), present different levels of difficulty, cater for different language levels and learning styles, provide forms of easily available interactive support and feedback and, possibly, look game-like to achieve an 'enjoy the ride perspective' (Moro 1997). The environment should be user-friendly and easy to explore, to prevent your learners from getting lost inside the software. You should provide a clear index, make all links easy to visualise, opt for a fairly linear content, use hypertextual facilities sparingly, design attractive pages (screen by screen as in a PowerPoint presentation, since scrolling is definitely unpleasant) and try to make the whole environment so enticing as to generate the wish to explore it.

## Conclusions

Creating a simple, tailor-made 'portable' VLE—ideal for 'blended learning'—is time-consuming but is worth the effort because, though inexpensive, it allows you to fully exploit the advantages and opportunities offered by ICT and can be very effective in increasing learner autonomy, boosting motivation and facilitating language leaning/acquisition.

Email: m.reguzzoni@virgilio.it

## References

Bertin, J.C. 2001. 'CALL material structure and learner competence' in A. Chambers and G. Davies (ed.). *ICT and Language Learning: A European Perspective.* Lisse: Swets and Zeitlinger.

Laurel, B. 1993. *Computers as Theatre.* Reading, Mass.: Addison-Wesley.

Moro, B. 1997. 'A pedagogy of the hypermedia' in A-K. Korsvold and B. Rüschoff (eds.). *New Technologies in Language Learning and Teaching.* Strasbourg: Council of Europe.

## 8.4 The use of audio and video software in giving feedback and training

**Sevhan Acar** *Sabancı University, Istanbul, Turkey*

The session aimed to define screen capture software, illustrate the ways it can be used in the context of ELT and discuss its further uses. Screen capture software, which can be downloaded to computers from the internet, allows one to record computer applications on the screen, record audio and webcam images and add captions to the recordings at the editing stage. The main areas this software can be used in ELT that were highlighted in the session were giving feedback to students' written work, learner training and teacher development.

One way the software can be used is giving feedback to students' written work. Once the soft copy of the students' written work is open on the computer screen and a microphone is plugged in, the teacher can record both his voice and the changes on the document by clicking on the 'record' button. The teacher can then stop the recording, save the file in a format s/he prefers (for example, Flash) and share it with the student. As the video recordings are relatively big files, emailing is usually not the best option. The sharing can be done by burning a rewritable DVD purchased by the student, transferring the video to the student's computer or iPod or posting it on a website which allows teacher to restrict the video view to that particular student only.

Some of the advantages of using this medium for giving feedback to students' written work are as follows:

- It is different and has the 'wow' effect even on digital natives!
- It's authentic listening.
- Students can save it on a writing folder and see their progress over time.
- It allows the teacher to deliver the feedback anytime, anywhere where there is a computer and a microphone.
- It allows the student to listen to the feedback as many times as they wish, anytime, anywhere.

A common concern highlighted by colleagues is that the recording might take a long time. However, it is a good idea to remember that there are editing options and a pause button.

The use of screen capture software in creating training videos is nothing new. It has been used in sales and marketing and in IT training. However, its use in ELT is relatively new. At the IATEFL Conference in Aberdeen, the idea of using the software to give feedback to students' written work was introduced. Once having taken this idea from the conference, it was possible to think of further ways that the software could be used in an ELT context. The two major areas introduced in my presentation were learner training and teacher development.

Learner training videos, such as training videos on IT skills (for example, formating documents in Word), or study skills (recording vocabulary) allow students to follow audio and visual examples. Students can also record videos using the software, such as the PowerPoint slides they have prepared for a class presentation with their voice-over. Some types of software also have additional features, such as adding captions (Figure 8.4.1) or video images (Figure 8.4.2) to enhance the recordings.

Based on the idea of learner training videos, one can also record teacher training and development videos. In-house teacher development videos (for example, using the internal website) can be used for giving technical assistance to colleagues. Also, the software can be used to share conference presentations or missed workshops. Once the PowerPoint slides or the soft copies of the handouts used in the presentation are recorded with voice-over, they can be posted internally or externally on a website medium. This could, for example, be a helpful medium for the next IATEFL online website, as it would allow ELT professionals from all over the world to not only hear the presentation, but also follow the slides and handouts as the speaker delivers the presentation.

*Figure 8.4.1: Turkish website tutorial for non-native Turkish speakers with English subtitles. (Especially good for Equal Opportunities)*

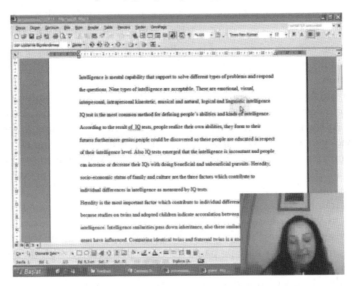

*Figure 8.4.2: Tutorial with webcam*

Furthermore, testing advisors can benefit from the software by producing institutional standardisation videos or teachers delivering distance learning courses can give feedback to students' work or provide them with general orientation. In sum, screen capture software offers endless possibilities in contributing to learner and teacher development in ELT.

Email: sevhan@sabanciuniv.edu

## 8.5 English for tourism services by cell phone

**Frank Farmer** *Universidad de Quintana Roo, Cozumel, Mexico*

### Introduction

This paper presented an overview of how cell phones are being used in an English for Specific Purposes project for tourism service providers in Mexico. The technological aspects of the project are discussed elsewhere (Juarez Manny, González Flores and Farmer 2007; Juárez Manny, Coot Bacelis y Novelo Granados 2007) and this paper focuses on the pedagogical design. The project uses cell phones as telephones, computers, game consoles, text message transmitters and cameras.

### Materials presented

Demonstration hyperlinked material was presented to illustrate the project: a sample transactional dialogue, a reference list of functional language and a dictionary of semi-technical vocabulary. These form part of a comprehensive set of materials including audio files accessed through menus, and printed user instructions. Activities designed for cell phone use are to be linked to interactions with other learners and tutor support from self-access staff through chat rooms, email, SMS text messaging and using camera functions, to provide a full learning experience in a local context.

### Learning activities

Hyperlinked material supports the following learning activities:

- Choose a situation from the menu.
- Choose a dialogue or catalogue of functional language.
- Choose to read and/or listen, and/or check dictionary.
- Choose a simulation or game.
- Choose a simulation partner according to feedback needs, either peer or tutor; arrange parameters, partner, date, time of simulation by SMS text or email.
- Clarify difficulties: chat room.
- Extend vocabulary: use cell phone camera function to see if anyone can name object/activity.
- Use language in real/simulated situations.
- Reflect on feedback from peers and tutors.

### Design of learning support

An analysis of the parameters for evaluating the learning support offered was presented:

- Typology of technology (Levy 1997)
  - Tool for apprehending and for engaging in appropriate discourse and communication.
  - Tutor for receiving feedback on accuracy and effectiveness of communication.
- Typology of learning experience (Laurillard 2002: 90)
  - Attending, apprehending: written and spoken texts.
  - Investigating, explaining: hyperlinked information, dictionary, glossary.

- Discussing, debating: chat room dedicated to programme.
- Experimenting, practising: simulation of situations aurally or in written form.
- Articulating, expressing: initiating and concluding a simulated transaction.
- Typology of language learning activities (Chapelle 2001: 55)
  - Language learning potential: focus on form.
  - Learner fit: opportunity for engagement maximised in m-learning.
  - Meaning focus: simulated situations prioritise successful communication of meaning.
  - Authenticity: simulated situations reflect real communication needs.
  - Positive impact: m-learning (using mobile technology for learning) is compatible with emerging social and cultural contexts.
  - Practicality: the appropriate use of technology, human and paper resources.
- Learning objectives (Hutchinson and Waters 1987: 59)
  - Why is the language needed? For work.
  - Medium: reading, writing, listening, speaking, oral presentations.
  - Channel: telephone, face to face, email, SMS text.
  - Text types: business, formal, informal.
  - Who will the language be used with? Native (mainly North American) and non-native speakers, service providers, clients
  - Where will the language be used? In travel agencies, hotels and restaurants, car hire firms, in Mexico.
  - When will the language be used? Parallel with learning.
- Digital, human and paper resources (Farmer 2004)
  - Digital resources: presentation of hyperlinked information, facilitation of communication.
  - Print resources: general instructions, maps of materials, suggested activities.
  - Human resources: peers' and tutors' participation in simulations, feedback, explanations.
- Learning evaluation
  - Self evaluation of functionality and accuracy of communication based on feedback from peers and tutors and success in simulations and real life transactions.

## Conclusion

In Bax's paper calling for moves towards the normalisation of CALL, he notes two prevalent fallacies (2003: 25–6): the belief that computer technology can do more than it really can, and the idea that the key factor in the implementation of technology is the technology itself. The English for tourism services by cell phone project is not concerned with stretching technical boundaries, but rather assigning feasible roles to technology, people and paper. The use of technology is firmly grounded in the tool mode (Levy 1997) and the necessary tutor functions are designed into the whole teaching and learning package much as conceptualised by Egbert's CALL equation (2005: 5):

Learners (with their thoughts, behaviours, motivations, experiences, and understandings)
+
Language (including its status and structure)
+
Context (physical and temporal environment and the social, economic, cultural and linguistic influences)
+
One or more tools (and the affordances the tool provides)
+
Tasks/activities (content, structure and organisation)
+/-
Peers and teachers(or others who can affect the process)

= CALL

The next step is to seek funding to make the system operational and carry out controlled and documented trials to evaluate not just learning and materials, but also social issues including the empowerment of users that m-learning may promote.

E-mail: frank@uqroo.mx

### References

Bax, S. 2003. 'CALL—past, present and future.' *System* 31/1, 13–28.

Egbert, J. L. 2005. 'Conducting research on CALL' in J. L. Egbert and G. M. Petrie (eds.). *CALL Research Perspectives*. Mahwah, N.J.: Lawrence Erlbaum.

Levy, M. 1997. *Computer Assisted Language Learning*. Oxford: Clarendon Press.

## 8.6 Are you goggling or Googling?

**Todd Cooper** *Toyama National College of Maritime Technology, Imizu, Toyama, Japan* and
**Valentina Dodge** *University of Naples l'Orientale, Naples, Italy*

World Wide Web version 2.0 has been both blessing and curse. The blessings for educators and students alike are innumerable; it has never been easier for them to access ICT tools and incorporate them into their work. Not too long ago, using web pages, blogs and international telephony was restricted by initial costs and expensive connection charges. Web 2.0, through its general absence of software and licensing fees, has done its part to decrease the Digital Divide.

But herein lies the curse. The limitless supply creates the huge dilemma of deciding which tool is best. Then, once dependent, educators become surprised when the 'free' software expires, or disappointed when the software company wants to make a profit. And then there are the endless numbers of accounts, passwords, login screens, and newsletters required for each application.

What if there was one website with one account, which would allow access to enough applications to satisfy any educational requirement? What if the company did not operate on the 'free-trial, then sell-for-profit' model? Well there is such a place. One username, one password, and one ubiquitous educational platform: welcome to Planet Google!

## Overcoming distance with Google

The purpose of our presentation in Exeter was to raise awareness of the multiple tools that Google offers beyond its search engine. We wanted to help teachers discover how flexible and simple Google applications are for classroom use. While any of the activities can also be used by students at adjacent terminals, the presenters actually met online during a training programme. They were actually 10,000 kilometres apart but continued working and developing educational ideas, including their presentation, via Google.

## Creating keys

The simple task of opening a Gmail account lands you on Google's generous platform. Immediately displayed in the Inbox (Figure 8.6.1) is a banner of options including Calendar, Documents, and Reader.

*Figure 8.6 1 Screenshot from cooper.td@gmail.com*

Clicks on the 'more' and subsequent 'even more' pull-down menus reveal forty-three different applications, among these, YouTube, Maps, Images, Books, Blogger, and their 'technology playground' called Google Labs.

## Creating doors

At the Toyama National College of Maritime Technology, students visit the instructor's blog regularly for assignments, quiz answers, podcasts and instructional videos, etc. This online gathering place highlights the versatility of blogging and provides an example for when students make their own.

The start page named iGoogle offers a different door to the internet. More web page than blog, iGoogle works well with small groups who want to individualise their learning through creation of an individual virtual learning environment (VLE). Gadgets and RSS feeds are easily 'dragged and dropped' onto the page, without requirement of substantial computer knowledge.

## Collaboration and control

Google Docs combines the power of word-processing software with the speed and real-time accessibility of the internet. Students can work together on the same document, presentation or spreadsheet at the same time. Educators can watch what students write, as they type, from their own monitor. Tasks, such as cloze exercises and group-writing, are easily and effectively set-up.

A great tool for in-class management is Chat or Talk. Both are online messaging services accessible from the Gmail inbox and offering voice and group chats. Talk features animated emoticons and voicemail. Either is excellent for stimulating in-class feedback. Calendar can also be used for control (set-up schedules for administrative purposes) or for collaboration (complete an information-gap activity).

## Co-APP-erating

Access to a 'one-stop shop' means it is much easier to design and complete tasks incorporating several applications. Here's an example using the well-worn 'giving directions' lesson under Google treatment. Partner A sends a Gmail requesting directions, partner B locates the place though Google Earth and gives oral instructions through Talk (in real-time with Call or recorded through Voicemail). Partner A confirms understanding by using Maps and drawing a line from start to finish. Once students have used the software, they will easily count giving and understanding directions among their skills.

## In summary

Google is undeniably the most famous search engine, but many educators are not aware of the wealth of applications available by signing up for a Google account. True, there are other options which may surpass it here and there. But overall, in our view we think you will be amazed at what 'one password' can do for you.

We hope that our presentation opened a path for exploring and enjoying Planet Google in any local or global context. We also hope that we have given teachers the information they need to stop just goggling at Google and really get Googling.

Email: cooper.td@gmail.com, valentinadodge@24hours.it

## 8.7 Online education that delivers: it's a matter of standards

**Marjorie Vai**  *The New School, New York City, USA*

Universities and other educational organisations can no longer ignore or dismiss the reality and promise of offering courses and programmes online. To excel they must also ensure that these courses are interactive and well-designed in both pedagogy and presentation. Where and how do they start?

Online courses have been rapidly progressing from the first 'read and discuss' models to learning units that are interactive, engaging, and multilayered. The tools and techniques for creating effective and engaging online learning environments are out there though not always easy to access.

In my presentation I argued that customised standards should be the first step in adapting or developing curriculum and content for online. Standards can provide a framework for planning and development. They also encourage consistency, clear learner expectations,collaboration and community-building, and overall quality across courses.

Below is one possible framework for standards with brief explanations.

## Content

- Course content for the online course is challenging and sufficient to meet the same clear outcomes as its onsite equivalent. The course is up-to-date and relevant.
- Language is as clear and accessible as possible to achieve the outcomes which themselves are written in a definite and clear style. The tone is supportive and conversational. Jargon and colloquialisms are avoided. Special terms, abbreviations and acronyms are glossed.

### Pedagogical design and organisation

- Material is logical and straight-forward in its presentation.
- Students know what is required of them.
- Content is broken up and varied in ways that are optimal for online learning.
- Learning Resources are accessible, accurate, up-to-date, varied in format and sufficient to support outcomes.
- Accuracy is emphasised throughout.

## Form

- Texture: course content is textured and interactive, presented in a variety of media and programs (for example, audio, video, images, web pages, wikis, blogs,…) which enhance understanding of the topic.
- Interactivity: course material is engaging, motivating, varied and challenging. (We now make distinctions between interaction and interactivity— *interaction* referring to the all-important student to student and student to instructor contact that has become the hallmark of online learning; *interactivity* meaning the inclusion of material that helps to create active learning online, such as the use of multimedia. 'Read and discuss' online classes are no longer seen as the best way to deliver content (Palloff and Pratt 2005) .)
- Accessibility: course material and resources are easy to access and, when possible, portable. Navigation tools are obvious in intent and consistent in use.
- Visual design: the visual presentation is attractive, uncluttered and enhances clarity and learning.

## Evaluation and assessment

- Evaluation is ongoing, transparent and equitable in process and timing.
- Assessment is varied in format and supportive of outcomes.
- Class participation and collaborative activities account for 20–35 per cent of the final grade.
- Students are able to track their progress.

## The human factor

- Collaboration and community. The interrelationship of students to teacher and students to students is of critical importance. It can make or break the online experience.

## Support

- Faculty: faculty need to feel that they are supported both by the institution and department through training in online technology, online pedagogy and multimedia. Support is also available while they are teaching and through the evaluation process. Faculty to faculty communication and collaboration is encouraged and supported by the institution.
- Student: students are trained to develop strategies for online learning and provided with easily accessible technical support. Forming online communities and collaborating with students, instructors and the larger institutional community is enabled and encouraged.

## Standards to framework

- Certain standards can be worked on early in the process and embedded throughout the programme such as *visual design* elements (for example, icons) and tools for navigation and *access* (for example, clickable glossed words, links).
- Pedagogical design and organisation standards define elements in the syllabus that will appear in each unit (for example, headings, activity types, instructions).
- Elements of interactivity and active learning, such as variety of presentation models, can also be determined early on and added to throughout development.

This type of planning, especially if done at the departmental level, simplifies course writing process while assuring a certain level of interactivity and quality.

Email: marvai@mac.com

## References

Palloff, R. and Pratt, K. 2005. *Collaborating Online: Learning Together in Community*. San Francisco, Calif.: Jossey-Bass Guides to Online Teaching and Learning.

# 9 English for Academic Purposes (EAP)

## 9.1 So you want to teach EAP?

**Olwyn Alexander, Sue Argent** and **Jenifer Spencer** *Heriot-Watt University, Edinburgh, UK*

Teaching English for Academic Purposes (EAP) is a growing field as more and more people require support to study, teach and communicate research through the medium of English. The demand for appropriately trained EAP teachers is growing. However, the field has yet to standardise its body of knowledge and skills and use this to train teachers. Evidence from a survey of 175 EAP practitioners in the UK (Alexander 2007) suggests that EAP teacher training remains largely an informal process. Survey respondents reported that they mainly learned to teach EAP through course induction sessions or by using coursebooks, but many had to discover for themselves what was appropriate in their context. The main challenges reported by over half the respondents involved understanding texts and students' needs in unfamiliar disciplines.

In spite of the informal nature of initial training, many inexperienced teachers in the survey reported that it had taken them about one year to feel confident teaching EAP. In contrast, the majority of experienced teachers said they had needed five years or more. Perhaps the inexperienced teachers had a narrower range of courses with more prescribed materials, which allowed them to feel confident sooner. However, they may also be using coping strategies that are not appropriate for EAP. One common misconception is that EAP involves teaching study skills, for example, skim reading, taking notes, giving presentations. This approach neglects the important academic language that students need to achieve their study goals.

Another misconception is to confuse *content* with *topic*. Inexperienced teachers may believe that if the topic of a lesson is academic, the content will meet EAP students' needs. This misconception was illustrated in our presentation using a case study comparing different treatments of the same topic in EAP and EFL course books. The topic was the nature-nurture debate, examined through the lives of identical twins separated at birth. However, the reading texts and the associated lessons were very different.

The EFL text was people-focused, had a journalistic style, starting the narrative with scene setting and ultimately taking a neutral stance on the issue of whether character is determined by genes or environment. In contrast, the EAP text from an academic textbook was concept-focused and reported research. It began by defining the terms and finally arrived at a stance supported by the research findings. In the EFL lesson, students learned to follow a narrative and studied language for describing life events, leading to the presentation of a personal narrative. In the EAP lesson students identified the writer's stance and the language associated with stance. The outcome was a short written text requiring critical thinking. That particular EFL lesson gave students oral fluency practice, whereas the EAP lesson enabled them to read and write in an academic way. Although the EFL lesson may have felt more familiar and safe, it did not meet students' academic needs.

Students' needs can be met more effectively by involving them in choosing texts. Although texts from unfamiliar disciplines can be daunting because of their technical content, the teacher can focus on features of academic genre and style, which will help students to understand how ideas and the relationships between them are presented. This approach was illustrated using the abstract from an electronics article (Kwok *et al.* 2003). Students identified the 'advertising' purpose of the abstract, in the authors' claim that their solution 'improves efficiency'. They noted the concise style of the abstract, achieved using long noun phrases which carried the topic from one sentence to the next. They found the longest noun phrase and tried to unpack its meaning. Finally, they identified the rhetorical function, *problem–solution*, used to achieve the persuasive purpose, and its related vocabulary. The outcome was a list of transferable problem–solution vocabulary which the students drew on to write parallel texts: abstracts of research they had done or read about.

Teachers who are new to EAP bring with them assumptions about what constitutes a good lesson and how to exploit texts. However, in EFL, the text is sometimes simply a vehicle to stimulate oral fluency practice. In EAP, it is central for understanding ideas and the way they are viewed in the discipline. Students are usually very motivated to work with their own texts and pleased when their EAP teacher shows interest in the content. Texts can be exploited through a collaboration in which the teacher contributes awareness of genre and text features and students contribute subject knowledge and expertise.

Email: O.Alexander@hw.ac.uk

## References

Alexander, O. 2007. 'Groping in the dark or turning on the light: routes into teaching English for Academic Purposes' in T. Lynch and J. Northcott (eds.). *Teacher Education in Teaching EAP*. Edinburgh: IALS, Edinburgh University.

Kwok, C., D. Fox and M. Meila. 2003. 'Adaptive real-time particle filters for robot localization'. Proceedings ICRA '03, IEEE International Conference on *Robotics and Automation*, Vol. 2: 2836–41. Abstract retrieved 11.06.08 from http://ieeexplore.ieee.org/xpls/abs_all.jsp?arnumber=1242022.

## 9.2 'So what?' Evaluation in academic writing: what, where, why, how?

**Edward de Chazal** *University College Language Centre, London, UK*

### Context and assumptions

I opened my talk with the observation that, while academic writing takes place in a teaching and learning environment where critical responses are valued, researchers (for example, in Hunston and Thompson 2000; Cotton 2004) conclude that tutors and assessors frequently do not see enough appropriate critical evaluation in students' written texts. Students may lack confidence, not realise its importance, or appear unfamiliar with the appropriate language. I argued that it is the role of academic writing teachers to address these imbalances. The talk explored evaluation, where it occurs, why and how we evaluate, the language involved, and teaching approaches.

## What?

At the heart of 'evaluation' is 'value'. Evaluation consists of value judgements. It is essentially subjective and inherently comparative. Numerous terms exist for similar or related phenomena, including among others, criticism, (authorial) stance, opinion, appreciation, perspective, attitude. Evaluation is a critical response to evidence, and distinct from other textual functions or moves: description, the presentation of evidence itself, exemplification, explanation and definition, exposition, analysis, argument and assertion. Writers and speakers can both evaluate and report others' evaluation. Crudely put, evaluation answers the question 'So what?'.

We evaluate texts: their quality, authority, reliability, intelligibility, context, partisanship, balance, influence, impact, comprehensiveness. Also we evaluate the entity (or 'thing', typically expressed by noun phrases), or proposition (or 'suggestion', typically expressed by clauses): their desirability, likelihood, significance, truth, credibility, usefulness, validity, relevance, feasibility, workability, purpose, effectiveness, cost, uniqueness, originality, safety, sufficiency, success. An audience member added 'generalisability'.

## Where?

Evaluation can be found throughout academic texts, particularly in essays, reports, reviews and critiques. Logically it follows evidence and exemplification. In certain scientific texts evaluation comes at clearly identifiable points or in conventional sections. In journalistic writing it appears from the headline onwards. One essay type explicitly calls for evaluation: 'situation, problem, solution, evaluation' (SPSE). Although helpful, this label causes confusion in that essays at large require evaluation. We do not compare and contrast without evaluating. I proposed reverting to SPSE's original incarnation, 'problem–solution', alongside a concerted effort to promote evaluation in essays generally.

## Why?

Hunston and Thompson (2000) emphasise that evaluation not only expresses the writer's opinion but also constructs and maintains relations between writer and reader, and organises the discourse. I added that as readers we crave evaluation. Information is ubiquitous; a writer's stance is unique. The purpose of academic writing is to persuade; a text without evaluation reveals little of the writer. Evaluation contributes significantly to a text's originality, offering clarification, illumination, discovery, closure, and release.

## How?

Whereas spoken texts rely heavily on paralanguage to express evaluation, written texts rely on language alone: grammar, vocabulary, style and, I suggested, a text's underlying phonology and tone. Graphics and visuals may also contribute. Effective language is essential.

## Language

Evaluative language includes evaluative adjectives ('scholarly', 'effective'), adverbs ('carefully', 'regrettably'), lexical verbs ('succeed', 'overestimate'), prepositions ('as opposed to ...', 'despite'), passive structures ('It is argued/assumed/underlined ...'), plus modals. These and other structures are covered by Biber *et al.* (1999) in an entire chapter. They also discuss lexical choices generally, idiomatic and transparent adverbials ('no doubt', 'in my view'), complement clauses ('I feel that ...'/'There is little doubt that ...'), stance nouns ('significance', 'validity', 'risk'), and noun phrases ('a great deal of interest'). Finally, 'retrospective labels' allow the writer to encode in one short phrase ('this problem/issue/challenge') a stretch of material: with the label comes the evaluation.

## Teaching

At various stages in the talk I presented texts to evaluate. The piece of evidence, actually a newspaper headline, 'In the USA, 1 in 100 adults are currently in jail' yielded audience responses including, 'that's really shocking' and 'is it true?' With a simple language shift these convert into academic evaluative material. Participants then identified such stance language in the original text: 'inexorable', 'even more startling', 'sobering', 'undesirable'.

I proposed firstly a receptive then productive classroom approach. As in my talk, we can: introduce, clarify and explain the concept of evaluation; emphasise its centrality in academic writing; identify and recognise evaluation in texts; foster critical evaluative reading skills; build up examples of evaluation in text; and develop tasks and learning materials aimed at production. Central to the production of evaluation is a toolkit of questions derived from the target qualities given in the 'What?' section above. My audience converted stance nouns to serve as questions: 'authority' leads to 'what evidence can I find that this text is authoritative?' Thus by fostering a critical mindset we ask perceptive questions and get insightful answers to incorporate into our academic writing.

Email: e.dechazal@ucl.ac.uk

## References

Biber, D., S. Johansson, G. Leech, S. Conrad, and E. Finegan. 1999. *Longman Grammar of Spoken and Written English*. Harlow: Longman.

Cotton, F. 2004. 'Evaluative language use in academic writing: a cross-cultural study.' Paper presented at the Institute of Education. London, November.

Hunston, S. and G. Thompson (eds.). 2000. *Evaluation in Text: Authorial Stance and the Construction of Discourse*. Oxford: Oxford University Press.

## 9.3 Designing writing workshops for the classroom

**Lisa Nazarenko** *University of Vienna and University of Applied Sciences, Vienna, Austria* and
**Gillian Schwarz** *University of Vienna, Vienna, Austria*

The work we presented in our talk derives from our observations over the years that even when students write with 'correct' grammar and appropriate vocabulary, their writing is often disorganised, unfocused and fails to achieve its purpose. We therefore introduced a focus on pre-writing in our process writing classes for intermediate to advanced classes at university level, as well as in ESP classes of engineering students.

### Background

Although we have always presented writing as a process, with pre-writing stages (brainstorming and organising) to post-writing stages (editing and revision), students did not always follow this process in the assignments they wrote at home. They tended to write texts that did not have a clear focus and did not use logical linking devices.

Since these texts were disorganised, then the revision stage was demoralising; the students often had to change many parts of their texts, while we had put effort into detailed feedback which was not really made use of. Moreover, students did not seem to have any strategies to deal with their problems. They were not used to reflecting on their work, and thus had no idea why some parts of the writing process were difficult, or other parts easier.

We therefore decided to continue with our process writing approach, but to change the focus from the end of the process—revisions—to the beginning—pre-writing. We also had students do more of their writing during class sessions, so that we would be able to make sure that they were indeed using the pre-writing activities. In addition, we introduced them to the concept of reflection, and made time for that in class sessions as well.

### Pre-writing

Before students are expected to write anything, we 'set the stage'. First, we determine guidelines for the text type they are going to write, and make a list that will serve as a checklist for the students to follow. We decide how the task will be assessed, and, again, make up a checklist of these points to serve as our Feedback Sheet. Then we find, or prepare, sample texts as a model of these guidelines. We have created accompanying activities and exercises for the students to do in class, and at home, which are designed to highlight features of the model texts that make them 'work'.

### Writing sessions

The writing sessions in class focus on those pre-writing activities the students don't do at home, such as preparing an organisation plan. Exactly which further stages of the writing process we do in class, and for how long, depends on the group, the text type, the purpose of the text, and the time frame of both the class session and the course. In effect, we 'design' these writing workshops to suit these factors.

Two important features of these in-class writing sessions are peer discussion/feedback and reflection time. The students find it very helpful to discuss various stages of their work with their peers, which can add to their ideas or serve to confirm that their ideas are 'worthy', making them feel more secure about what they will write.

Time for reflection is important, we find, since this is a skill students are generally not familiar with. They need time to develop the skill before it can be an effective tool for them to understand themselves as writers. To help them practise it during the writing process, we give them a clear, simple form to fill out at various stages (both in class and at home); this focuses their attention on what they are doing and how they feel about it.

## Post-writing

After students have handed in their text, they have to be guided to develop skills for editing and revising. They are given the Feedback Sheet, which focuses specifically on those areas of assessment we have made them aware of, and indicates both what they have done and not done. This style of feedback allows us to give a response that is more specific, and also more clearly focuses on the positive aspects of the writing, not just the problems. Students are able to make better use of our feedback, resulting in a better return on investment of the time we put into it.

## Conclusion

Bringing writing into the classroom allows us to guide the students in all stages of the writing process. Results show that our students not only produce better texts in their first draft, but are developing a better understanding of the features of English discourse, including a clearer focus on their choices of vocabulary and use of grammatical structures.

Email: lisa.nazarenko@chello.at, gillian.schwarz-peaker@univie.ac.at

# 9.4 Essay-writing with new BA English Language Studies students

**Marion Colledge** *London Metropolitan University, London, UK*

## Introduction

The talk reported on a survey of student need and development of appropriate teaching strategies leading up to the first assessed essay in the first year of a BA English Language Studies degree in the UK, where the student population is diverse in respect of first languages, ethnicity, age and socio-economic status.

Fifty per cent of students have either EU status or International status. Even of the UK-status students, approximately half have English as a second language. Many students have not previously been assessed by coursework essay. Some have completed preparatory courses, where they have learned prescriptive notions unsuitable for our subject area, for example, that first person 'I' is not allowed.

Such student diversity presents challenges for production of the first assessed 1,200-word essay, the more so as the UK government guidelines for English degrees state that we are to produce efficient, literate communicators who can present sustained persuasive written arguments in essays, and other types of assessments.

The module in which our intervention took place is entitled 'Introduction to Texts: Spoken and Written'. In it students study various text types in English such as conversations (and their own accents), essays, news reports, and science reports. Generous contact time (3 hours a week over 12 weeks) and relatively small classes (20) make it possible to alternate between short lectures and group work.

We surveyed the concerns about academic writing of new students and carried out an analysis of the essays of one cohort. The project was part-funded by the 'WriteNow Centre for Excellence in Teaching and Learning' (UK-government funding) and was co-researched with Steve Jones.

## Teaching strategies

Both holistic and analytical strategies were adopted for developing the essay-writing skills of these students. We drew on constructivism, critical thinking (for example, Bean 2001) and the 'writing in the disciplines' approach to texts (for example, Swales and Feak 2004; Hyland 2006).

The survey showed that students were particularly concerned about writing with accurate vocabulary and grammar. We met this concern to some extent by providing a glossary of new linguistic terms for the module. Students added further items themselves, working in groups. We made available lists of words for different stances in citation, as well as different 'link' words. Students were very interested in using Haywood's *Academic Word List Highlighter* (http://www.nottingham.ac.uk/~alzsh3/acvocab/awlhighlighter.htm) at the editing stage of their work to check if their writing 'had an academic feel'.

Students' second main concern, and our principal one, was tackling the amounts of reading required. Weaker students had been plagiarising popular websites instead of using the material from their reading list. We collated essential reading material into an annotated Reader, saving students' time searching for, and through, books on the reading list. We related this reading material to students' current ideas and knowledge frame, distinguishing between linguistic-knowledge-based and opinion-based types of material, encouraging a sceptical stance towards the latter.

Our second main worry was the unevenness of evidence in students' arguments (though some Italian and Polish students, new to essay assessment, showed great strengths in written argument). Some of the ways in which we addressed weaknesses were by:

1. Collecting on a flip chart points made by the class on a topic of argument, for example, 'Does Received Pronunciation matter in London today?' We encouraged students to note the difference between the fragmented collection of class opinions and a structured argument in a written essay.
2. Encouraging structure within paragraphs: point, example, explanation.
3. Using an essay-writing frame in preparation for the assessed essay, incorporating the reading already undertaken. A sample section of such a frame is shown in Figure 9.4.1.

Introduction

Part 1: Point 1 in your description or argument          Source/s

Part 1: Point 2 in your description or argument          Source/s
Part 1: Point 3 in your description or argument          Source/s
Part 1:Conclusion and a link sentence to Part 2

Part 2 ...          ...

Conclusion encompassing all parts

*Figure 9.4.1 Sample section of writing frame*

After the experiment, the quality of argument in essays really improved. Some students still reported inability to evaluate the band that their own completed essay would fall into. We therefore made available a sample essay, asking students to apply the module mark scheme to it and to their own at hand-in time. Further essays were made available through the university's intranet system 'Weblearn'.

Email: m.colledge@londonmet.ac.uk

## References

Bean, J. C. 2001. *Engaging Ideas: The Professor's Guide to Integrating Writing, Critical Thinking, and Active Learning in the Classroom.* San Francisco: Jossey Bass.

Haywood, S. http://www.nottingham.ac.uk/~alzsh3/acvocab/awlhighlighter.htm (last accessed 12 June 2008).

Swales, J. and C. Feak. 2004. *Academic Writing for Graduate Students: Essential Tasks and Skills,* Second edition. Ann Arbor: University of Michigan Press.

## 9.5 English in the workplace: Speaking vs. writing skills

**Hans Platzer** and **Désirée Verdonk** *Fachhochschule Wiener Neustadt, Wiener Neustadt, Austria*

### Background

One crucial aspect of Business English which theorists and practitioners alike agree on is the centrality of needs analysis. Such needs analysis is meant to ensure that the acquired language skills are relevant to the situation in the workplace. By its very nature needs analysis is of course only feasible with in-service learners. However, it is also true that the vast majority of Business English instruction in Austria takes place in a pre-service context, typically in secondary and tertiary education. As a business university, the *Fachhochschule* (university specialising in particular subjects) *Wiener Neustadt* enrols pre-service as well as in-service students. So, in order to predict the future needs of its pre-service students and to adapt the curriculum accordingly, the Department of English at the *Fachhochschule Wiener Neustadt* has twice conducted surveys among its in-service students, once in 2003 and most recently in 2008.

## Method

The questionnaire survey conducted in 2008 was based on a sample of 242 in-service students, 165 (68 per cent) of whom need English in the workplace. The findings reported below relate to these 165 English users.

## Results and discussion

In the following section we will focus on the role of spoken vs. written English in the workplace.

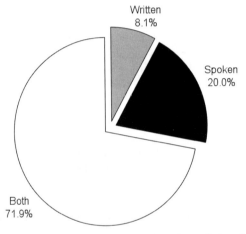

*Figure 9.5.1  Spoken and written English in the workplace (n = 165)*

Not surprisingly, the majority (71.9 per cent) of respondents use both spoken and written English. What turned out to be surprising, however, was that a substantial minority (20.0 per cent) reported that they used spoken English (almost) exclusively. On the other hand exclusive written use stands at less than half this figure (8.1 per cent). These numbers seem to support the case for highlighting speaking skills in a vocational context. In fact, an Austria-wide survey conducted in 2005 among over 2,000 personnel managers comes to a similar conclusion. While just over half of HR managers (53 per cent) reported that their staff needed written English, the figure was 70 per cent for spoken English (Archan and Dornmayr 2005: 58, Ill. 35). And similarly, only 39 per cent of executives felt that improvements were needed in their staff's writing skills, but almost three quarters (72 per cent) felt speaking skills needed improving (Archan and Dornmayr 2005: 64, Ill. 41). So in a professional context, users of English do not feel a particular need for more instruction in writing. Indeed it is becoming increasingly difficult to make business students see the relevance of formal writing. And to be fair, on the basis of the surveys cited above, it is difficult to argue that this is a skill which is in particular demand among employers.

A further look at the individual situations in which our respondents use English should provide additional data on whether skills in formal writing are indeed less crucial in a vocational context. The top two uses, cited by roughly three quarters of our respondents, are telephoning (75.2 per cent) and correspondence (73.9 per cent). As the overwhelming amount of correspondence nowadays tends to be conducted by email, there does not seem to be a pressing need for formal writing here. Moreover, writing is no issue at all when it comes to meetings (38.8 per cent) and social contacts (35.2 per cent), both of which are mentioned by over a third of the respondents. On this basis it is certainly doubtful whether a focus on formal writing is justifiable.

*Figure 9.5.2  Speaking and drafting in English (n = 165)*

It is only the next three text types (reports 28.5 per cent; minutes 26.1 per cent; technical documentation 22.4 per cent) which demand skills in formal writing. However, only about one quarter of the respondents require such skills. And finally around 15 per cent use English to conduct negotiations (17.0 per cent) and give presentations (15.8 per cent), where formal writing again is hardly relevant.

So from a purely vocational perspective, such as at secondary vocational schools, a special highlight on formal writing may not be a tenable position. At an academic level, on the other hand, sidelining written skills is probably not an appropriate response, as one of the mainstays of academic discourse is formal texts. Consequently, confining English instruction in tertiary education to merely suit the vocational sphere is unduly restricting and may eventually prove shortsighted. For universities and *Fachhochschulen* to limit English teaching in this way would mean risking their academic standing and being mistaken for vocational institutions pure and simple - which can hardly be in their interest.

Email: hans.platzer@fhwn.ac.at, verdonk@fhwn.ac.at

## References

Archan, S. and H. Dornmayr. 2005. *Fremdsprachenbedarf und -kompetenzen. Unternehmensbefragung zu Ausbildungsqualität und Weiterbildungsbedarf.* (ibw-Schriftenreihe; Nr. 131) Vienna: Institut für Bildungsforschung der Wirtschaft.

## 9.6 Self-assessment and learner autonomy in EAP

**Susan Esnawy** and **Mohga Hafez** *The American University in Cairo, Egypt*

It is essential to find ways to develop English as a Second Language (ESL) /English for Academic Purposes (EAP) learners' autonomy, especially if they come from educational contexts where learner autonomy is minimal, which is the case for our students. Self-assessment is an 'integral part of autonomous learning' which most learners experience, even if they are unaware of it and do not know its benefits and the way to do it 'effectively' (Gardner 2000). The learner needs to be aware of this process (Coombe and Canning 2002) and the strategies he uses, to modify his beliefs and attitudes towards learning (Wenden 1998). Therefore a self-assessment study was conducted to reveal students' perceptions of their abilities, and to determine the skills they need to help them become autonomous. A brief description of the study, including the results and their implications for the classroom, is followed by activities to enhance learners' self-assessment of their performance.

Our study was conducted in a university freshman EAP programme. It involved 135 subjects. The instrument was a 30-item questionnaire on reading comprehension, writing, summarising, research and test-taking skills, which was administered at the beginning and end of one semester. The analysis of the data compared their sets of responses and their responses with their performance on exams, which showed statistical significance (using T-Test and Gamma). The results showed significant differences between their evaluations of their abilities at the beginning and end of the semester, reflecting more capability at the end, especially by successful students. For example, there was a significant difference between their satisfaction with their performance at the beginning and end of the semester in reading comprehension, $t(134)$ = 3.07, $p$ = 0.003, and writing, $t(134)$ = 4.37, $p$ = 0.000. In summary, there was a significant difference in items about accurate communication of author's purpose, $t(134)$ = 3.18, $p$ = 0.002, and writing a concise and non-wordy summary, $t(134)$ = 3.02, $p$ = 0.003, and in research skills, in comparing and contrasting information from different sources in their writing $t(134)$ = 3.09, $p$ = 0.002. There were also significant correlations between their evaluations of their abilities and their performance on exams, for both students who went on to the next level and those who needed another semester. On the whole, approximately 70–75 per cent of the subjects passed and the rest failed the course; the passing students were better evaluators of their abilities, and some of the failing students also evaluated their abilities quite accurately, but the rest of them tended to overestimate their abilities. This happened in the different skills, such as finding the main idea ($\gamma$ = 0.35; $p$ = 0.006, 69 per cent of passing students) and relations between ideas in reading comprehension, organisation ($\gamma$ = 0.31; $p$ = 0.015, 83 per cent of passing students), planning and proofreading in writing, identifying the ideas and summarising them, managing time, preparing and worrying about exams in test-taking skills, and citing sources accurately in research.

The results implied that there is a need for raising students' awareness to enable them to assess their abilities and improve their skills. Thus, some activities can be used to achieve this and they fall into two categories: analyse product and evaluate product. In analysing product, using a rubric, students analyse their writing, evaluate their findings and discuss their analysis with their teacher. For example, they analyse a paragraph by writing the main idea, finding the supporting ideas and the details, examples, and then evaluating them as to their effectiveness and completion, while considering adding information that would improve the paragraph. In evaluating product, using correction criteria, students grade their own essays and summaries, or peer grade each other's. In a group activity, students write a summary in groups, and then using an OHP, they read and grade another group's product. The teacher can also have students come up with their own criteria, after discussing the course's criteria, and use it in evaluating their product. When students did so, they actually came up with very similar criteria, but phrased in their own way, and their evaluations of the product were quite similar to the teacher's.

The study showed that freshman EAP students, with minimal or no guidance, were able to assess their abilities in different skills to a certain point, which implied that giving them more guidance in how to assess their performance would help them in becoming better at evaluating their abilities and being more independent learners. Further research is needed to determine the effects of this guidance on their performance and ability to become more autonomous learners.

Email: sesnawy@aucegypt.edu

## References

Coombe, C. and C. Canning. 2002. 'Using self-assessment in the classroom: rationale and suggested techniques'. *Karen's Linguistics Issues*, February. (Retrieved 28 November 2007 from http://www3.telus.net/linguisticsissues/selfassess2.html.)

Gardner, D. 2000. 'Self-assessment for autonomous language learners'. *Links & Letters* 7: 49–60. (Retrieved 28 November 2007 from http://www.bib.uab.es/pub/linksandletters/11337397n7p49.pdf.)

Wenden, A. 1998. *Learner Strategies for Learner Autonomy*. London: Prentice Hall.

## 9.7 Meeting students halfway: generating greater commitment in EAP classes

**Clare Anderson** *Freelance, Cambridge, UK*

EAP students need and want to succeed, so why do we experience commitment problems? The notion of meeting students halfway indicates a willingness to look at the causes and to ask if this apparent lack of commitment is all it seems. This issue emerged at my talk on interactive approaches, tasks and materials in EAP given in 2006 (IATEFL Harrogate 2006). While a later article (Anderson 2007) goes some way to addressing how this approach may be implemented, the question of how to maintain a commitment in an EAP context where the classes may well not be the student's main course of study is the focus of attention here. This workshop aimed to give EAP practitioners an opportunity to share their experience and successful strategies for generating commitment. It was a lively, even noisy session for which the participants must take credit for taking part so enthusiastically at the end of a very full day.

There were four interactive tasks to be done in groups. These included:

- defining commitment and what is expected from the teachers, students and institutions;
- focusing on the solutions to problems and categorising them into course content/materials/classroom management and pastoral.

## Expectations

Regarding institutions' and teachers' expectations, what emerged was a rather disturbing mismatch between what was often offered in terms of EAP course materials and aims and what the students could offer in terms of their undoubted intelligence, but lack of linguistic range. It was thought by some that the information transfer and 're-gurgitation' approach was used when actually universities wanted the skill of information transformation or synthesis. Furthermore the level of language required may be too high and the culture of the receiving institution 'irrelevant' to low level learners. The shock of being away from home and in an unfamiliar culture, and issues of not wanting to lose face are often overlooked, and students may feel overwhelmed by what they have taken on. These factors could all contribute to teachers (and presumably students) having unrealistic expectations.

## Suggestions for generating greater commitment; solutions to problems

### Course content, materials and classroom management

- establish clear boundaries,
- learner contracts and attendance sheets for persistent latecomers,
- review of student satisfaction and motivation,
- portfolio assessment with regular tests and quizzes,
- news review first thing in the morning; gets students there on time,
- clear long term goals broken down into smaller attainable targets,
- demonstration, enforcement and reinforcement of learner independence strategies,
- learner journals,
- encouragement of student collaboration,
- encouragement of healthy rivalry: harness peer pressure, for example, peer demonstrations of competence,
- involving students in decision-making in *everything*: course and lesson planning, materials, assessment,
- clear explanations,
- consistent feedback; finding time for tutorials when returning essays,
- fun activities,
- subject-specific material that is relevant, motivating, interesting, and intellectually stimulating.

### Pastoral

- being available for problems, i.e. show them you care,
- being pro-active: responding to repeated class absences,

- befriending the student support network officer,
- promoting student clubs,
- taking culture shock into account.

## Analysis

An emerging theme was the need for learner independence, and training in this area. As participants said 'the students need failure before they'll believe us!' and 'if you wait for me to teach you, you won't learn much!' Teacher dynamism was important but so was 'class synergy, self-responsibility, self-evaluation and reflection'.

Materials needed to be more relevant: 'dry materials! We're all bored—*we* write materials! It's the hardest ELT I've ever done!'

The expectations of institutions and staff, the desirability of more training for EAP teachers (which Alexander *et al.* (2008) have, most recently, done much to remedy) also emerged as key issues, as did pastoral issues. If staff address these points students could indeed be met halfway and enabled to make the progress needed.

Email: clareanderson1@gmail.com

## References

Alexander, O., S. Argent and J. Spencer. 2008. *EAP Essentials: A Teacher's Guide to Principles and Practice*. Reading: Garnet Education

Anderson, C.G. 2007. 'Enabling interactive teaching and learning methods in EAP classes and assessing some students' views of effective learning' in M. Krzanowski (ed.). *Current Developments in English for Academic, Specific and Occupational Purposes*. Canterbury, IATEFL.

## 9.8 Thai postgraduate students' identity negotiation in British university classroom participation

**Singhanat Nomnian** *University of Leicester, UK/ Mahidol University, Thailand, Bangkok*

The rapid growth in the numbers of international students in UK higher education increases linguistic diversity in academic and social contexts in a British university, and that raises issues regarding the extent to which multilingualism influences interactions and inter-relationships between tutors and international students within classroom settings. The study on which I reported in my presentation explored the factors affecting the ways Thai students position themselves in relation to their tutors and peers with regard to oral participation in postgraduate classrooms. The data was collected from seven Thai students by means of semi-structured interviews, classroom observations, and English speaking logs from October 2005 to April 2006.

The theoretical framework of this study draws upon Creese and Martin's (2003) concept of *multilingual classroom ecologies*. This concept recognises the significance for classroom environments of not only psychological aspects such as perceptions and attitudes of speakers towards their own language use, but also the sociological aspect of different languages used within the particular classroom. Communication in multilingual classroom settings in my study was influenced by the impact of language ideologies and power relations embedded within local classroom practices, as well as wider socio-political institutions. Consequently, the Thai students regarded 'standard' English as a 'legitimate' language and considered speakers of other 'non-standard' varieties as 'non-legitimate'. Pavlenko and Blackledge's (2004) work regarding *negotiation of identities in multilingual contexts* claims that linguistic minority speakers in multilingual contexts are likely to encounter a conflict between their identities, linguistic ideologies and power relations. In such circumstances the minority language speakers may struggle to claim rights of linguistic legitimacy. *Positioning theory* (Davies and Harré 1990), as an analytical framework, offers critical insights into understanding the complexity of power relations, linguistic ideologies, linguistic legitimacy, positions of the minority language speaker students and those with whom they interact.

Based on the Thai students' interview transcripts, the findings suggested key factors that stem from lecturers' linguistic diversity, the inclusion of students from other subject disciplines, and the recent dramatic increase in student numbers and class size. Firstly, the lecturers' linguistic diversity causes negative attitudes from some Thai students who strongly believe that studying in the UK should involve studying with 'native-speaker' lecturers rather than 'non-native' ones. Secondly, Thai students' attitudes towards the inclusion of students from MBA and MSc Management programmes during their second term are rather mixed; some Thai students enjoy listening to mature and experienced students who share their business knowledge in class and group discussions while others feel intimidated by MBA students' dominance. Accordingly, Thai students are likely to withdraw from discussions and allow those mature students to take the floor and share their valuable experience. Finally, the large class size undermines Thai students' confidence to engage in discussions as they develop anxiety about their Thai accent which they believe does not sound 'native' or 'standard' compared with other varieties of English spoken by European students. Thai students thus sometimes position themselves as 'illegitimate' speakers in these circumstances. Interrelated and complex factors, such as, students' academic expectations, lecturers' teaching styles, classmates' relationships, English language proficiency, and the Thai students' personal identities and agency also seem to impact upon this situation and demand appropriate action from the postgraduate programme co-ordinators and course designers to ensure quality and equality, rather than quantity in terms of student numbers.

My study suggests that tutors in pre-sessional courses should be aware of the increasing multilingualism in British universities and inform students about potential linguistic issues, such as pronunciation of other English varieties and accents, which they may encounter while studying in postgraduate classrooms. Thai students should be informed that other English varieties are equally valued, and this could enhance self-confidence, self-esteem, and ownership of their spoken English. More use of English as an international language (EIL) pedagogy could help to broaden Thai and other international students' viewpoints regarding multilingualism in British academic settings and would have the potential to encourage them to become 'legitimate' speakers of EIL. Accordingly, they might feel more empowered, confident, and proud of their spoken English, which could lead to more positive learning experiences for them in UK higher education. It is also vital to raise awareness of issues relating social inclusion and tolerance towards international students amongst native-speaker students and academic staff, since a multilingual student body contributes to a positive intellectual and social climate in the British university landscape.

Email: snomnian@hotmail.com

## References

Creese, A. and P. Martin (eds.). 2003. *Multilingual Classroom Ecologies: Inter-relationships, Interactions and Ideologies.* Clevedon: Multilingual Matters.

Davies, B. and Harré, R. 1990 'Positioning: the discursive production of selves'. *Journal of the Theory of Social Behavior* 20/1: 43–63.

Pavlenko, A. and A. Blackledge (eds.). 2004. *Negotiation of Identities in Multilingual Contexts.* Clevedon: Multilingual Matters.

# 10 Assessment and examinations

## 10.1 The Common European Framework and functional progression in materials for ELT

**Anthony Green** *University of Bedfordshire, Luton, UK*

The Common European Framework of Reference for Languages: learning, teaching, assessment (CEFR) (Council of Europe 2001) is intended to provide common terms for learners, teachers, publishers and language testers to communicate about language learning and levels of language ability across borders, target languages and educational sectors. The CEFR has been widely adopted around the world as a means of helping users to set targets for learning, teaching and assessment. However, its value is limited by the lack of clear specifications of linguistic features associated with performance at each of the levels it describes.

The Council of Europe envisages that more detailed Reference Level Descriptions (RLD) will be required to expand on and exemplify the CEFR scales for specific languages to inform the planning of language programmes and for assessment. The purpose of RLD is 'to describe or transpose the [CEFR] descriptors that characterise the competences of users/learners at a given level in terms of linguistic material specific to that language and considered necessary for the implementation of those competences' (Council of Europe 2005). My presentation described one strand of the work of a cross-disciplinary team aimed at developing RLD for English.

The CEFR describes language in terms of *communicative functions* or 'What people *do* by means of language … things such as describing, enquiring, denying, thanking, apologising, expressing feelings, etc.' (van Ek and Trim 2001); *notions* or the concepts that are communicated; and the *lexical and grammatical exponents* that are used to express these. In the research described here, the focus was on the language functions that characterise performance at the C1 and C2 levels of the CEFR (levels for which no detailed specifications for English have yet been published by the Council of Europe) and features of language use that might distinguish these from the B2 level.

A wide range of documents including published course books, national curricula, syllabuses, proficiency scales and examination specifications was analysed. From these materials, lists of language functions and can-do statements were collected, reflecting the expectations of language educators of learners' ability to use English as they move above the B2 level. These were categorised using Wilkins' (1976) extensive list of communicative functions.

Corpus analysis tools including WordSmith Tools (http://www.lexically.net) and the Compleat Lexical Tutor (www.lextutor.ca) were used to explore ways in which descriptions of the C level differed from B2. By highlighting the specific vocabulary that characterises a text in comparison to a corpus of general language (the Brown corpus in this case), *keyword analysis* is often used to provide an indication of the topic of a text. In this study the keywords analysis was used to identify functions that were particularly associated with the C level of the CEFR. Once these words had been identified, *concordance lines*, which show every instance of a selected word in a text or corpus, were generated to compare the contexts in which function words such as 'argument' or 'instruction' appeared in can-do statements or descriptions of language functions at the different levels in the materials we had collected.

Analysis suggested that, in spite of the diverse materials, it was possible to abstract a broad set of claims about the distinctive features of C level performance that could be refined, enhanced and recast as a coherent set of communicative functions. These claims could then be tested against both the perceptions of educators and the analyses of learner language corpora towards the development of RLD for English.

Our analysis suggests that sets of functions such as arguing, criticising and evaluating; editing, refining and structuring; defining, defending and justifying; abstracting, interpreting and integrating are salient at the C level, together with increasing sensitivity to the relationship between choices of linguistic form and contexts for use. It is also notable that the materials we analysed included very few functions at the C levels concerned with what Wilkins (1976) terms 'personal emotions'. This may reflect the academic and professional bias of higher level materials, but seems a curious oversight nonetheless as careful choice of language of the kind that seems characteristic of the C level would seem to be important in expressing personal feelings.

In future phases of the project, a set of functional descriptions defining salient features of the C level for English will be drafted. These must then be tested against and contextualised by learner-language empirical evidence collected from naturalistic settings.

Email: tony.green@beds.ac.uk

## References

Council of Europe. 2005. *Guide for the Production of RLD. Version 2.* Retrieved 23 April 2008 from http://www.coe.int/t/dg4/linguistic.

Wilkins, D. 1976. *Notional Syllabuses.* Oxford: Oxford University Press.

van Ek, J. A. and J. L. M. Trim. 2001. *Vantage.* Cambridge: Cambridge University Press.

## 10.2  Using action research to improve a TOEIC preparation course

**Jo Mynard** *Kanda University of International Studies, Chiba, Japan*

### Background to the research

TOEIC (Test of English for International Communication) is widely used in Japan by colleges, universities and employers as a standard for entry and an indicator of progress. At the women's college where I was previously employed, a high emphasis was placed on TOEIC scores, yet little research was available indicating how students can be helped to achieve higher scores. As I was one of the instructors responsible for delivering the English for TOEIC course, I was interested in making changes to the course in order to help students get better test scores.

## Action research cycles

Action research is useful in situations where an educator wants to improve an aspect of a teaching/learning situation. A cyclical approach like the one presented by Coughlan and Brannick (2005) highlights that often just making one set of changes is not enough; the research needs to be ongoing—see Figure 10.2.1. This is the approach I adopted to inform change in the English for TOEIC course.

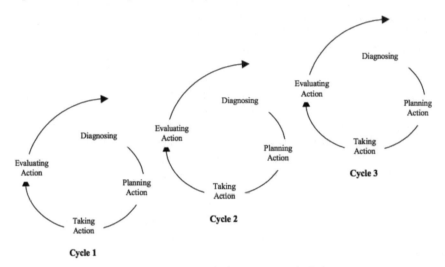

*Figure 10.2.1 Spiral of Action Research Cycles*
*(reproduced with permission from Coghlan and Brannick 2005: 24)*

## Participants and context

Participants were all English majors at a two-year women's college in Japan. There were 45 first-year students and 5 second-year students.

## About the original TOEIC course

Initial research highlighted a number of problems with the original 'English for TOEIC' course. Firstly, the focus was on listening skills in the first semester and reading skills in the second semester. Students mainly had problems with reading skills. Secondly, the textbook was designed for more advanced students. Thirdly, there were no self-study activities. Also, the course was very teacher-centred. Finally, the students were not clear about exam study techniques.

## Phase 1: Changes made over a one year period

Based on the initial research, four main changes were implemented in the following academic year. Firstly, a new textbook was introduced which included Japanese grammar explanations and some self-study material. Secondly, the syllabus was revised to incorporate elements of goal setting, record-keeping and reflection. Thirdly, the new syllabus focused more on students' weaknesses. Finally, there was more use of technology and access to computerised self-study practice materials.

## Results of implemented changes

Research showed that the changes that were implemented had a positive effect on the learners. Students enjoyed the course, benefited from the self-study component and were clearer on what they needed to do to prepare for the test. However, despite the positive changes, students were still disappointed with how little their TOEIC scores improved.

## Phase 2: Research into how students study outside of class

Phase 2 of the action research cycle focused on reasons for continuing low scores and investigated how students prepared for the exam outside class time. The data showed that students mainly relied on the teacher-assigned homework and textbooks to improve their English outside class. Evidence showed that students did not use the textbooks effectively for self-study. In addition, there was very little evidence to show that students could identify activities which they could do apart from ones in the textbook. Students were passive listeners to English songs and relied on Japanese subtitles when watching English language movies. There was evidence that students worked hard, but the activities did not necessarily help them to improve their overall English abilities and get a higher score in the test

## Phase 3: Implemented changes

Phase 3 saw the implementation of further changes to the course based on the research findings. Firstly, a textbook with substantial self-study material was chosen. In addition to focusing on reading and listening skills and strategies, class time was spent on the following activities: accessing and effectively using motivating authentic texts such as movies, music and websites, setting realistic goals, identifying weaknesses, organising notes, learning how to use the textbook efficiently and plotting progress. Initial observations indicated that students were using more effective ways of learning English outside class time which would hopefully be reflected in their TOEIC scores in coming semesters. This research is ongoing.

Email: mynardjo@hotmail.com

## Reference

Coghlan, D. and T. Brannick. 2005. *Doing Action Research in Your Own Organisation*. London: Sage Publications Ltd.

# 10.3 Learners' IELTS strategies and perceptions: a preliminary study

**Yi-Jen Tsai** *University of Warwick, Coventry, UK.*

## Introduction

Currently, there are over 130,000 international students in British higher education. Before the international students can get an offer from a university in the UK, they are

generally required to obtain an overall band score of 6.5 to 7 in the IELTS examination. Without effective support, it is especially difficult for non-English major students
to pass the requirement of the IELTS examination. While most previous research has
focused on IELTS content and development from the perspective of testing theory,
little research has examined candidates' own perceptions and strategies in relation to
this important gate-keeping test.

## Research design

My study aimed to discover Chinese-speaking learners' strategies and perceptions relating to the IELTS exam. The investigation combined qualitative and quantitative
approaches. It began with the analysis of 150 forum transcripts, as learners usually seek
help to prepare for the exam on an online forum. After registering as anonymous forum
members, learners ask questions about the IELTS exam and preparation and successful learners share their experiences. In the second stage, six interviews were conducted
for further investigation based on the forum analysis. Finally, eighty questionnaires,
designed in the light of the interview outcomes, were collected. The main findings of
learners' strategies and perceptions will be discussed in the following paragraphs.

## Findings: learner strategies

The results concerning learner strategies were classified into three categories: the four
skills (listening, reading, speaking and writing), metacognitive strategies and social-affective strategies.

- For listening and reading skill strategies, learners tended to practise with IELTS
  materials, make use of online English news, find keywords and guess meanings from
  context. For speaking skill strategies, learners often practised with the questions from
  previous exams, joined a study group, talked to friends in English, recorded and reviewed their speeches. For writing skill strategies, learners tried to memorise 'model'
  sentences which they could use in their essays. Some students wrote everything in
  English such as journals, dairies, emails or MSN as often as they could. Practising
  with the questions from previous exams and joining a study group for peers' feedback were also useful.

- In terms of metacognitive strategies, learners discovered their strengths and weaknesses by doing mock tests. Some students reviewed and learned from mistakes when
  doing exercises, while others made study plans to arrange their learning schedule.

- With respect to social-affective strategies, many learners tried to understand the context of British culture since they would like to study in the UK. Discussing and practising with peers in a study group or on the forum helped them to gain support.

## Findings: learners' perceptions

The findings regarding learners' perceptions of the IELTS exam indicate that learners believe the exam can generally reflect their language abilities accurately and fairly.
However, they may improve their marks simply by focusing on test-preparation and
test-taking skills. Even though preparing for the exam makes them aware of a variety
of strategies, they feel it is a practical exam which reflects ability for *general* language

use more than for their *academic* study. During the exam preparation, they were more motivated by listening and speaking practice because listening is the easiest area in which to improve marks and speaking encompasses interesting topics. They suggest that writing and listening are frustrating as they are not used to analytical writing, or to the British accent.

## Conclusion

The results of this investigation might be of interest and benefit to learners and a wide range of practitioners. Discovering students' perceptions and strategies for IELTS can provide essential assistance to prospective learners, not only to understand the exam format and to prepare for the exam but also, more importantly, to be conscious of effective learning strategies for EAP. By identifying successful learner strategies, teachers can integrate training in a range of strategies into their IELTS and EAP curricula. By understanding learners' perceptions of the exam, test writers may discover potential problems, and gain perspectives to improve future EAP test development. Test developers can then provide more support for learners' academic study through a process of EAP exam preparation. After evaluating the preliminary study, an exploration on a wider scale will be implemented and examined from more angles.

Email: Y-J.Tsai@warwick.ac.uk

## 10.4 Bringing exam tasks to life: things we've tried that work

**Peter Beech** *Anglo-Hellenic Teacher Training, Corinth, Greece*

This presentation reported on a series of lessons in which trainee teachers used tasks from past examination papers as the basis for their teaching practice. For the trainee teachers, it is useful experience to devise interesting and creative lessons while gaining familiarity with exam tasks. For the students at the beginning of their exam preparation, these lessons provide an accessible way to work with authentic exam materials, developing their exam skills while also building their language competence.

### Reading

A reading lesson generally consists of several stages, and there is no reason why a lesson based on a reading comprehension task from an exam should be different. One lesson, based on a text about a memory test, started with Kim's game, where students have a minute to memorise a list of words and then have to recall them. Next, the students took a memory test on the BBC website, which introduces a memory training technique similar to the one described in the exam task. Having practised this, the students were primed to read the text. The preparation made it more meaningful but the actual exam task was unchanged.

Similarly, a lesson based on a cloze passage, although this eventually becomes an exercise in lexico-grammar, started out as a reading lesson, with a warm-up and gist read before the gap-fill. The same principle applies to any passage in the Use of English paper.

To prepare students for an exam task that involves putting paragraphs in position in the text, once again the first stage was to set the context. A text about the life of an artist is accompanied in the practice test book by a detail of one of her pictures. This and additional pictures were used to stimulate students' interest in the topic. As this text is a biography, it is organised chronologically, so the gist read task was to arrange the missing paragraphs on a timeline in rough chronological order.

This gist activity activated the students' existing knowledge of the world (schemata) while taking a top-down approach to the text as a whole. This allowed them quickly to decide roughly where in the text each paragraph belonged. The main reading activity, which was the actual exam task, completed the task of allocating each paragraph to its precise position using bottom-up processing to identify specific reference links.

## Listening

As with reading, the listening lessons included pre-listening activities to make the topic more accessible. For example, a task where candidates have to decide which travel guide each statement refers to was introduced by a discussion of whether the students ever use travel guides, followed by a task where each group was given an actual guide and had to:

- discover what kinds of information it contains,
- find some specific information,
- discuss why each type of information is important for tourists, and
- decide if the guide is a good one or if they would make any changes.

## Writing

For writing tasks, we firstly demonstrated a topic-based approach, where the teacher began with a discussion of the topic and introduced relevant vocabulary before linking this to the writing task. The other approach which we illustrated began with an examination of the features of some of the genres which candidates are required to produce, before drafting an outline for a text in one of these genres.

## Conclusion

Allocating tasks from past exam papers for trainee teachers to use as the basis for some of their teaching practice has proved to be an effective way of encouraging their creativity. As these materials are designed to test, not teach, the trainees are obliged to create other activities to complement them, and in doing so gain a good insight into the staging of a lesson. It also gives them a chance to gain some experience of working with exam preparation classes, which is particularly valued by potential employers in our context.

One effect of presenting the exam tasks in this type of lesson framework is that they are made considerably easier. This approach would not be suitable for candidates who are just about to take the exam, but it does give students a gentle introduction to the requirements of exam tasks, building their confidence while developing their ability to handle such tasks.

Email: mail@peterbeech.com

# 11 Learner language, teacher language

## 11.1 Teaching spoken grammar—is 'noticing' the best option?

**Christian Jones** *University of Central Lancashire, Preston, UK*

In recent years, research within corpus linguistics has demonstrated that speech has a grammar that is often distinct from writing. Research by McCarthy and Carter (1995) Carter and McCarthy (1997, 2006) for instance, has highlighted specific features of this grammar, particularly in regard to speech of a spontaneous nature.

These features include: ellipsis ('_____ you going out?'), discourse markers ('You know' 'I mean', 'like', 'Mind you', 'So', 'Right', 'Ok') , vague language ('sort of', 'that kind of thing'), backchannels ('Mmm' 'Yeah'), hesitation ('Err', 'Umm'), heads ('My brother, he lives in London'), tails ('He lives in London, my brother').

At the same time, there has been only a small amount of debate about how spoken grammar should be approached in the classroom. An early suggestion was to use an Illustration-Interaction-Induction (III) framework (McCarthy and Carter 1995: 217) helping to develop learners' language awareness and helping them to notice features of spoken grammar and how they differ from written grammar. This framework suggests that helping students notice features of spoken grammar but not to practise or perfect them in class may be a helpful approach.

Research into second language acquisition provides some evidence that noticing does help and this has been applied to studies of classroom pedagogy but the evidence is limited. A similar point can be made about research into the benefits of giving learners language practice. However, the main problem with all the research evidence is that learners are not asked which approach *they* believe helps the most. Given that it will always be difficult to provide conclusive evidence regarding which teaching approach seems to aid acquisition the most, it seems worth considering learners' subjective views.

My talk discussed the findings of a pilot study involving eight intermediate learners in the UK. Two groups were formed and each group was taught spoken discourse markers. One group was taught using a language awareness approach, which required them to discuss and analyse the language but not produce it. The other group was taught using a presentation/practice framework, which required them to practise the discourse markers. Learners' use of the discourse markers was measured using an objective pre- and post-test and their views of each class were measured through diaries and follow up interviews.

Results indicated the following:

- Both approaches led to an increased use of discourse markers in a paired format speaking test, when compared to their use in a pre-course test.
- This increase in use was not reflected equally across all students.

- The presentation/practice group used a marginally wider range of the target discourse markers in their post-test. The difference, is not, however, significant enough to suggest that one approach was more beneficial than the other in this regard.
- Students from both groups could demonstrate explicit knowledge of what was studied.
- Amongst all students there was a more positive evaluation of a language awareness approach but practice was also seen as useful, providing it was not rushed and there was time to prepare.
- Practice within the classroom was not seen as essential for all students, though many felt it was helpful.
- Both approaches seemed to enhance students' ability to notice the discourse markers focused upon. This was reflected in diary comments, interviews, and if we are to accept the claims made for noticing, we could argue it may have contributed to the increase in the use of discourse markers pre and post test.

The small scale nature of this study must be acknowledged but these results seem to indicate that learners, at least in this context, may prefer a language awareness approach even if this does not always seem to increase their production of discourse markers. Overall though, the results indicate the need for a larger scale study to provide more qualitative and quantitative data in order to measure the effect of different teaching approaches in relation to the acquisition of discourse markers and draw firmer conclusions.

Email: Cjones3@uclan.ac.uk

## References

Carter, R. and M. McCarthy. 1997. *Exploring Spoken English*. Cambridge: Cambridge University Press.

Carter, R. and M. McCarthy. 2006. *Cambridge Grammar of English*. Cambridge: Cambridge University Press.

McCarthy, M. and R. Carter. 1995. 'Spoken Grammar: what is it and how can we teach it?' *ELT Journal* 49/3: 207–18.

## 11.2 Do students learn grammar the way we think they do?

**Yasemin Birgan** *Bilkent University, Ankara, Turkey*

### Introduction

This talk presented findings from a study of Turkish students' preferences and experiences of learning grammar, in order to better understand how different ways of grammar teaching impact on students' learning. These findings were then incorporated into a framework for teaching and learning grammar which may serve as a guide for teachers to adopt a principled approach to helping their own learners learn grammar effectively.

## Grammar learning in L2

Despite decades of research and numerous new methods claiming to be the best, there is still no conclusive evidence that any one way of teaching grammar is best for all learners and in all contexts (Ellis 2006). This may be because every brain is unique and needs different conditions in which to learn and different contexts may require different ways of teaching.

Nevertheless, there is mounting evidence from psycholinguistics and cognitive psychology that certain conditions are necessary for learners to learn grammar effectively in the classroom. Learners need to notice input so that it becomes intake. This intake then needs to be restructured in the brain and linked to learners' existing knowledge, ideas and experience. Learners also need plentiful opportunities to re-notice and to use the grammar point so that it can be retrieved more quickly.

There are many different ways in which teachers can create these conditions to help learners learn grammar; the choice should depend on individual learners' needs and preferences. Learning is, therefore, likely to be more effective if teachers understand their learners' preferences in learning grammar.

## Study

My study aimed to find out students' perceptions of how they learn grammar, aspects of grammar teaching which help/hinder their learning, and their preferences for different types of grammar lessons. Five sources of data were collected from two upper-intermediate mono-lingual classes:

- students' essays about their grammar learning;
- initial questionnaires (open-ended questions based on student essays);
- post-lesson questionnaires of five grammar lessons (two initial presentations, three remedial presentation lessons);
- two focused discussion groups of five students each;
- follow-up questionnaires with both discussion groups (open-ended questions based on focused discussions).

## Results

Firstly, the findings showed that students seem to view their learning in terms of noticing/restructuring/proceduralisation. On the whole they seem to think that:

- lots of examples, memorable rules and variety of deductive/inductive presentations through a story/dialogue/text help them notice new grammar;
- personalisation, teacher feedback, analysis/comparison/translation, and plentiful opportunities for practice help them restructure new grammar;
- making their own examples, using grammar in speaking/writing and learning through real-life tasks help them proceduralise better;
- feedback on their speaking/writing through error correction, and revision lessons help them to re-notice the grammar.

Secondly, the findings show that despite individual differences, students generally have different preferences depending on whether a grammar point is being presented for the first time or not. For example, they prefer PPP, inductive and long lesson(s) in initial presentations, and TTT, deductive and short lesson(s) in remedial lessons. However, in both cases students benefit from lots of examples.

Thirdly, the findings show a pattern to students' learning preferences. For example, in initial presentations they want to start with a dialogue/story/example sentences, then see rules, whereas in remedial lessons they want to start with rules first then see example sentences. This might be because they need a context when something is new for them. They also prefer to compare the grammar point with L2 in initial presentations and with L1 in remedial lessons, perhaps because they feel insecure without L1 support when they are revising a grammar point, especially if they want to focus on rules out of context. Interestingly, they prefer to do writing for freer practice with new grammar and speaking with remedial grammar, possibly because they find speaking more challenging and therefore they feel safer with writing using new grammar. In both cases, they want gap-fills, personalisation, translation and feedback on their use of grammar, as well as lots of revision and recycling.

## Implications

The findings show that we need to help our students learn grammar by taking their process of learning into account, and to help them notice, restructure, proceduralise and re-notice the grammar point they learn. Although these are some common points that we need to consider, there are also different ways of achieving these. Students have shown us that we need to vary our grammar teaching according to the grammar point itself, learner readiness, and learner preferences. One way of doing this is to use a principled eclectic approach to cater for individual learners through PPP, TTT, translation either inductively or deductively.

Email: birgan@bilkent.edu.tr

## References

Ellis, R. 2006. 'Current issues in the teaching of grammar: an SLA perspective'. *TESOL Quarterly* 40/1: 83–107.

## 11.3 Using an English learner's dictionary on CD-ROM

**Birgit Winkler** *Internationales Sprachzentrum Graz, Austria*

Reporting on a study I carried out in 2008, my presentation showed how dictionaries are used in general and, in particular, for writing. Fourteen Austrian students took part in the study, all of whom were preparing for the Cambridge First Certificate exam. The *Longman Exams Dictionary* and accompanying CD-ROM, *Longman Exams Coach* 2006 (*LEC*) were chosen. The study had four parts:

- participants' general use of dictionaries (interview);
- participants' report on the book dictionary (after leafing through it);

- teacher's demonstration of and participants' report on *LEC* (including a short hands-on-session); and
- writing task: composing a short text utilising *LEC*.

## Part 1

The following five questions were asked and answered:

1.  How often do you use a dictionary?
    Eight participants were using a dictionary when work demanded, three used one regularly, three rarely.
2.  Which dictionary/dictionaries do you use?

    They clearly favoured the bilingual version and internet dictionary, *Leo*, an online English–German and German–English translation dictionary developed by the Technical University in Munich, Germany. Three said they needed a bilingual and monolingual dictionary for their studies. Three preferred the book dictionary. Interestingly, hardly anyone was familiar with the CD-ROM and none of them had used Longman's free online dictionary.

3.  When do you use a dictionary?
    The dictionary was mainly consulted for translation, reading and, occasionally, for writing essays or letters to check spellings and look up phrases.
4.  What has your experience of using dictionaries been so far?
    The information provided seemed helpful and look-ups online fast but partly confusing, especially when various translation equivalents were given without further explanation. Generally, dictionary work appeared time-consuming, so had to be limited. Problematic areas were phrases, meanings and usage, academic English, collocations and subject-specific terms.
5.  What should the ideal dictionary look like?
    The ideal dictionary should be comprehensive, electronic, up-to-date, possibly combining a bilingual and monolingual dictionary plus translation tool, without being too big; should be more colourful and interesting, including more phrases, sayings, examples, grammar and pronunciation—elements in fact already in the latest of the various English learner dictionaries.

    Answers suggested respondents' dictionary awareness was low.

## Parts 2 and 3

Positive and negative aspects mentioned by participants are shown in the tables below.

| Book dictionary | |
| --- | --- |
| positive | negative |
| clear layout (colour) | too bulky to carry, too much to read |
| clear guide, user-friendly | not enough photos |
| word-families, study notes, thesaurus, grammar | too little subject-specific vocabulary |
| Writing Guide: phrases, samples, topics | Writing Guide not so good as a coursebook |
| good paper quality. | no page-marker ribbon. |

*Figure 11.3.1 Participant reactions to using a book dictionary*

| CD-ROM dictionary | |
|---|---|
| **positive** | **negative** |
| fast interaction; more colour | less familiar than book |
| spellchecker | partly too much info (overwhelming) |
| audio and recording (pronunciation) | partly confusing (search facilities, results) |
| hyperlinks | time-consuming |
| more info, more thinking: better | not enough subject-specific vocabulary |
| link to other applications (e.g. WORD) | technical problems (e.g. copy functions) |
| exercises: fun, useful ('private teacher') | look-up facility and answers for Exercises |

*Figure 11.3.2 Participant reactions to using a CD-Rom dictionary*

## Part 4

Using *LEC*, participants wrote a short text on: 'Can alternative medicine be a real alternative to traditional medicine?' Approximately 20 minutes were available. Participants thought aloud, to enable me to understand the look-up processes and note-taking. The activity focused mainly on participants' use of the CD-ROM dictionary, not on text length and quality.

The following functions of *LEC* were found helpful: spellchecker, subject area (to find expressions and gather ideas), copy function (definitions, example sentences) and even the audio facility and exercises (although not immediately relevant for the writing task). The additional features of *LEC* allowed users to find more information, thus encouraging thinking and fostering memorisation. Yet how can you look up an unknown word form? In such cases, participants would have liked to peruse a bilingual dictionary ('*Bachblüten*' in English?). Advanced searches, for instance, combining search terms, in most cases also failed because the list provided was either too long, unhelpful or void of any result. Similar problems also occurred when checking the subject area facility. Uncertainty as to whether expressions like 'school medicine' existed remained unresolved, but participants also erred in integrating dictionary information textually, for example, adding 'the' to 'Chinese medicine'. Some participants overused the copying function, becoming distracted by *LEC*'s various features.

The bilingual dictionary is still the preferred form because students consider it to be fast and easy, 'for the lazy', though its information is sometimes unhelpful. Students are more familiar with book than electronic versions of English learner's dictionaries. Look-ups are felt to be very time-consuming. However, dictionary-using skills depend on individual users, their language skills and motivation, since looking-up entails seeking, finding, reading, interpreting and applying information: this needs time and effort, as well as perseverance.

Email: birgit_winkler@hotmail.com

## 11.4 Nuts and bolts: the parts of words our learners need

**Rob Ledbury** *Izmir University of Economics, Izmir, Turkey*

My workshop involved participants in discussion and practical activities related to four key questions.

### Why is a knowledge of prefixes and suffixes useful for students of English?

The following points were elicited from, and discussed with, workshop participants:

- Most suffixes and some prefixes change the part of speech.
- Some affixes, especially prefixes change the meaning.
- Students expand their *word knowledge.*
- Students expand their vocabulary.
- Students word guessing skills improve.
- Students get high rewards for learning effort.

### How do you decide which word parts to teach, and when?

#### Frequently used prefixes

According toHodges in a booklet entitled *Improving Spelling and Vocabulary in the Secondary School* published by the *ERIC Clearinghouse on Reading and Communication Skills* (1982: 30) 'if you were to examine the 20,000 most used English words, you would find about 5,000 of them contain prefixes and that 82 per cent (about 4,100) of those words use one of only fourteen different prefixes out of all available prefixes in the language'.

#### Research into affixes

A number of studies have been carried out on affixes that may provide a sound basis for teaching and learning. Bauer and Nation (1993) established seven levels of affixes based on the following criteria: *frequency* (the number of words in which the affix occurs), *regularity* (how much the written or spoken form of the stem or affix changes as a result of affixation), *productivity* (the likelihood of the affix being used to form new words) and *predictability* (the number and relative frequency of the different meanings of the affix).

#### Three hundred useful affixes

Sinclair *et al.* (1991) is an excellent resource for learners. This *Cobuild Guide* is a reference book on word formation for higher intermediate level learners and it is also an invaluable resource for teachers and course designers. It provides information on 300 inflectional and derivational affixes and includes a list of words for each affix.

### How can we help students recognise word parts?

Practical classroom techniques and a number of activities were demonstrated:

1. Raise students' awareness of affixes through classroom techniques such as effective boardwork, questioning techniques and eliciting.
2. Use colour and underlining to highlight prefixes and suffixes.

3. As an alternative to automatically putting up word information such as the part of speech for the students, ask questions and elicit the information from them: 'Is it a verb or a noun?' 'What's the verb?' 'Can you make the noun?' 'How do you know it's a verb?' ('It ends in "–ise".') 'Do you know any other words ending in "–ise"?'
4. Write up a word students (think they) do not know, perhaps as a warmer or filler, or as it arises during a lesson. Then, break the word up into its parts with the help of the learners.
5. Set 'research-a-word' mini-projects for homework that can be checked with classmates and the teacher the following day.
6. Train students in how to use a dictionary to check predictions of form and meaning.
7. Raise students' awareness that the underlying meanings of words within a family are not necessarily the same.
8. Include affix and word formation items regularly in tests.

Email: robert.ledbury@ieu.edu.tr

## References

Hodges, R. 1982. *Improving Spelling and Vocabulary in the Secondary School*. ERIC Clearinghouse on Reading and Communication Skills.

Sinclair, J., G. Fox, S. Bullon, J. Bradbury. 1991. *Collins Cobuild English Guides 2, Word Formation*. London: Harper Collins.

Ledbury, R. 2007. 'What learners need to know about prefixes and suffixes' in P.Davidson, C. Coombe, D. Lloyd and D. Palfreyman (eds.). *Teaching and Learning Vocabulary in Another Language*. Dubai: TESOL Arabia.

## 11.5 Investigating learner language through the Role-Play Learner Corpus

**Andrea Nava** and **Luciana Pedrazzini** *University of Milan, Italy*

In 2002 a project was initiated at the University of Milan to compile a small-scale corpus of spoken learner language. The corpus started as part of an action research process: we had introduced the use of role-play technique in the oral exams of first-year students of English and wanted to assess how effective the new approach was. The purpose of our research was both linguistic and pedagogical, as summarised in the following research questions: (1) What features of learner spoken language are produced by our students through role-play tasks? And (2) Does the language in the corpus offer any evidence for what teachers of English generally and rather vaguely consider major and unacceptable errors?

Data for the Role-Play Learner Corpus were collected according to a specific format:

• the participants were all Italian mother tongue first-year university students of English, at different levels of proficiency: B1—B2—C1 (Council of Europe 2001);

- they worked in pairs. They were given one role-card each. After reading it, they carried out a short conversation;
- the role-plays were about familiar topics, such as planning holidays among friends;
- the data were transcribed according to the LINDSEI (Louvain International Database of Spoken English Interlanguage) corpus guidelines.

So far 114 first-year undergraduate students of English have been recorded while interacting in 57 role-plays. The Role-Play Learner Corpus currently stands at approximately 28,000 words, but data assembly is still going on.

The first research question that we set out to investigate was aimed at identifying the features of spoken discourse that first-year students at our university produced in carrying out role-plays. The role-play tasks were designed in such a way as to trigger production of transactional language. However, it is a fact that no natural interaction is exclusively transactional, and features of what O'Keeffe and McCarthy (2007) call 'relational language' appear to crop up in any sort of oral communicative exchange. It was thus of some interest to explore to what extent our participants resorted to 'relational' linguistic features in carrying out the role-play tasks.

An example of relational language is the use of listener response tokens (minimal units, such as 'mmm', 'yeah', and longer tokens, such as 'right', 'fair enough', 'is that so?'), whose overarching function is pre-eminently affective. Research seems to indicate that response tokens tend to be underused by non-native speakers of English (cf., for example, Prodromou 2003). Preliminary investigation of the Role-Play Learner Corpus data pointed to a dearth of listener response tokens in the output of first-year students at our university. In the following extract, for instance, some sort of affective response would have been expected from B2 after B1 has explained that she cannot afford the type of holiday proposed by B2. Instead, B2 rather abruptly asks a question about the length of the holiday:

> <B1> I don't know we we have to ask the a=agency how much it cost because you know I can't spend too much because . I haven't earned a lot this year <\B1>
> <B2> and how many weeks we can … <\B2>

(Role-Play Learner Corpus)

The second research question was an attempt to view the interlanguage samples gathered in the Role-Play Learner Corpus from the EFL teacher's point of view. Preliminary findings indicated that while instances of those that are usually regarded by EFL professionals as serious mistakes (dropping the third person present simple morpheme, placing adverbials between verb and direct object, use of the determiner 'the' for general reference, ellipsis of the subject pronoun) were widely represented in our corpus, so were errors of which EFL teachers are often less aware—see the following extract:

> <B2> em well em we visit three countries and erm . it's a shame that you: didn't come  . it was beautiful really <\B2>

(Role-Play Learner Corpus)

What is going on here is that the speakers do not seem to have realised that 'beautiful' is not semantically co-extensive with Italian '*bello*'. Indeed, unlike Italian '*bello*', 'beautiful' is not usually used to express a generic positive appreciation of an event such as a trip; 'nice' would have been a better choice.

It is evident that even a small learner corpus such as the one we have been compiling may re-orient both researchers' and teachers' perspectives on learner language and learning/teaching priorities. We are currently exploring possible implications that the Role-Play Learner Corpus learner corpus may have for both language teaching methodology and teacher development.

Email: andrea.nava@unimi.it, luciana.pedrazzini@unimi.it

## References

Council of Europe. 2001. *Common European Framework of Reference for Languages: Learning, Teaching, Assessment.* Cambridge: Cambridge University Press.

O'Keeffe, A. and M. McCarthy. 2007. *From Corpus to Classroom: Language Use and Language Teaching.* Cambridge: Cambridge University Press.

Prodromou, L. 2003. 'In search of SUE: the successful user of English'. *Modern English Teacher* 12: 5–13.

# 11.6 Let your body do the talking

**Geoff Costley**  *RSAF Technical Studies Institute, Dhahran, Saudi Arabia*

When the Blu-Tack has lost its grip on the jazzy wall posters or the dreaded power cut has reduced your hi-tech classroom to a wasteland, fear not! Get physical!

The purpose of this workshop was to explore the potential of the teacher's body as a vital stage prop with visual impact. Demonstrating mime techniques gleaned from experience in physical theatre companies, I attempted to show that easily learned slick movements can intrigue and amuse a class of students as they learn English, or indeed any other subject.

Many teachers cower at the prospect of 'acting' and dismiss it as irrelevant. I'm not sure if this is prompted by shyness or cynicism, but to me all teachers are performers. Why shouldn't we make the most of whatever talents and potential we possess to convey our 'message'? You don't have to be slim or fit to master basic mime techniques. You can then build your own 'library' of moves and gestures.

Thirty workshop participants threw themselves enthusiastically into a variety of physical activities and sharpened their illusionary mime techniques. We began with physical 'loosening' exercises, including a 'hips, chest, neck' roll during which everybody froze on cue. As an ice-breaker, they then held that stance, took a character from it, and moved around the room interacting.

### Essential techniques in illusionary mime

1. A 'toc' or spasm of energy in the wrists is used to manipulate imaginary objects. It defines the exact moment objects are grasped and released. Without the 'toc',

objects will seem elastic. The resulting confusion will produce boredom and disinterest.

2. An object's shape and weight is conveyed by tension in the body. For lifting a box, right angles should be made with the hands. The actual lifting experience should be simulated, including counter balance, such as leaning in the opposite direction when lifting a heavy suitcase.

3. The location of fixed objects must be memorised. If a glass is taken from a counter it should be replaced at the same level. Ignoring the logic which flows through mimed actions can result in walking through cupboards and windows! When pulling a rope, both hands should show the same diameter.

4. Tricking oneself into being surprised is important for the realistic portrayal of being tripped, pushed, pulled, burned, etc. For tripping, the right foot comes forward and strikes the heel of the left foot, forcing a stumble. The trick is to look nonchalant. If anticipation is visible the trip will look contrived. When a dog on a lead shoots off in a different direction, the dog walker's wrist will turn first, pulling the arm then the torso until balance is lost and 'catch up' is underway! Such situations are useful for teaching the passive.

5. A series of actions can be reduced to its essence and clarified with a slight exaggeration. For example, the left index finger can be used as a bolt while the right hand tightens a nut on it, using increasing tension and resistance. Fastening a shirt button can be shown by a simple twist of the fingers. When miming getting dressed, care should be taken to avoid touching one's own clothes.

## Body language

Besides illusionary mime techniques, we experimented with different aspects of body language. Character and mood can be convincingly portrayed, not simply by facial expression but by the way we move. This helps in teaching adverbs.

Limping or displaying other injuries resulting from accidents can enhance the teaching of the present perfect.

Beware of the cultural inappropriateness of some gestures!

## Conclusion

I believe learning should be fun. The international appeal of Mr Bean urges us not to underestimate the power of visual humour in the classroom, including the use of incongruous sound effects.

I wish the skills I learned when retraining as an actor had been included in my PGCE and TEFL courses, because since returning to teaching they have been my survival package for twenty-five years. From demonstrating the functions of aircraft parts, such as ailerons and retractable landing gear, to creating comic mimed narratives for discussion and writing, using the body as a stage prop has served me well.

If even one of the workshop participants was hooked into applying the techniques to their own teaching needs, it was worthwhile.

Email: geoffcostley@yahoo.com

# 12 Social issues in ELT

## 12.1 British Council Signature Event: Frameworks for diversity and equal opportunity in ELT

**Mike Solly** and **Liam Brown** *British Council, London, UK*

This *British Council Signature Event* marked a first at IATEFL. The themes of diversity (D) and equal opportunities (EO) have not had such a high profile at the event before, and an added 'first' was through the *Exeter Online* initiative where we engaged in real time with people globally. The lead-in discussion and subsequent panel formula led to trenchant interactions as questions were raised from the floor and via the internet. The event aimed to demonstrate a commitment to promote equality of opportunity and diversity in ELT.

There was a brief period of silence as we were invited to watch a series of powerful images, flashed on screen. These were intended to mark the territory of the discussion and forced us to picture the issues we were debating. Fiona Bartels-Ellis, Head of Equal Opportunity and Diversity at the British Council, took the lead in presenting the ground, bringing in some wider perspectives which were challenging in themselves as they were not always high-agenda items in the ELT context.

Fiona Bartels-Ellis first defined the terms and suggested:

- Equal opportunity = legislating against unjustified discrimination. In other words: *It means treating people fairly, removing barriers to equal opportunity and redressing imbalances.*
- Diversity = harnessing and maximising potential to the benefit of the organisation. In other words: *The recognition that people are different in many ways, and valuing this difference.*

She explained, that just as with a salad, the ingredients with their distinct flavours and colours add the richness we require, and are individually selected for their unique contribution to the end product. While we look for variety of shape, colour, texture and flavour, we want them to work well together but not be all the same.

This cannot be a passive commitment. Managing diversity means seeking, valuing and capitalising on difference. And it is not just about the obvious big ticket issues of gender, age and race but also the less obvious, such as life experiences, behaviours and work-styles. *We are all different. We all have something to offer.*

Fiona Bartels-Ellis stressed that this approach is new and not yet widely practised. Workplaces now consist of individuals bringing different perspectives, with distinctive needs, expectations and life-styles, and there have been quite significant changes from the past.

The most evident changes—more women in a variety of jobs, the inclusion of people with disabilities, widening age groups and multiple 'racial' and ethnic identities—sit alongside the less obvious ones. The thing to recognise is we are *all* members of a diverse workplace and 'We have diverse customers too!'

Turning to the issue of diversity, 'harnessing and maximising potential to the benefit of the organisation', we were asked to consider what drives diversity.

Among the contenders, Fiona Bartels-Ellis offered globalisation, demographic changes, climate change, politics of recognition, persistent inequality, unfair treatment of workforce, urbanisation, polarised and segregated communities.

Each of these impacts differently on our working lives according to where we find ourselves as individuals and how our organisations respond. Fiona Bartels-Ellis concluded with describing three relevant strands to responding to diversity in ELT: business, moral and legal.

The first strand, *business*, is about the rationales underpinning an organisation's case for investing resources in equality and diversity. It may, for example, wish to be an 'employer of choice' able to select from the widest possible talent pool. From the customer perspective we might add that creativity is released, and staff are supported to innovate, innovative products can become more relevant to customers' needs and customers in turn recognise their needs are reflected, which promotes loyalty.

The next strand, the *moral* case, centred on *social justice* reasons, specifically that it is a basic human right to be treated with dignity and fairness, and that we see greater attention to ethics, especially in research.

The last strand, the *legal* case, focuses on the *statutory requirements/obligations,* specifically the growing number of equality laws which require employers and service providers to take account of different needs, and the shift in emphasis from anti-discrimination to active promotion of equality.

The ground was now set for discussion. Mike Solly, the Global Issues SIG Coordinator, suggested that we ask ourselves how these agendas impact upon our definitions of good and best practice in ELT. The four other panellists, all experts working directly in the field of ELT in a variety of contexts, briefly raised issues of concern to them in relation to EO&D.

Catherine Walter from the Institute of Education at the University of London, directly related EO&D to IATEFL Exeter by pointing out that the titles and abstracts of sessions in the conference programme greatly under-represented some EO&D areas such as gender and disability. Dr Walter invited the audience to reflect on the representation of people with disability in ELT materials and on the provision made for teachers and learners with disabilities, asking how much they are seen and heard and to what extent the profession was successfully promoting them and meeting their needs. Harry Kucher, national pedagogic inspector at Cameroon's ministry of basic education, highlighted the reality of the context for most teachers of English around the world, and the fact that coursebooks rarely reflect this reality. He stressed that in many cultures where English learning takes place, gender equality is not respected. Also that untrained teachers, who meet an essential need, should be valued and respected. The third panellist, Tricia Thorlby, a teacher trainer with the British Council in Malaysia, added that the profession also needed to think about equality of opportunity for access to training. Tricia Thorlby also stressed that as classrooms become increasingly diverse, issues are raised for us as teachers/educators and we need to be aware of our ethical and legal responsibilities in this context. The final panellist, Rod Bolitho, Academic Director at NILE (Norwich Institute for Language Education), began on an optimistic note by saying that a decade ago, when he was working as a consultant to textbook writers, issues were voted off the agenda as being too sensitive in their contexts (for example, the treatment of Roma people and bullying). Some of these same writers recently produced a human rights book in which all these issues were included. But Rod Bolitho also reminded the audience that the height of the glass ceiling for women differed from context to context and ended by raising the issue of the ethical choice we have to make in working in countries with regimes that we may find repellent.

Questions and comments were then invited from the present and virtual audience. These covered, for example:

- A suggestion that if literacy in the first language was not developed, it would inhibit the learning of a second language.
- Concerns about managing diversity and about the potentially contradictory concepts of diversity and equal opportunities.
- Global coursebooks as non-homogenising influences; they can enhance awareness of diversity by shedding light on people and issues around the globe.
- The issue of age discrimination at both ends of the age spectrum.

At the end of the event the facilitator echoed Catherine Walter's point about certain EO&D issues being neglected in programmed talks, but hoped that next year we would see a marked difference. The discussion continued for another two months on Exeter OnLine.

Email: Liam.Brown@britishcouncil.org, mike.solly@yahoo.co.uk

## 12.2 The application of critical race theories to English language teaching

**Kelly King** *Akita International University, Akita, Japan*

The purpose of my talk was to discuss the impact of race as it applies to English language teaching (ELT). I believe most white ELT professionals think uncritically about race. In doing so, we fail to acknowledge the continuance of institutionalised racism, particularly within our own field or practice, or our role/s as agents in supporting or resisting white supremacy.

Critical Race Theory (CRT) is a lens through which we can discuss the impact of race. Thus I began my talk with an explanation of some of the key tenets of CRT. Developing from US legal scholarship, in particular the writing of Derrick Bell and Alan Freeman, CRT began as a critique of the post civil rights context in which institutionalised racism persists, often in newer, subtler forms. CRT scholars insist that racism is not an aberration, but the 'common, everyday experience of most people of color' (Delgado and Stefancic 2001: 7). Moreover, because white interests are supported by the system, whites have little motivation to change it. Finally it should be understood that although CRT originated in the US, racism, and the system of white supremacy which produces it, are global phenomena: 'White supremacy exists and interrelates at multiple geographical levels: local, state, national, international and global' (Allen 2006: 11).

Although individual whites are not privileged equally, as a group we receive privileges; we benefit both materially and psychologically from institutionalised racism. Thus, the focus of Critical White Studies (CWS) scholarship is on the meaning of 'whiteness'. McIntosh (1988/1997), a white feminist, was one of the first to re-examine her power and privilege *vis-à-vis* people of colour. She came to understand that whites have unearned privileges they are 'taught not to recognise,' and which she characterises as 'an invisible weightless knapsack of special provisions, assurances, tools, maps, guides, codebooks, passports, visas, clothes, compass, emergency gear and blank checks' (1997: 291). McIntosh wrote a list of forty-six ways in which she has been privileged by her racial status. They include being able to live in an area she can both afford and wishes to live, reading the newspaper or watching television and 'see[ing] people of [her] race widely represented,' (1997: 293) being listened to when she is the only white member of a group, being able to ignore issues, problems or positive actions taken by minority groups without fearing negative consequences, and being able to receive medical help without fear that her racial background will 'work against [her]' (1997: 294). She further notes that her children receive educational materials in which people of their race are fully represented and that she doesn't have to teach them about institutional racism in order to protect them.

Although critical of McIntosh's claim that whites do not perceive our unearned privileges—see Zeus Leonardo's work, for example—I have made a list of my own. As a white US female who has spent approximately sixteen years in Japan, I know I receive unearned privileges, privileges compounded by my status as a native English speaker (NES). Although we have deconstructed the notion of the native speaker, there continue to be real, material benefits given to/taken by those of us whose English is considered 'natural'. In a 2005 issue of TESOL's *NNEST Newsletter* Shin describes how race factors into our understanding of what a native English speaker looks like and sounds like; how NES connotes whiteness and conversely, how being 'Asian' comes to signify that one is a non-native English speaker (NNES). My experiences in ELT in Japan support Shin's statements. I know qualified Japanese nationals who receive lower salaries than less qualified white 'native English' speaking colleagues. Moreover, I know African-Americans and Asian-Americans whose experiences mirror those of non-native speakers. CRT tells us that personal stories have the power to transform. It is only when I compare my experiences with colleagues who do not have white privilege that I come to a better understanding of how racism benefits me personally.

We in ELT rarely discuss race and racism. Yet my experiences, as narrow as they are, have taught me that racism is not an abstract issue happening to 'other' people, but something I participate in and benefit from on a daily basis. The challenge all white ELT professionals must ultimately face is to act in ways that disrupt racism and our own privilege. We need to have this conversation.

E-mail: kellyking@aiu.ac.jp

## References

Allen, R. L. 2006. 'The race problem in the critical pedagogy community' in C. A. Rossatto, R. L. Allen and M. Pruyn (eds.). *Reinventing Critical Pedagogy: Widening the Circle of Anti-oppression Education.* Plymouth: Rowman and Littlefield Publishers, Inc.

Delgado, R. and Stefancic, J. 2001. *Critical Race Theory: an Introduction.* New York: New York University Press.

McIntosh, P. 1997. 'White privilege and male privilege: a personal account of coming to see correspondence through work in women's studies' in R. Delgado and J. Stefancic (eds.). *Critical White Studies: Looking Behind the Mirror.* Philadelphia: Temple University Press.

## 12.3 Cross-curricular issues in Spanish primary education and published ELT materials

**Diego Rascón Moreno**  *University of Jaén, Jaén, Spain*

### Introduction

Some research I conducted across primary English classrooms in Jaén for my master's dissertation led me to conclude that the vast majority of teachers in this Spanish city use published materials widely and stick to the syllabus provided by the publishing house when teaching their classes. Therefore, it can be argued that analysing the materials they use is an objective way to find out if the cross-curricular issues (CCIs) considered in Spain under the *Ley Orgánica General del Sistema Educativo* (*LOGSE*) are addressed in this context.

### Objective

The investigation briefly described here aimed to discover through the analysis of published materials the situation in English classrooms in the third cycle of primary education of the city of Jaén with regard to the teaching of the CCIs mentioned in the *LOGSE* curricula.

### Procedure

From February to April 2006 I borrowed the sets of published ELT materials exploited in 33 classes at levels 5 or 6 of primary education (Key Stages 6 or 7 in England and Wales). These groups of pupils came from 26 out of 30 of the institutions in Jaén offering the third cycle of primary education. I took the *LOGSE* CCI guidelines as the basis for deciding on the cross-curricular contents that were supposed to be taught in upper primary education at that time. The data was gathered using a checklist that I myself had created and analysed in the following months.

### Analysis

Peace education is the CCI most commonly covered in the units of the published materials used in schools. Around half of the units in these materials deal with it. It is followed by moral and civic education, which is present in nearly 40 per cent of them.

Environmental and health are the next most frequently addressed issues. Consumer, road safety and gender education are the items with the least presence in the materials, together with sex education which is approached in only one unit of the published materials used in the 33 groups.

Nevertheless, only some of the peace education and moral and civic education contents in the guidelines are included. Peace topics like family, friendship, help, NGOs and intercultural education are often broached, but rarely others such as dialogue as the way to bridge differences, disarmament, love, respect for other young people (versus bullying) and religious diversity education. As for moral and civic education, tolerance to other people's opinions and following rules in society for a happy coexistence are promoted, but building one's own system of values that does not threaten other people's happiness, tolerance to other people's conditions and knowing about and agreeing to the Universal Declaration of Human Rights and the Spanish Constitution are only touched on.

On the positive side, all the sets of materials analysed deal with gender, peace and moral and civic education through the inclusion of pictures and photographs of both boys and girls or men and women, pictures and photographs of people from different races and cultures, and pairwork and groupwork activities. However, I did not consider this in the analysis described above because of there being no definitive attempts to deal with these issues.

The analysis of the published materials exploited in the groups also focused on the way each CCI is taught, the communicative skills that are most thoroughly worked on when they are approached, the promotion of their teaching by means of ICT, and their evaluation.

## Conclusions

Primary teachers of English in Jaén use published materials almost exclusively, so these provide insights into CCI teaching in their lessons. Among the several conclusions that can be drawn from analysing materials used in a significant number of fifth or sixth level classrooms across the city, are that peace and moral and civic education to a greater extent, and environmental and health education to a lesser extent are sufficiently dealt with in terms of frequency. However, the same cannot be said concerning depth of coverage. Sex education is by far the least addressed CCI.

This study is particularly interesting because the results obtained shed light on the integration of the cross-curricular approach in the primary English classroom in the last years of the *LOGSE* period. These results can perhaps be generalised to other parts of Spain if the same sets of published materials were used as widely elsewhere.

Email: diegorascon@hotmail.com

## 12.4 The language of colonialism or that of conflict mitigation?

**Zarina Subhan-Brewer** *British Council STEPS Programme, Colombo, Sri Lanka*

In English Language Teaching (ELT) there are many specialist English courses: English for academic purposes, business, hotel management, medicine, science, engineering and law. There is an equal variety of organisations that work in the development field: voluntary organisations, non-governmental organisations (NGOs), humanitarian agencies and charities. Surprisingly, of the many ELT courses, none fits the bill for working in development. Perhaps a variety of courses can be patched together, but nothing tailor-made exists commercially for the areas of governance and the developing world. I would therefore like to highlight the need for and propose the requirements of a new area of ELT.

### Working in development

From my work in Nepal, Ethiopia and Sri Lanka, I have witnessed a need for national staff, who work in development, to not only function efficiently in English, but also to understand the governance points of views of international staff. Additionally the international staff are truly international, hence they are likely to be second or third English language speakers themselves. Therefore the likelihood for misunderstandings or miscommunication is great.

### The Sri Lankan context

It was therefore of interest to me when I joined a project supported by the German government's organisation for development cooperation, GTZ, in Sri Lanka, to improve efficiency of local government through English language in the North and East (NE) of the country. Due to a combination of its history and the Asian Tsunami of 2004, the Northern and Eastern Provincial Councils found the need for working in English paramount.

### Language policy

The British Empire ensured that the language of governance became English, but it remained so even after independence in 1948. By design or default, many Tamil-speakers were proficient enough in English to hold important positions in government. Tamil-speakers are a minority in Sri Lanka, hence the situation was not well-liked. Some say this resulted in the language policy of 1956: *The Sinhala Only Act.* This meant that the education system favoured Sinhalese speakers. As Medawattegedara (2008) says, 'If you disadvantage one group of people over another, then you have conflict'.

### The present status of English

After years of conflict between Tamil separatists and the Sri Lankan government, the Indians brokered the Indo-Lanka Accord in 1987. This led to the 13th amendment to the constitution, an important provision of which was that both Sinhalese and Tamil became official languages, with English being defined as a link language. Hence when the Tamil-speaking Northern and Eastern Provincial Councils communicate with central government, and vice versa, they often communicate in English.

Due to decades of war, development (and ELT) in the NE has been hampered. Hence the GTZ Performance Improvement Project (PIP), funded by the German Federal Ministry for Economic Cooperation and Development (BMZ) and the British government's Department for International Development (DFID), came into being. The tsunami further highlighted huge problems in communication with aid agencies, so English was recognised as an important tool in improving efficient management, coordination and monitoring.

## Skills Through English for Public Servants (STEPS)

As part of a GTZ-British Council team, I co-wrote a tailor-made one-month course for public servants—*Skills Through English for Public Servants* (*STEPS*). Its aim is to improve English, critical thinking skills while increasing the awareness of development and governance issues. The course uses the Content and Language Integrated Learning (CLIL) approach and tackles difficult but thought-provoking themes, such as globalisation, conflict and children, microfinance, disaster preparedness. The language is part of the thinking process, so it is used to answer a question or discuss a point rather than practising language for the sake of it. The course also follows Krashen's (Krashen and Terrell 1983) input theory; language is learned by understanding messages that the learner is interested in.

## A new role for English?

English is no longer an enforced language of colonialism, but a tool that is a part of a wider process of effective communication, leading to a greater understanding and engagement with alternative concepts or values. *STEPS* has brought together public servants from the Sinhalese, Tamil-Hindu, Tamil-Christian, Tamil-Muslim and Burgher communities. English is being used as a tool to break down prejudices. It can be a tool to develop individual skills, organisations, society and in the long-term nations, which can lead to political stability, as in Singapore. Why then is there such a lack of interest and materials in what could be an ESP field in its own right, English for Development?

Email: zsbsteps@gmail.com

## References

Krashen, S. and Terrell, T. D. 1983. *The Natural Approach*. San Francisco: Alemany Press and Pergamon Press.

Medawattegedara, L. 2008. 'Can language provide a bridge for peace?'. Paper presented at the Galle Literary Festival, Sri Lanka.

## 12.5 Forging peace through ELT: utopia or reality?

**Radmila Popović** *University of Belgrade, Serbia*

> Language teachers all over the world may ultimately prove more efficacious in establishing good permanent relations between the nations than the Peace Congress at the Hague.
>
> Otto Jespersen *How to Teach a Foreign Language*

In recent years there has been considerable controversy over the role of English in the globalised world. While some have criticised it as an instrument of colonisation and linguistics imperialism, others have seen it as a possible arena for addressing social, political and environmental issues. A number of language educators have pushed the boundaries even further, claiming that English has peace-building potential that could be employed to reduce violence and prevent wars. This paper explores ways of bringing peace education into English language classrooms in diverse teaching contexts, and identifies complexities and contradictions inherent in those efforts. It also provides a story of the professional and personal involvement of the author of the text, who was prompted and motivated to ponder on teaching English and peace by sheer force of circumstances—living and teaching in Belgrade during NATO's military intervention against Serbia in 1999.

### Teaching peace and language: historical background

Peace education brings together multiple traditions of pedagogy, theories of education, and international initiatives. From the point of view of teaching, it can be determined as the employment of theory and teaching models or approaches to explicitly teach towards greater peace in the world. If learning is taken as a starting point, then peace education can be said to encompass the knowledge, skills, and attitudes needed to achieve and sustain a global culture of peace. Regarding aims, many peace theorists and practitioners emphasise that their primary goal is contributing towards changing the world by eliminating structures of violence in human relations, in all areas of society and between states.

Peace education emerged as a new discipline in the period between the two world wars, drawing strength and theoretical grounding from the works of John Dewey and Maria Montessori. The first academic peace studies programme was set up in 1948 at Manchester College, Indiana, while the professional association International Peace Research Association, founded in 1964, marked peace studies becoming legitimate research subject matter (Harris 2001). After 1980, the peace agenda received significant support from various international organisations (UNESCO, Institute for Peace in Washington, DC, UK World Peace, World Peace Society Australia, etc.) which focused their efforts on producing policy documents, mission statements and recommendations that gradually seeped into school curricula in several countries. They also ran projects in conflict zones aimed at eliminating prejudice against 'perceived' enemies. These initiatives increasingly brought an awareness of the potential of language education for promoting peace. Thus, in 1987 Linguapax was formed by UNESCO as an international programme dedicated to the preservation and promotion of language diversity, multilingual education, and teaching peace through foreign languages (UNESCO 1987), while in the 1990s several national and international teacher's associations, such as JALT, TESOL, IATEFL, set out to work towards raising awareness of the necessity to include peace issues in language instruction. In 1999, peace and language studies acquired a theoretical framework in 'peace linguistics', an interdisciplinary branch of linguistics and peace studies which concerns itself with the relationship between language and communication, while the interface between language education and peace became the subject proper of 'applied peace linguistics' (Gomes de Matos 2000, 2001, 2002; Friedrich 2007).

As can be seen from this overview, both peace education and peace linguistics are new, hybrid fields that developed out of a sense of urgency to incorporate peace issues in education. Since the mainstream disciplines - language pedagogy, linguistics and education theory, did not seem to offer solid theoretical foundations for further practice, peace education proponents went beyond discipline boundaries, seeking knowledge which would assist them in adding a new dimension to teaching.

It is also possible to identify several premises underlying the new subfields:

- Language is seen as an apt tool for fostering peace.
- English has a great potential to contribute to the advancement of the peace cause and the development of tolerance among nations because it is a language of international communication spoken by one billion people.
- Teacher neutrality is neither desirable nor possible. Educators, especially English language teachers, are seen as leaders of society, who have the power to bring about positive changes.

## Teaching peace and language: challenges

I have previously stated that peace education initiatives received considerable backing from international organisations which supported a number of seminars and workshops on teaching language and peace. However, in spite of this considerable support, peace education remained a peripheral area, on the fringes of school life in the USA and Western Europe. According to Harris and Freudenstein, teacher educators actively involved in these programmes, this can be ascribed to:

- lack of interest, (other issues, such as use of technology, seem to be more appealing to teachers);
- lack of administrative and faculty support;
- strict curriculum requirements and standardised tests that leave no time for peace topics (Harris 2001; Freudenstein 1997, 2003).

One cannot fail to notice that invested efforts are at odds with actual outcomes. A valid question to ask at this point is whether there are other reasons for this discrepancy. In the following text I will look more closely at the factors underlying the complexity of incorporating peace education in language curricula. For that, I will resort to the framework designed by the educator David Hawkins (1974), frequently employed as a starting point for exploring key elements in the teaching /learning enterprise, as well as their relationships: *I*—the teacher, *thou*—the learner, *it*—subject matter, and *context*—the environment in which teaching takes place.

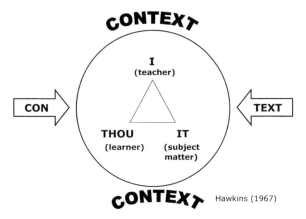

*Figure 12.5.1*

## It—the subject matter

The subject matter of peace education is vague and abstract. First, it is hard to define peace (the most frequent definition being 'the absence of war'), determine objectives (What competences does 'peace proficiency' comprise?), and assess achievement (Is it a movement along the peace illiterate–peace knowledgeable axis? What can a 'peace proficient' person do?). Apart from this, the integration of peace education and English language teaching is seen by some as another instance of linguistic imperialism, the promotion of a hidden political agenda shaped by dominant classes (Kazmi 2004). Finally, for many, peace has become just a buzz word, a compromised idea much talked about, or at best a lofty ideal hard to achieve.

## I—the teacher

Teaching language and peace requires additional knowledge and mediation skills that are usually not taught (at least in a systematic way) in teacher education programmes. Therefore, teachers bent on practising it must undergo special training, and that necessitates additional resources, frequently difficult to secure. Also, the implementation of the peace curriculum implies a specific role of the teacher—her commitment to being a 'transformative intellectual' (Giroux) or a 'critical educator'. Let us consider what such an orientation involves:

> A critical educator is someone who is personally and professionally committed, who understands him- or herself as a specific rather than a universal educator, who is engaged with both the local context and the global domain, who works with other cultural and political workers, and who listens while always acknowledges the difficulties and partialities of those listenings.
>
> (Pennycook 1994: 306)

This quotation is indicative of the complexity of the ELT profession: teachers are expected to possess numerous competences, complex knowledge and a range of sophisticated skills. Yet, at the same time, this profession is practised by those with no or minimal training. Can such teachers be expected to be critical educators? Also, given the increased influence of commercial factors in the field of ELT, is it realistic to expect that teachers will resist pressures to conform to the requirements of the global market (including, in an extreme case, meeting with photographers and fashion stylist, wearing miniskirts and high-heeled shoes, because these are 'selling points': *The Guardian Weekly* December 2007), and become actively engaged in promulgating critical and peace education?

## Thou—the learner

In the predetermined classroom hierarchy, the teacher is assigned the part of knower who is supposed to impart a body of information to her learners. In the language classroom, it is very clear what that knowledge comprises (grammar, for instance), while the situation is not so apparent with regard to peace education. If the teacher is taken as an authority on peace issues, then students are implicitly accorded the position of 'peace ignorant' who are to yet to become proficient in thinking and acting peacefully. Needless to say, such an assumption does not stem from peace education tenets, but is nevertheless inherent in the power distribution in the classroom.

## Context

Everything outside the classroom can have an impact on it. Hence, teachers wishing to incorporate educating for peace in their curriculum may possibly face an unsympathetic attitude from parents and/or school authorities. Also, it should be noted that the current climate in general is not particularly conducive to peace learning: we live at a time in which violence is taken as natural (Chilton 1998). Moreover, peace and language educators are faced with mission almost impossible, since they are to teach language, in which war metaphors for example, 'argument is war', 'sport is war', and, conversely, 'war is sport') pervade many aspects of everyday life (Chilton 1998; Schaffner and Wenden 1995; Thorne 2006).

As demonstrated above, pursuing peace as an enterprise in the language classroom is full of pitfalls: the subject matter is complex and vague, it requires additional training and resources, as well as specific commitment on the part of teachers. However, if language teaching is to go beyond language instruction, mere imparting of linguistic information, and become language education that socialises learners in the social order and gives them means to change it (Kramsch 1993), then the key issue is not whether to teach peace and language or not, but rather *how* to teach it (Friedrich 2007). After all, language teaching is a form of social and cultural action, and it is about producing, not just reflecting realities (Pennycook 2001: 53). Therefore, a next step in this discussion is to examine what can be learned from those who have ventured into producing new realities, both in theory and practice.

## Language and peace in theory: peace linguistics

The term 'peace linguistics', coined by Francisco Gomes de Matos, came into circulation at the end of the 1990s. David Crystal (1999) endorsed it by including it in his dictionary of language, defining it as 'the climate of opinion … in which linguistic principles, methods, findings and applications were seen as a means of promoting peace and human rights at the global level'. Peace linguistics sets three general goals for linguistic peace education: teaching empowerment, offsetting imperialism, and de-focusing on conflict - focusing on peace (Friedrich 2007: 59). A common thread uniting these aims concerns the 'responsible use of language' (Gomes de Matos 2000, 2001, 2003). If they want their students to become responsible language users, language teachers should:

- promote the use of positive language (respectful language, optimistic vocabulary, positivisers);
- avoid the negative (prevent verbal harm and humiliation, monitor communications for their moral, social values, make a list of potentially harmful words which are to be avoided);
- teach for tackling conflict constructively (Gomes de Matos 2000, 2001, 2003).

Such a position rests on the belief that the insistence on the positive will bring about the desired change.

Two questions arise: is it possible to change reality by changing language? Will the students become peaceful people if they are taught peaceful language? As a matter of fact, this is a much larger issue and concerns the relationship between language and thought. Possible answers to these questions can be found in linguistic literature. Since it has been established that loaded words can have an influence on perception (Bolinger 1980), it can be assumed that the insistence on positive vocabulary and avoidance of negative terms might bring about a similar effect. As for structural metaphors (for example, 'argument is war'), they do not exist in our belief systems as separate ideas, but are systematically organised into conceptual metaphors at an even higher, ideological level (Schaffner and Wenden 1995). Likewise, it is logical to suppose that non-violent metaphors will generate different—peaceful—ideology. Finally, one should not lose sight of the fact that one campaign for language change—the feminist movement against sexist language—has met with some success (Cameron 1995). However, it is not clear whether an altered way of referring to different issues makes any difference to the way they are perceived. It is not my intention to disagree with ideas and ideals promoted by peace linguists (and in a way, these ideas are difficult to disagree with). Rather, I would like to pose a series of critical questions trying to evaluate the contribution of this approach, in an attempt to answer the central point of the paper—to what extent these ideas are utopian /realistic.

First, is it possible to avoid negative words and replace them with the positive ones? Cameron holds the view that it is, but up to a point: 'discursive drift transfers not only the words but also the passions associated with a particular concern' (Cameron 1995: 34). As previously stated, the feminist campaign has met with some success. However, attempts to replace the war metaphor with less violent ones cannot be said to have brought fruitful results. For instance, it has been suggested that the expression 'take apart', a realisation of the metaphor 'argument is war' be replaced by expressions derived from less violent conceptual metaphors. Thus, the sentences 'She *took apart* every one of his arguments' should be replaced by one of the following positive counterparts: 'She *disarticulated/erased/unglued* every one of his arguments' (Hardman 2002). These examples indicate that changes in language not coming up from below or from within may not succeed.

Instances of 'top down' language changes are numerous in language policy, and are frequently associated with attempts to impose 'right' ideological positions and influence the way language users think. I am going to illustrate this claim by two examples. In 2004, American president Bush started a campaign worth 4.5 million dollars aimed at supporting education in Afghanistan. The donation included the introduction of new textbooks which 'will teach tolerance and respect for human dignity, instead of indoctrinating students with fanaticism and bigotry'. The other example dates back to a more distant past, a speech given by the Yugoslav President Tito on possible solutions to the cold war. He argued that a remedy for the cold war would be the removal of certain expressions, such as 'block division' from the international vocabulary. Needless to say, these efforts did not bring about the desired outcomes. A discussion as to why this may be the case is beyond the scope of this report. Suffice it to say that many people resent such campaigns because they see in them the politicising of words against their will. Hence, it is very possible that the promotion of 'positive language use' will lead to similar results—a backlash reaction. Furthermore, there is no guarantee that positive speech reflects peaceful thoughts and attitude. Also, what assurance can a language teacher get that learners with L2 mediation skills will transfer them to L1?

To sum up, peace linguistics has highlighted the need to focus on the responsible use of language in the language classroom, and the importance of cultivating critical language awareness. However, the idea that the peace cause can be advanced through the use of positive language is somewhat removed from reality. True, the clash between ideals and reality does not invalidate the effort required by such dedication (Friedrich 2007). Nevertheless, I would venture an opinion that ideals are more likely to be put into practice if the gap between them and reality is not too wide.

## Insights from practice: teachers' stories

In order to further illuminate issues related to teaching language and peace, in the following section I am going to present the results of a meta-analysis of stories recounted by teachers who have attempted to teach language and peace. The data analysed include published articles and unpublished theses, direct and indirect accounts and several qualitative analyses of reflection-on-peace-teaching-action. In them, I looked for recurring themes in the stories of teachers who recognised the importance of going beyond the linguistic development of their students.

## Motivation

A large number of teachers considered it important to explain what inspired them to become engaged in this difficult enterprise. Most of them mentioned a sense of urgency, commitment, their own spirituality, concern about word affairs and injustice: 'I was very aware of the limitations of demonstrations and so on … I wanted to have a better understanding of the nature of war' (Bjerstedt 1993). Secondly, teachers appear to have been more motivated to bring peace issues into the classroom if they experienced them as relevant and achievable in their workplace, and if the training they received seemed to offer concrete solutions to their problems (Harris 2001). Thirdly, most of them highlighted that they would not have persevered in their efforts if it had not been for the support of family, friends, colleagues and, on some occasion, school authorities.

## Context, content, objectives

Teachers discussed the whats, hows and whys of teaching peace through language at great length, emphasising that the overall success of the implemented programmes depended on:

- Students' age: there is a unanimous agreement that it is easier to work with younger learners. After the age of 16, students seem to become less open to different views, and resist being challenged.
- Relevant instruction content, which is determined by a broader context. In *ESL situations* the most frequently mentioned learning focus was conflict management, because it was perceived as a most pressing need of ESL students. In *EFL 'tension free'* contexts (countries such as Germany, Italy, etc.) the prevailing goal was discovery about other cultures, while in *EFL 'tension laden'* environments language and peace educators were mostly concerned with dealing with burning issues (stereotyping, causes of war, etc.).

## Successes and challenges

As for successes and challenges, they seem to have been identical. In most instances, teachers shared success stories and pointed to difficulties involved in dealing with stereotypes, efforts aimed at teaching *both* language *and* peace, and problems related to topic and task selection.

### Dealing with stereotypes

Several teachers reflected on challenges associated with addressing stereotypes in the language classroom. The main dilemma seems to have been how to confront them without antagonising the students. Some teachers reported that after a while they dropped such discussions altogether, because they realised they lacked skills that would enable them to deal with the negative reactions of their students. What appears to have been effective in certain situations was working on awareness raising:

> I was not trying to eliminate stereotypes ... I wanted the students to become more conscious of them, in order that their prejudices not get in the way of learning English.
>
> (de Mas and Ryan 2001)

Rather than engaging in rectifying stereotypes, this teacher decided not to threaten the learners' self-image or their perception of the group self-image so that they would feel safe to bring their points of view out into the open.

### Teaching language and peace

The most frequent complaints coming from language teachers relate to the apparent subordination of the language component to the peace content. A possible solution to this problem lies in finding ways to connect language pedagogy and critical pedagogy. This can be achieved through aligning explicit focus on form, meaning and use to promote language learning (Larsen-Freeman 2003), and explicit focus on the word and the world to promote peace learning (Freire 1970). The union may result in a specific form of language practice which could be called output practice with an attitude. As a way of illustration, I can offer an example from my own teaching practice. After discussing Whitman's poem 'I hear America singing', I focused the attention of the students on the pattern 'verb of perception + –*ing*' and then asked them to write what they see and hear in Serbia nowadays. They embraced the opportunity to express their views of the current political situation:

> I hear Serbia mourning for Kosovo,
> I hear Serbia crying for financial help,
> I hear Serbia singing folk songs
> about fur coats,
> diamonds and Ferraris,
> I hear Serbia boasting
> about its glorious past,
> I hear Serbia dread to think
> about its future.

*Topic and task selection*

Peace and language educators also dwelt on difficulties involved with choosing topics challenging enough to push the students towards confronting issues that might be painful. A number of them emphasised that in certain situations it would better to avoid certain topics so that students would not have to live through their unpleasant experiences (Cheffou 2004). This does not amount to a refusal to face burning issues. The immediacy of a challenging situation or violent event may make it hard for students to talk about it; however, they may be willing to approach the topic in a roundabout or metaphorical way. For example, following demonstrations after the declaration of Kosovo independence in February this year, it was difficult to talk about what was going on around us, and yet impossible to ignore. Inspired by an article on Serbian aphorisms recently published in the New York Times, I asked the students to translate their favourite witticisms. This is what they came up with:

> Our country is in transition. It vanishes from the political map.
> Our homeland is in danger. From rescuers.
> Serbia is like Nokia. It's getting smaller and smaller.

## Signposts for praxis

In the final section, I am going to highlight main points and variables that ought to be taken into consideration in opting for an appropriate treatment of peace issues in the language classroom. The suggested framework is designed to serve as a signpost for critical praxis and an ongoing language-and-peace teaching practice.

Peace education aligned with language pedagogy can take many different forms. To achieve the cross-fertilisation of the two fields, teachers should make use of constructs from ELT and peace education, combining them in a principled manner. This approach can be metaphorically represented as adjusting lenses:

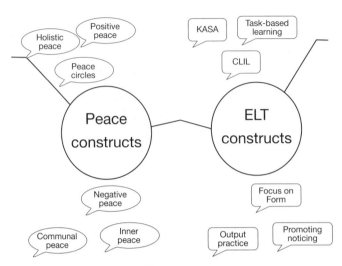

*Figure 12.5.2*

The glasses combining ELT and peace education foci would hopefully help teachers look beyond the horizon of language teaching into the area of peace studies, but also retain language learning objectives in their field of vision.

- Materials should connect with the learners' lives and match their psychological and sociological realities, so that affective engagement can be achieved. It ought to be borne in mind that the culture of peace cannot be imported or imposed from outside, but must develop out of the culture of the people concerned (Groff and Smoker 1984).

- Teachers should identify their sphere of influence and work within it. For that, it is important to outline realistic objectives. Different contexts pose different challenges and require different strategies.

I hope that my talk contributed to understanding how to make teaching peace through language a viable reality, and suggested some answers as to how to make English both a means and a site of struggle (Pennycook 1994). The entire effort represents an attempt to pave the way to educative learning – that which gives a broader value and meaning to the learner's life (Williams and Burden 1997).

Email: rpopovic27@yahoo.com

## References

Bjersted, A. (ed.). 1993. *Fifty Peace Educators: Self-portraits in Passing from Twenty-two Centuries.* Lund University: Malmo School of Education.

Bolinger, D. 1980. *Language, the Loaded Weapon: The Use and Abuse of Language Today.* New York: Longman.

Cameron, D. 1995. *Verbal Hygiene (Politics of Language).* London: Routledge.

Cheffou, I. 2004. *Designing Peace and Disarmament Education Tasks for Elementary Schools of Niger.* Unpublished Master's Thesis, School for International Training, Brattleboro, Vt.

Chilton, P. 1998. 'The role of language in human conflict: prolegomena to the investigation of language as a factor in conflict causation and resolution' in S. Wright (ed.). *Language and Conflict: A Neglected Relationship*. Clevedon: Multilingual Matters.

Crystal, D. 1999. *The Penguin Dictionary of Language*. London: Penguin.

de Mas, E. and P. Ryan. 2001. 'Stereotypes of Americans: foreign language learning research'. Accessed on 31 May 2005 at www.eric.org/articles/deMasRyan.

Freire, P. 1970. *Pedagogy of the Oppressed*. London: Penguin Books.

Freudenstein. R. 1997. 'Peace education? No, thank you!' *Global Issues in Language Education* 26: 14–15.

Freudenstein. R. 2003. 'Teaching communicate peace in second language classroom'. *Worldnews 59*. Assessed on 15 June 2005 at http://www.fiplv.org/news/news59.htm.

Friedrich, P. 2007. *Language, Negotiation and Peace. The Use of English in Conflict Resolution*. London: Continuum.

Gomes de Matos, F. 2000. 'Harmonizing and humanizing political discourse: the contribution of peace linguistics'. *Journal of Peace Psychology* 6/4: 339–44.

Gomes de Matos, F. 2001. 'Applying the pedagogy of positiveness to diplomatic communication' in M. Kurbalija and H. Slavik (eds.). *Language and Diplomacy*. Malta: University of Malta, Mediterranean Academy of Diplomatic Studies: 281–8.

Gomes de Matos, F. 2002. 'Teaching peace-promoting vocabulary: a new frontier'. *Glosas Didacticas* 8/I.

Groff, L. and P. Smoker. 1984. 'Creating global-local cultures of peace'. Assessed on 25 October 2007 at http://www.gmu.edu/academic/pcs/smoker.htm.

Hardman 2002. 'The language of peace: constructing non-violent metaphors'. Assessed on 24 June 2005 at http://grove.ufl.edu/~hardman/peace.html.

Harris, I. 2001. ' Challenges for peace educators at the beginning of the 21st century'. Paper presented at the Annual Meeting of the American Educational Research Association, Seattle, 10–14 April.

Hawkins, D. 1974. *The Informed Vision; Essays on Learning and Human Nature*. New York: Agathon Press.

Kazmi, Y. 2004. 'The hidden political agenda of teaching English as an International Language'. Assessed on 21July 2007 at http://www.tesolislamia.org/articles.

Kramsch, C. 1993. *Context and Culture in Language Teaching*. Oxford: Oxford University Press.

Larsen-Freeman, D. 2003. *Teaching Language: From Grammar to Grammaring*. Boston: Thompson and Heinle.

Pennycook, A. 1994. *The Cultural Politics of English as an International Language*. London: Longman.

Pennycook, A. 2001. *Critical Applied Linguistics*. Mahwah, N.J.: Lawrence Erlbaum.

Schaffner, C. and A. Wenden. 1995. *The Language and Peace*. Brookfield, Vt.: Dartmouth Publishing Company.

Thorne, S. 2006. *The Language of War*. London: Routledge.

UNESCO. 1987. *Content and Methods that Could Contribute in the Teaching of Foreign Languages and Literature to International Understanding and Peace*. Paris: UNESCO.

Williams, M. and R. Burden. 1997. *Psychology for Language Teachers*. Cambridge: Cambridge University Press.

# Index of authors

# Index of topics